EVOLUTION TOWARD EQUALITY

EVOLUTION TOWARD EQUALITY

Equality for Women in the American West

Teresa S. Neal

iUniverse, Inc.
New York Lincoln Shanghai

EVOLUTION TOWARD EQUALITY
Equality for Women in the American West

iUniverse books may be ordered through booksellers or by contacting:

iUniverse
2021 Pine Lake Road, Suite 100
Lincoln, NE 68512
www.iuniverse.com
1-800-Authors (1-800-288-4677)

ISBN-13: 978-0-595-38702-1 (pbk)
ISBN-13: 978-0-595-83084-8 (ebk)
ISBN-10: 0-595-38702-0 (pbk)
ISBN-10: 0-595-83084-6 (ebk)

Printed in the United States of America

Contents

Preface

The western frontier experience was important to the growth of equality for women, but it was different for young women and girls than it had been for their mothers. Historical studies by Lillian Schlissel, John Mack Faragher, and Julie Roy Jeffrey indicate that older women and women in the prime of their maternal years found the westering experience oppressive, regretful, and even deadly.[1] Many women became weak and sickly along the trail as they migrated west. They mourned their lives back home and death was not uncommon. These accounts, however, limit the history of western women to the migrating generation. The oppressive misery should not be assumed true for the daughters and granddaughters who grew up in the West.

The western women described in the historical work of Schlissel and Faragher have few similarities with the western women I heard about while growing up, read about in family and community histories, and continued to discover during my historical research. With the exception of the migrating generation, western women were more likely to possess the characteristics described in Teresa Jordan's *Cowgirls*: strong, hard-working, high-spirited, independent, often negligent in household cleaning, and more likely to be found at work and play in the outdoors than inside the house.[2]

One of the major differences between the older generation of migrating women and the younger generation who either grew up in the West or migrated there by choice was their attitude toward the West. The migrating generation had homes, friends, and lifestyles they were forced to leave behind. These could not be easily replaced in the sparsely populated, uncivilized homesteads and communities of the West. Their daughters, on the other hand, had little or none of the old eastern life to interfere with their lives in the West. To them, the frontier environment was the norm. Gender structures were also different between the two generations. Daughters were freer to experiment with both "male" and "female" work, privileges, and responsibilities.

Girls growing up on the western frontier spent more time with fathers, brothers, and father-substitutes and were more apt to identify with male role models than were girls who were brought up in more cultured urban centers where Victorian ideals defined a stricter gender division of labor and relationships. The western daughter did not see herself simply as "daddy's girl." She was special to him not because she could serve as his little darling who dressed to please him or cooked his favorite pies and dinners or sat quietly on his lap to admire him. A daughter of the West often played and worked with her father. She learned to identify with his behavior and attempted to imitate his activities. This was especially true when her mother appeared weak, denigrated, and depressed or was absent altogether.

This study counters the oppressed, domestic female that Schlissel (1977, 1982) describes in her historical accounts of westering women.[3] It will also reveal an alternative to the mother-daughter relationships that Nancy Chodorow (1978) found to dominate American culture.[4] While I respect the work of Schlissel and Chodorow, I do not believe their work represents the complete experience. There were a large number of western women who were neither oppressed nor weakened by the American West. Likewise, not all American women have been brought up to emulate their mothers' domestic, maternal lives. During the latter part of the nineteenth century, many young women in the East protested the inferior, domestic status of their mothers by going away to college, creating female institutions, and otherwise segregating themselves from their mothers' traditional role. Similarly, young women in the West also protested the traditional weak identity assumed for women but did so by including themselves in the male-dominated world of politics and economics. As a result of a less rigid social structure, western women gained a sense of gender equality.

Sources for this investigation consist of biographical sketches and theoretical discussions of self-reliant, independent women of the American West. [A selected list has been included in the Appendix.] In the hundred or so biographies, diaries, sketches, and letters of women of the American West that were included in this study, I found a distinct pattern of male influence, especially by fathers, brothers, and father-substitutes. As second generation women grew up, they emulated male figures as much as, if not more than, their mothers, aunts, and other women. In a majority of these cases, mothers were sickly, depressed, unavailable, or otherwise unlikely role models for the development of the frontier daughter's positive self-identity. Daughters, therefore, turned to the more self-assertive and goal-oriented behavior of their male parents and mentors.

In this book I use *daughter* to signify the exceptions to Schlissel's view of the oppressed, older generation, or "drudges." *Daughter* seemed appropriate because the women of my study either grew up in the West or identified their lives, goals, and independent aspirations more as daughters than as wives or mothers.

My choice of the modifiers *independent* and *assertive* are in direct contrast to the ideal feminine qualities of the nineteenth century woman which have been defined in Barbara Welter's classic essay as "purity, piety, submissiveness, and domesticity."[5] Where the ideal woman was supposedly submissive, women of my study were assertive. While the majority of nineteenth century women were considered dependents of their fathers, husbands, or families, my investigation concerns women who were relatively independent. Where the majority of women remained in the private, domestic sphere, the assertive women who grew up in the West or moved there by choice were more inclined to expand their interests beyond domesticity and enter the public sphere traditionally reserved for men.

Examples of assertive women in this study represent predominately white, middle- to lower-middle class women. There is a definite influence of non-white culture in the West, especially in regard to the Native American and Latino populations living among or in close proximity to the white settlers. However, since the subject comparison concerns conventional Anglo-American culture, the women of this study are primarily Caucasian and usually at least second generation North Americans living in U.S. and Canadian territories and states,[6] though many of them were concerned with other cultures already present in the West.

The geographic location of the study has not been limited to a specific place or time. The *West* and *western frontier* of this study represent an environment rather than a specific locale. During the nineteenth century, the American West referred to different locations at different times, beginning in the Midwest during the early part of the century, expanding to the Mississippi River and quickly beyond to Texas, Oregon, and California during mid century, returning to the plains states of Kansas and Nebraska, and finally filling in the Rocky Mountain Region with Colorado, Wyoming, Montana, Utah, and Idaho by the end of the century. The *West* or *western frontier* is used in this study, therefore, to refer to various, newly settled territories that did not yet have the population base and organization in which Victorian divisions of gender, class, culture, and ethnicity could dominate behavioral patterns.

Patricia Limerick (1987) has asserted that the impact of the West as a region did not end in 1890 as Frederick Jackson Turner suggested.[7] Life and law in the nineteenth century western United States continued to affect the rest of the country well into the twentieth century. The experiences of assertive western women as described in this study should be included in this formula. Their story is pertinent to both the development of the American West and to the nineteenth century woman's rights movement. Their experience also sheds light on childhood development that did not follow traditional patterns.

The lives of second generation western women reveal that there was a moment in western settlement when women achieved unparalleled equality and freedom. This study explores how that period came about and in what ways it influenced ongoing social behavior in the United States. Specific topics of this analysis include the differing attitudes toward the environment between the migrating generation and their children who grew up in the West, father-daughter relationships and male influence on western women, work as an important factor in western women's status, legal rights and political participation of women, and the reinstitution of eastern conventions and Victorian culture as the West became more urbanized. As Walter Prescott Webb points out, there was indeed a "peculiar psychology which developed in a region where population was sparse and women were comparatively scarce and remarkably self-reliant."[8] The interesting result was the positive impact of that experience on the rest of the country.

Material for this study include both published and archival sources. During my research, the Huntington Library in San Marino, California offered an abundance of resources and a remarkable atmosphere. Dr. Emmett Chisholm and his staff at the University of Wyoming's American Heritage Center were extremely helpful in providing valuable files on women of Wyoming and neighboring states. The records at the Historical Research and Publications, Division of Parks and Cultural Resources, Cheyenne, Wyoming supplied the final touches I needed to supplement my research on women of the West. Published sources include letters, journals, diaries, memoirs, essays and autobiographies by western women. Many of these were discovered and brought to public attention by the growing interest in women's history during the 1970s and 1980s. This new interest stimulated the publication of many new, non-traditional sources including those of pioneer women and their daughters. I have also used biographies of women from both the East and the West. Biographies of eastern women such as Elizabeth Cady Stanton by Lois Banner, Catharine Beecher by Katherine Kish Sklar, and Alice James by Jean Strouse have provided an analytical base to compare to and contrast with women of the West.[9]

I have selected sample material primarily from two contrasting states—California and Wyoming. California was admitted to the Union in 1850 and soon became one of the largest and more urbanized of the western states, while Wyoming was not admitted into the Union until 1890. Wyoming continued to be one of the more rural and sparsely populated states, but it is important to this analysis because it took the lead in women's rights when it became the first state to grant woman's suffrage and to appoint and elect women into public office. I include material from other states as well to suggest the extent and variety of western experiences in regard to woman's rights.

Chapter One

Beyond Domesticity

When God has given a woman the ability to do the highest work and in equal measure, she ought to be as free as man to do it and to be well paid for it.

~Superintendent O.P Fitzgerald, 1870

While participating in the National Woman's Congress held in Cheyenne, Wyoming in 1916, Harriott Stanton Blatch made this observation: "Here all you men and women sit together, you have always voted, and you women think no more about it than the men do and you do *not look unladylike.* You ought to *look masculine.*" She concluded, "You upset all the suffrage arguments…Here you are, womanly, beautiful women! Strange!"[1] Blatch was amazed at the degree of harmony in Wyoming where men and women worked and voted together. It was a considerable contrast to the East, especially New York, where Blatch did most of her campaigning for woman's suffrage. As the daughter of Elizabeth Cady Stanton, the founding mother of the woman's suffrage movement, Blatch was excited to see the application of goals for which she and her mother had worked so long and so hard.

While mother and daughter had been busy campaigning for suffrage for several decades, Wyoming women had been voting for forty-seven years by the time of the national conference. It is no wonder that Blatch exclaimed, "Up here in this great mountain state Freedom grows in the mountain air." She also noted that Wyoming women "had a different sort of man to appeal to."[2] Equality in this environment seemed more natural; and a different psychology of non-typical, cross-gender relationships was part of the formula.

At the same meeting, Dr. Grace Raymond Hebard, a professor at the University of Wyoming reported on the status of suffrage in her state over the 47 year period of its existence (1869 to 1916). She claimed the territorial government had adopted woman's suffrage as a "by-product" of the Civil War, and citizen's had "cherished it sacredly." Wyoming citizens enjoyed the attention and publicity but did not believe their state to be rebellious: "We have not turned the world upside down," Hebard declared, "nor have we intended to do so. We have tried *not to be radical*, because we did not want the gentlemen of your states [referring to Blatch and other conference attendees]…to point the finger of scorn against the women of Wyoming…"[3]

Map of Woman's Suffrage, 1915*

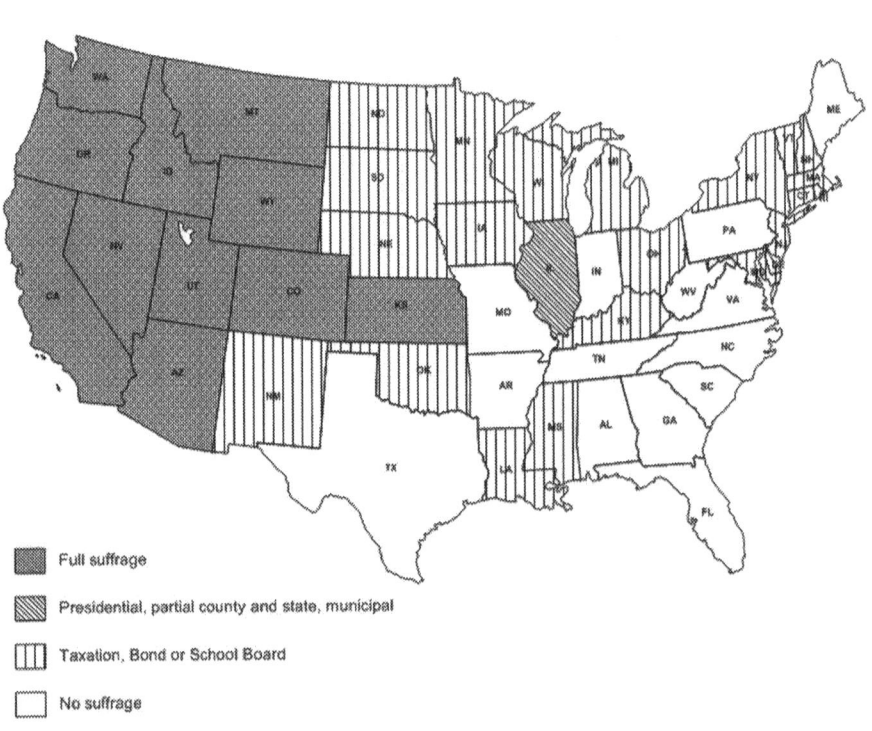

Full suffrage

Presidential, partial county and state, municipal

Taxation, Bond or School Board

No suffrage

* Data by J. B. J. Gerety

Woman's suffrage was first granted in western territories fifty years before the ratification of the Nineteenth Amendment to the United States Constitution in 1920. Wyoming and Utah included full suffrage rights for women in the territorial organizations of 1869. Utah, however, revoked that right a few years later.[4] The first state constitutions officially began to include woman suffrage in 1890 when Wyoming was admitted into the Union. Three other Rocky Mountain states enfranchised women soon after: Colorado in 1893 and Utah and Idaho in 1896. By 1916 when Blatch attended the National Woman's Congress in Wyoming, women in every state west of the ninety-eighth meridian except Texas had some level of voting privileges, at least in terms of school or municipal elections. Over half of these states had granted full suffrage. In contrast, no state east of the Mississippi River had yet granted full suffrage to women. Only sixteen of the thirty-one states in the eastern half of the nation had allowed partial female participation in taxation, bond, or school suffrage.[5]

Suffrage was not the only dimension of women's equality where the West took the lead. Co-education was instituted in frontier states even earlier than suffrage rights. Oberlin, Ohio, which was part of the western frontier up until the 1840s,[6] paved the way when the college opened a female department in 1836–37. Other western states followed with the first eight co-educational state universities: Iowa (1855), Wisconsin (1867), Kansas, Indiana, Minnesota (1869), Missouri, Michigan, and California (1870).[7]

Western legislatures moved more quickly than eastern states to legalize property rights for married women. In 1850 Oregon Territory passed the Donation Land Law which included provisions for wives of settlers to claim 320 acres in their own name. Other western states and territories provided some legal codes to allow women to own property, operate businesses, or homestead land in their own behalf.[8] Laws in eastern states, however, remained patriarchal.

In terms of economic opportunities, the West again took the lead. Proportionally more career women practiced their professions west of the Mississippi than in the East. T.A. Larson's analysis of the 1890 census reveals that while the national average of women workers in professional occupations was only eight percent, it was fourteen percent in the West. While the West was populated by a mere four percent of the women in the country, that region encouraged a higher percentage of professionals per capita. For example, in the more "learned" professions, the West had "11 per cent of the women authors and scientific persons, 14 per cent of the women lawyers,…and five per cent of the women professors." In the creative fields, the West also produced a disproportionate number of career women: "17 per cent of the actresses,…11 per cent of the women artists and art teachers, ten per cent of the women journalists, seven per cent of the musicians and music teachers."[9]

These statistics show that, per capita, western women were almost two times more likely to work in professional occupations than were women in the East.

They also reveal an important phenomenon which occurred in the frontier regions of the United States during the mid to late nineteenth century: westerners supported a move toward equality for women. In addressing this movement, it is important to consider how the West's leadership in the evolution toward equality affected the daily lives of women including social relationships, male-female interaction, and public involvement.

A listing of all the women who were among the first to serve in various public office would reveal that western states promoted women into office more rapidly than did eastern states. The central concern, however, should be an attempt to understand why this difference occurred. First of all, why did these women choose to run for office, and why did they believe they could win? More importantly, why did their communities and states support them when their eastern counterparts were seen as radicals and social deviants? What modifications in feminine behavior were required? Where did these individuals find the strength and confidence to do what no woman had done before?

Some of the women were married, others were single. Some were pioneer emigrants while most were second generation westerners. Some of these women were assertive and campaigned for their elections while others seemed to merely fall into the position. The two factors that each of these women had in common, however, was the encouragement of male role models and community acceptance. Western communities supported women who pursued more "masculine" jobs and political goals in ways that eastern culture found unacceptable. The less restrictive social environment of the western states, therefore, allowed women to advance more rapidly in the political arena than did women in the East.

The concept behind the West's leadership in implementing laws and practices of equality for women was introduced by Frederick Jackson Turner in 1893. In his address to the Chicago meeting of the American Historical Association he introduced the idea that the American West was essential to the character of the American people. He asserted that the continuous availability of relatively cheap western land strengthened the independence of the frontiersmen. This translated into a rugged individualism which evolved a new American population clearly distinguishable from its European influence.[10]

While his theory did not specifically address the impact of the West in facilitating an elevated status of pioneer women and the increasingly egalitarian opportunities available to their daughters, he did suggest why this might have occurred. Turner claimed that "the peculiarity of American institutions is, the fact that they have been compelled to adapt themselves to the changes of an expanding people." He claimed that the uniquely American characteristics of social development was the result of frontier influences, particularly "the fluidity of American life," the "expansion westward with its new opportunities," and America's "continuous touch with the simplicity of primitive society."[11]

Although Turner believed that "each tier of new States has found in the older ones material for its constitutions,"[12] he might have clarified that the citizens of the frontier did not simply imitate older, established institutions. They brought their own interpretation of laws and culture with them from the East, and then modified these to satisfy their personal needs and the conditions of their new frontier society. This is perhaps what he meant when he claimed that "line by line as we read this continental page from West to East we find the record of *social evolution*."[13] What Turner suggested but did not clarify was that without the freedom permitted by the continuous opening of new frontiers, experimentation with new ideas might not have taken place as rapidly.

This can be applied to new equality rights for women. Turner did not address the woman's* movement specifically; however, his theory can be applied to woman's suffrage. The Seneca Falls Convention of 1848 which took place in New York was the beginning of the woman's movement. At this convention, Elizabeth Cady Stanton proposed that women be granted the right to vote. This was a highly controversial issue which the majority of the attendees did not support, and it was not a proposal that the New York legislators would consider for several decades. It was an issue, however, that began to grow and spread to other parts of the United States. By the time Wyoming became a territory in 1869, suffrage was included in the constitution of the new territory.

The American West promoted equality and a higher status for women as suggested by greater numbers of educated women, earlier suffrage rights, higher divorce rates, and greater frequency of women working outside the home. The mutuality and sharing between women and men of frontier areas with their new roles, responsibilities, and ideas were a central part of the change. This change, however, could only occur when assertive women were able to overcome the traditions that limited them to domestic lives.

---

* Note: The woman's rights movement of the late nineteenth and early twentieth centuries was referred to as woman's rights in much the same way that mankind's rights were referred to as man's rights. By the time of the women's rights movement of the late twentieth century, the emphasis had changed to contrast with the rights of men (plural form). I have chosen to refer to the movement as expressed in the original time period: woman's rights.

This evolution toward equality occurred in four stages. First, assertive women rejected the old model of domestic traditions that subordinated their mothers and grandmothers. Second, assertive daughters found new role models to provide new directions for them to achieve equality. This often required the positive relationships with fathers and other male mentors. Third, the open expanse of the West—both literally and figuratively—inspired women (as well as men) to connect to something much larger than themselves. Finally, the blending of gender roles in the West helped promote the concept of equality rights for women.

To meet the first requirement, the assertive women of the nineteenth century realized the need to overcome the domestic traditions and ideals which were full of obstacles and restrictions that impeded their aspirations. In order for them to pursue a life beyond their traditional role of domesticity, they had to convince their families or their communities or both that an alternative life style was suitable for them. Sometimes this meant that parental wishes had to be discarded, marriages avoided, or new, more accepting communities sought. Generally, independent women had more leeway in the West where traditional lifestyles were frequently rejected or modified. However, even western women had to deal with parents or husbands who still clung to Victorian ideals.

Even if parents were supportive of the girl's non-domestic pursuits, at least to some degree, the social environment, especially when influenced by traditional standards, often made her development difficult. A father who encouraged his daughter to become highly educated or professionally trained often found that the community would not accept a woman accomplished in male-dominated occupations. Or a mother who allowed her daughter to seek higher education in the East often discovered that women were denied admittance. Once trained in her profession, some women found that potential clients or patients were biased against women who competed with men. Husbands and suitors also posed a threat to the woman's aspirations when they demanded that she give up her career, wages, and independence to become dependent upon them, to take care of their homes, and to raise their children.

The transition to the expected feminine adult behavior was especially difficult for Catharine Beecher (1800–1878), daughter of the famous Calvinist leader of the Second Great Awakening, Lyman Beecher, and sister of Harriet Beecher Stowe, renowned for her novel, *Uncle Tom's Cabin*. Catharine Beecher had been her father's favorite child. She grew up imitating his style of leadership, becoming interested in his profession, debating theological topics with him, and avoiding most of her domestic responsibilities. She believed she would achieve a career of public work similar to her father's. However, when she reached marriageable age, her father suddenly insisted that she prepare for a life of marriage and mother-hood. She resisted to the point of severe depression, but her father persisted. Not until the accidental death of her fiancé was Beecher finally released to pursue a public career. Because her advanced ideas in female education proved too radical for eastern communities, she was forced to look to the West to find people so desperate for teachers that they were willing to work with her revolutionary notions.[14]

There were a variety of situations in which the non-domestic generation faced opposition; however, in each case the problem was based upon old conventions that restricted female behavior. There were still ties to old, Victorian social customs, but these were not strongly enforced, especially when they no longer carried any obvious value. For example, when Prairie Rose Henderson, daughter of a Wyoming rancher, decided in 1908 to compete in a "bronc busting contest" at the Cheyenne rodeo, her request was denied. She sought out the rule book and discovered that there was nothing in the rules specifically about women, so she convinced the officials to allow her to compete. She did not perform well, but she set the precedent to allow women to participate in more rodeo events.[15]

Often the western daughter learned to combine Victorian culture with her outdoor interests. In *Daughters of the West*, Anne Seagraves describes Kittie Wilkins as "a well-educated woman who could ride the range, consummate a shrewd business deal, or sit at the piano to entertain guests." Wilkins was born in Oregon in 1857 and grew up in several western states where her parents raised horses and cattle. Her mother sent her to the finest schools, but she learned horse trading from her father. She became know as "the Horse Queen of Idaho" after she and her family settled in Idaho where they "broke and shipped 154 horses every two weeks" under her leadership. When Wilkins visited eastern stockyards for business, she traveled with "two trunks, one for her work-clothes and the other for her fancy outfits, which were worn with a flair." While trading horses in the stockyards, she "pulled her golden hair up under a hat and dressed in skillfully tailored mannish attire, something that was unheard of in that era."[16] Later, she would be found in public "dressed in a svelte, tailor-made costume, her blond curls surmounted by a dainty Parisian creation."[17]

The non-traditional generation of assertive western women was able to overcome most obstacles. Sometimes it took incredible persistence while other times it required long, enduring patience. For women of the first generation, new opportunities were open to them when they moved to the West but additional opportunities became available to their daughters. Being in the right place at the right time was important. Eastern communities did not need and did not want female doctors. Doctors in the frontier West, however, were so scarce that even female doctors were warmly received and highly respected. During the early years of statehood, Nebraska welcomed Dr. Georgia Arbuckle Fix (1852–1918) who set up a productive homestead and a steady medical practice. Her primary obstacle was her old-fashioned husband, Gwynn Fix. After they married, he expected her to give up her homestead to move in with him and turn over her wages to be used as he thought appropriate. Later, he demanded that she give up her practice in order to concentrate solely on her domestic and wifely responsibilities. Fortunately for Dr. Fix, the community did not support his Victorian attitude. After the inevitable divorce, she re-established her practice and became a highly respected professional member of the community.[18]

In some cases, marriage itself was an official act of rebellion against parental wishes. Bertha Muzzy (1871–1940), whose pen name was B.M. Bower, married Clayton Bower in 1890 to spite her parents. She hoped a life apart from them would allow her to control her own destiny. The marriage ended in divorce, but during her first eleven years of marriage, Bower was able to begin her writing career. That was something she had been unable to achieve in her parents' home.[19]

Desire to use marriage to open the door to new opportunities was not uncommon. Phoebe Apperson (1842–1919) married against her parents' wishes. As a child, Apperson had dreamed of travel and perused every book, almanac, and catalog she could find. She longed to ride on a steamboat or train like the ones her visiting cousins described. When she heard her cousins and neighbors talk of young men who had left for California, "she cried once or twice to think she was n't [sic] a boy so she could run away to California, too."[20]

One of Apperson's childhood heroes was George Hearst, a neighbor twenty-two years older than she. He was one of the young men who had left for California when she was seven. When he returned to be with his mother during her final days, he became reacquainted with Apperson, now beautiful at seventeen. George and Phoebe decided to marry, but Mr. and Mrs. Apperson did not approve. They wanted their daughter to marry someone younger and remain close by. They did not want her to be carried off to the other side of the continent to live in wild and dangerous territory.[21] That, however, was one of the attractions of the marriage for young Apperson; she had always longed to see the world. Eventually the couple convinced the Appersons to agree to the wedding which took place in 1862 in Steelville, Missouri. Soon after, her dream came true as she rode a steamboat and visited the exciting cities of Chicago and New York on her way to the streamliner that would carry her to her new home in San Francisco.[22]

Second generation women successfully proved to their families and their society that they had a right to pursue a life beyond the normal path of domesticity. For most, the struggle began during adolescence when they were pressured to give up their tomboyish dreams as they matured. For others, the rebellion involved marriage, and they used their marriage to make their own decisions and claim independence from their parents. In other cases, marriage itself was the problem when the woman's self-identity was threatened by a tradition-minded husband who demanded a strictly domestic wife.

Moving Beyond the Restrictions of Domesticity

According to the popular Cult of True Womanhood of the nineteenth century, the ideal woman was pure, pious, submissive, and domestic. She was selfless and dedicated to her family—first her father and mother and later her husband and children—and her church. She was physically fragile and intellectually inferior, but she was morally superior because her family and God always came first.[23] A woman's life was molded by her family and church, by marriage and mother-hood. Male physicians of the Victorian Era supported this view by insisting that a woman's destiny was determined by her reproductive organs. She accomplished her duty to humanity only through motherhood. According to these doctors, female intellectual pursuits would over stimulate the brain and cause disorder to a delicate physiological balance.[24]

During the first half of the nineteenth century, promoters of woman's rights discarded neither the virtues of the Cult nor the male physicians' basic under-standing of women. Instead, they attempted to expand the definitions. They still believed that motherhood was a priority for women, but childrearing took up only a part of their lives. The nurturing skills women learned for and by mother-ing, along with their moral superiority, could be transposed into the public world. "More pious and domestic than men, the efficient housekeepers of the Nation," Smith-Rosenberg summarizes, "True Women could not confine their efforts to their homes and families. They must extend their 'home rule' to encom-pass the world—wherever children and other women needed their ministra-tions."[25]

Women's "moral superiority" was a social construct of the settled regions of the older, more established states of the East. Catharine Beecher (1800–1878) and many of her contemporaries of the Northeast advocated women's subordination. They translated self-sacrifice into a public good. They believed that submission, purity, and domesticity were not the natural order of life; however, these feminine virtues should be adhered to for the general good of society. Women's moral supe-riority would thereby give them authority and a central purpose in society.[26]

Although she supported the virtues of the Cult in theory, Catharine Beecher was one of the first women to publicly pursue alternatives to the Cult of Domesticity. After her fiancé was shipwrecked and died at sea in 1822, Beecher chose the life of a single woman. Because her father could not continue to sup-port her indefinitely, Beecher was encouraged to begin her career as an educator.

Other opportunities for marriage arose, but she always turned them down. She was never able to submit to the will of another nor did she particularly care for domestic chores. Beecher modeled her life after her father and learned her autonomy from him.

Catharine Beecher is recognized as one of the early leaders of female education. She spent most of her life organizing schools for girls and colleges for female teachers. In spite of her own inability to submit to domesticity and become submissive to anyone but her father, she believed that household duties and a moral home environment were essential to the public good. She asserted that women must be consciously and carefully taught domestic science. Beecher's treatises on domestic economy (the foundation of courses later known as home economics) were not, however, the extent of her beliefs in female education. She identified a moral superiority of women that began in the home which could be extended to the public sphere through the influence of female teachers.

Beecher's life was a contradiction of what she preached. The ideals she conferred upon others were not the ideals she upheld in her own life. She could be neither submissive nor domestic. Her seeming self-sacrifices for her schools held ulterior motives to improve her own status and living conditions. One biographer has pointed out, "Catharine's evangelical style and her covert upper class aspirations created a tension in her thoughts that was not resolved until she left New England *for the new social context of the West.*"[27]

As a young girl, Beecher lived to please her father and refused to have anything to do with the domestic work associated with her fragile, meek mother. This was true until her mother died when Catharine was 16. At that time, Catharine was only too glad to take over her mother's role to please her father. Lyman, however, remarried a year later and brought his new wife home to a jealous stepdaughter. Nevertheless, Catharine managed to control her emotions and show restrained respect for the new lady of the house.

When Lyman put pressure on Catharine soon after to move on to a separate domestic and married life, she resisted. As one form of protest, she avoided the commitment of marriage; and similarly, she prolonged the religious conversion experience her father believed was essential to those who were truly saved. Catharine's problem was that she was not ready for a separation from her father, nor was she willing to lose her autonomy by submitting her self to another person. She was more motivated by the ambitions of her father than the ideals of her mother. She idealized her father and had expected to model her life after his. His sudden persistence that she reverse her ideals and become a submissive domestic like her fragile mother had been seemed impossible to Catharine. The trauma to her psychological development created a pattern of instability that she was to struggle with for the rest of her life.

She finally agreed to marry a man of whom her father approved. Part of the reason for her compliance may have come from the pressure of being pushed out of the house in order to contribute to the family economy. With all his other children, Lyman could not afford to continue to provide Catharine's subsistence. Catharine may also have agreed to the marriage because her fiancé was much like her father: an intelligent, well-respected person and an honored public speaker. She perhaps unknowingly transferred her idealization of the man who had recently begun to reject her (as the more independent woman she wanted to be) to a new man who admired her and to whom she could idealize for many of the characteristics she had formerly admired in her father.

While Catharine agreed to the marriage, she nonetheless failed to achieve a full conversion experience. Even after much persistent persuasion from both Lyman and her brother Edward, also a Calvinist minister, Catharine's inner self simply refused to allow her to become a subordinate being. As a biographer pointed out, "Catharine…could hardly forget what the spirit of submission had meant to her own mother." She realized that while "[a] young man might exercise briefly his submission to God and then recover his sense of independence and self," a woman would have a different experience. Her "submission to God might be but the prelude to a lifetime of earthly submission to a husband."[28]

When it came down to choosing between her mother's life of submission and her father's example of personal autonomy, Catharine chose her father's model. The problem was that neither her father nor her society approved of this decision. Her father wanted her to have a conversion experience and then get married. Society had little use for unmarried women and gave them very few options for economic independence. Lyman refused to support her forever. Although she had plenty of nieces and nephews whom she could have helped raise, the spinster aunt was not a role she cared to play. Catharine knew well the limited freedom of unmarried aunts. She had loved and respected two maiden aunts during her own youth. Mary Foote, her mother's sister, had loved her, raised her, and taught her the romantic imagination of Scott and Burns. Unfortunately, Aunt Mary had been meek and fragile and had died young just as Catharine's mother had. Another aunt, Esther Beecher, helped manage the housekeeping in Hartford in 1826 when Catharine decided to set up a household with Mary, Harriet, and Henry Ward.[29] To Catharine, maiden aunts were symbols of restricted lives and subordinate domesticity.

Ultimately, Beecher was not obligated to submit to a husband. Her fiancé, Alexander Fisher died during a shipwreck. She lapsed into mourning accompanied by ill health. The conversion experience continued to be a source of contention between father and daughter. They used Fisher's death as a warning to her that she could not let earthly treasures get in the way of her soul. Neither her father nor her brother Edward would allow her time to mourn. After considerable resistance and a nervous breakdown, Beecher moved to Boston to live with her stepmother's sister and a distant cousin. Her health and strength returned and she gave up the conversion attempt in 1822.[30]

She then spent time with the Fisher family where she discovered the depth of her intellectual ability. She had promised to tutor Fisher's siblings. In the process, she read his notes and realized that she understood his advanced level of scientific knowledge. This gave her the confidence and interest to establish female schools which focused on higher levels of learning.

The emphasis of her school was different from the typical feminine schools of that era. She was too proud to comply with her father's recommendation that she observe the famed schools of his friend, Mr. Emerson of Saugus.[31] Instead, she established her own procedures and ideas. A young lady's ability to assume motherhood and domestic responsibilities should not be taken for granted, she decided. These were practical skills a girl must be taught. Gradually, a woman's moral upbringing became Beecher's priority.

The Hartford school for girls which she founded in 1823 was so successful that she converted it into the Hartford Female Seminary in 1827. By 1829 she was again dissatisfied with the school and wished to advance it to a new level of moral molding by adding a female associate principal. The project failed, and she collapsed into depression. In 1830 she returned to the school with a new plan to promote teacher training. Hartford was unwilling to support her project.

Her biggest problem was that the established communities of the East did not need nor want her. However, she found the less settled areas of the West more than willing to support her schools. After all, they had a shortage of teachers and administrators. In 1833 she established the Cincinnati Western Female Institute with the major goal of preparing teachers to instruct in the West.

During the 1840s she organized the Central Committee for Promoting National Education. She lectured and raised money in the East for this project which provided education in the West. In 1848, however, she broke with William Slade because he had taken over too much control of her organization. Her new society started in 1852 as The American Woman's Educational Association.

Still restless and always willing to initiate but never able to settle long with a project, Beecher moved farther West and founded the Milwaukee Female College in 1850. She dedicated her efforts there until 1856. When this community like all the others that hosted Beecher's female academies insisted on asserting their needs over her personal preferences, she again moved on. She gave up trying to establish any more schools and turned to writing about morality.

Separate Spheres

Catharine Beecher, like other women raised during the nineteenth century, looked for alternatives. It was a transitional period in religion, in science and technology, in industrialization and urbanization. It was also a transitional period in expanding the boundaries of womanhood. In essence, the advice literature for women attempted to recreate the Garden of Eden while man's exploration and science exiled humanity into new territories. New directions in the public sphere forced old domestic traditions into obsolescence. Separate spheres were created.

Initially, the separate sphere philosophy expanded rather than rejected the four feminine virtues defined by the Cult of Domesticity: purity, piety, submissiveness, and domesticity. Women were not encouraged to pursue individual ambitions but instead were advised to sacrifice their personal identity for the greater social good (rather than merely for the good of the family).

The separate sphere advocates of the woman's movement were further divided by differences in definitions of what that separate sphere should entail and what strategies should be followed. Basically, the differences can be classified into four levels. The most conservative advocates of the separate sphere can be identified as *Domestic Strategists*. They attempted to work within the culture that confined and constricted them. They did not wish to turn the world upside down, but chose merely to extend the virtues of womanhood into their communities. They hoped changes would evolve smoothly and rationally.

The other three levels supported revolutionary changes. At the second level, the *Separatist Strategists* created their own institutions such as women's colleges and settlement houses where there was minimal contact with men. The third and fourth levels challenged male power outright. Those who supported both the *Radical* and *Militant Strategies* sought revolutionary changes.[32] They wanted to radically change many social and political institutions. The difference in these two levels was the strategy of their approach. Radical Feminists irritated their opponents and forced people to consider new ways of viewing their society. Militant groups went a step beyond and were not afraid to resort to vandalism, hunger strikes, and other violent tactics. The militant approach was associated with labor unions, socialism, and European influence.

The distinctions in the developments of the "woman movement" has been classified by Nancy Cott (1987) in *The Grounding of Modern Feminism*. She clarifies that "Feminism" (referred to in the early years with a capital *F*) was not used in the U.S. until the 1910s and 1920s. Although it was in some ways an extension of the nineteenth-century woman's movement, "the new language of Feminism marked the end of the woman movement and embarkation on a modern agenda." Cott contends that "women's efforts in the 1910s and 1920s laid the groundwork and exposed the fault lines of modern feminism." She distinguishes the original woman's movement as having "three arenas of effort." The first and earliest arena was based on "service and social action, motivated by…neighborly or altruistic intent." Through "benevolent, charitable, social, welfare, and (eventually) civic reform efforts…women…discovered new strengths in collectivity and forms for self-assertion." The second arena focused more directly on campaigns for "'woman's rights'—rights equivalent to those that men enjoyed on legal, political, economic, and civic grounds." The third arena called for even more change that included "activity toward women's self-determination via 'emancipation' from structures, convention, and attitudes enforced by law and custom."[33]

Which level of strategy a group chose depended upon the time and the place. Cott points out that "these three arenas displayed not simply smaller and larger visions of the same thing…but also potentially conflicting visions, the first more, the second less loyal to the existing social order, the third not loyal at all."[34] The woman's movement tended to become more radical as it progressed over the decades. Cities attracted the more divisive and militant behavior while women in less sparsely populated areas were more likely to work within the system. In spite of vast differences in goals and strategies, the basic premise that all these groups had in common was belief in women's moral superiority as an impetus toward equality.

Domestic Strategists

Domestic Strategists were the most conservative of the separate sphere advocates. The spirit of Christian duty drove moral women into part-time public service. Women would not be submissively confined to the home when the community needed them. Historian Karen Blair identifies the smooth transition from limited domesticity to community involvement as "Domestic Feminism." Blair contends that "by invoking their supposed natural talents" through their work in benevolent societies and service-oriented women's clubs, "women took the ideology of the home with them, ending their confinement and winning influence in the public realm." In this manner, the domestic strategy "redefined the ideal lady"[35] as it claimed a limited and non-disruptive influence for women. Most nineteenth-century women believed their work to be a pragmatic shift in duties rather than a contentious uprooting of tradition. Female educators throughout the period and clubwomen who emerged after the Civil War chose to work within the system rather than radically overturning it.

The Beecher sisters were among the first to promote the moral superiority of women. Catharine Beecher, one of the first women to establish female education in the United States, and her sister Harriet Beecher Stowe, an abolitionist famed for her book *Uncle Tom's Cabin*, believed in the domesticity of women but advocated improvements in domestic science.[36] They maintained that a woman's foremost responsibility was to the Christian family. "The family state...is the aptest earthly illustration of the heavenly kingdom, and in it woman is its chief minister," Beecher wrote. "Her greatest mission is self-denial, in training its members to self-sacrificing labors for the ignorant and weak: if not her own children, then the neglected children of her Father in heaven."[37]

According to the Beecher sisters, women's Christian obligation extended outward to encompass the moral well-being of the entire community. In this manner, they began a movement that deviated from the traditional view of domesticity and True Womanhood. They did not believe women had to have children of their own to enjoy the "blessed privilege of the family state." With the help of a "properly qualified female associate," a woman could "institute a family of her own" and take care of the destitute. The woman's "motherly devotion" to the underprivileged would aid them not only in their earthly needs but would also "train them to follow the self-denying example of Christ." The orphan, the sick, the homeless, and the destitute could then find "true happiness" for both their life on earth and their eternal home.[38] To accomplish this, Catharine Beecher promoted higher education for women to be trained in the special womanly duties of nursing, housekeeping, and teaching. In addition, she suggested these women would become the best wives and mothers.

Although Catharine Beecher influenced the advancement of women into the public sphere, she refused to support woman's suffrage. She did not share the enthusiasm of other leaders of the movement who wished to push their way into the "political arena" or to crowd men out of the "learned professions." Instead, she proposed that "woman raise and dignify her own profession," to endow honor and prestige to domestic-based pursuits, and uphold the special "character and duties" of the feminine sex.[39]

Beecher idealistically believed that women could have an indirect but powerful influence on political reform merely because of the virtue of their moral superiority. As part of a good education, she recommended that women should be "prepared to communicate in an easy manner" and learn how "to regulate their own minds, tempers, and habits" so that they can use "their stores of knowledge" to "effect improvement in those around them" and thus change "the face of society."[40]

Beecher's philosophy reflects the evolution from the Cult of Domesticity to an expanded role encompassing community responsibilities. Women began to organize, form clubs, participate in community issues, and speak out publicly. Women continued to focus on education but gradually included other interests and goals.

One of the strongest organizations to develop during this period was the Woman's Christian Temperance Union. The W.C.T.U. was a national organization that had a strong and active following at the state and local levels. Members believed that abuse of alcohol often destroyed families and disrupted the community. The organization attracted women and men because its Christian base fit their moral sense of duty. While temperance was its central concern, the W.C.T.U. developed a much broader platform. For example, the California W.C.T.U. combined their activism against problems of alcohol abuse with their support of public education and promoted a Temperance Education Law in 1886 to keep alcohol out of public schools.[41]

At first the Temperance Union refused to support woman's suffrage. Eventually, however, members began to realize that women needed the vote in order to influence school laws and administration. Thus, franchise became an important issue. At their 1886 California State Convention in San Jose, W.C.T.U. members voted to support franchise and appointed Sarah M. Severance as superintendent. In 1890, the Union increased publicity by running a weekly paper with Severance editing the suffrage section.[42]

By 1893 W.C.T.U. members were actively lobbying legislative efforts for school suffrage for women. To increase publicity, Severance wrote a powerful satire for clubs to perform. Entitled *An Extra Session of California Legislature*, the drama reversed the male and female roles so that women played the role of legislators and discussed whether men deserved school suffrage rights. The ludicrous scenario made it all too obvious why the power of school franchise should be granted to women.[43]

From initial refusal to deal with the issue of franchise to full-fledged support, W.C.T.U. reflected the changing attitudes about women's rights. The expanded moral obligations promoted by the domestic strategy required women to turn to political solutions. Moral duties of women eventually outweighed older ideas that politics were too rough and too dirty for women. In fact, this corruption was exactly what women believed they were obligated to overturn. This meant that women needed voting power. Ironically, the arguments by the opposition that politics were too corrupt for women only strengthened the drive for woman's suffrage.

During 1895 and 1896, the California W.C.T.U. financed Severance's lecture tour of the state to promote woman's suffrage.[44] California women's widespread involvement in the state's education system convinced enough legislators that women deserved the right to vote on school issues. In 1899, California passed a school suffrage law. The success, however, was short-lived when Governor Gage vetoed the bill.

California women did not give up, but they did change their strategy. Sarah Severance and others continued to travel, write, and lecture. Only this time, they pushed for full suffrage rights. California women finally won the battle late in 1911. "The war has ended," wrote Severance, "and we have captured the flag." For her as well as other women, it was a hard-won moral fight. With a sigh of relief she wrote, "I feel like saying, Now lettest thy servant depart in peace, O Lord!"[45]

Other women's organization gave women collective power to influence their communities. Women's clubs that formed during the latter half of the nineteenth century were not merely relics of proper society. Instead, they were reform oriented. The domestic strategy was reflected in clubs because they appealed to a woman's sense of a Christian extension of the home and moral obligations to the community. Mrs. Caroline M. Severance (not related to Sarah M. Severance), known as "the mother of clubs," described the club as "only a larger home which welcomes and harmonizes; it strives to bring into broader and finer relations to each other all varieties of taste, temperament and purpose, so these be only helpful and noble."[46]

Madame Severance (as she was respectfully addressed) founded the first woman's club in Boston in 1868. The idea for the club had come to her while she and her husband lived in Ohio in the 1840s. The frontier town had a few schools and churches and a library association but few other intellectual resources. When she returned to Boston in 1855, Severance was starved for a literary association she could share with other women.[47]

After she moved to Los Angeles with her husband in 1875, she again recognized the need for a woman's club. "I find women's clubs a great moral force," she once told an acquaintance. "Sometimes the only conspicuous moral force in a city; where there is no moral grip on anything, a woman's club furnishes it."[48] In May 1878, Caroline Severance organized the Los Angeles Woman's Club. Membership was composed of responsible Los Angeles women and included the honorary membership of Mrs. Jeanne Carr who at the time was serving as State Deputy Superintendent of Public Instruction.[49]

The object of the club, according to the constitution and by-laws, was "the intellectual and social improvement of its members, and any kindred work approved by the society."[50] Special emphasis was given to education, art, literature and women's work. For supplemental reading material the club ordered *New England Journal, New England Journal of Education,* and *The New Education.* In addition, club members relied on newspaper articles to inspire topics of discussion. Caroline Severance compiled a varied list of topics including such issues as "Past and Present Housekeepers," "Religious Morality," "Kindergarten Addresses," "Women and Peace," "Suffrage," "Mothers Congress," "How to

Teach Morals in School," and "What Will Socialism Do for Women?"[51] The club had a broad agenda, but as this list suggests, Los Angeles women were interested in the same issues of good education and community morality that educated women and the W.C.T.U. promoted.

Because memberships in women's clubs included women teachers and often overlapped membership with other organizations, strong networks of support groups were possible. Several organizations working on similar projects, especially in education and suffrage, strengthened the overall influence of women.

One particular project that received wide support from various groups was kindergartens. Caroline Severance and her L.A. woman's clubs were instrumental in bringing kindergartens to Los Angeles. They studied the work of Frederick Froebel, a German who started the first kindergartens in 1837. They were particularly interested in his methods of play as an instructional device. Both Boston and St. Louis experiments using this method with very young children had been successful. Los Angeles women believed kindergartens could be a valuable asset to their community. As the work progressed, the California W.C.T.U. assigned a kindergarten committee and appointed Caroline Severance to the chair.[52]

To begin the project, Severance invited Miss Emma Marwedel, a German native well acquainted with the kindergarten system, to come to Los Angeles. Marwedel was working in Washington at the time but agreed to help the L.A. women. Miss Kate Douglas Smith, a house guest of Severance who was looking for a career, took advantage of the situation. She became Marwedel's first student-teacher. When Marwedel left L.A. to establish new kindergartens throughout the state, she left Smith in charge of managing the Los Angeles kindergartens. Later, Marwedel again called upon the assistance of Smith (who had become Mrs. Kate Smith Wiggin) to help instruct kindergarten teachers at the State Normal School in San Francisco.[53]

Severance was a key figure in support networks of women in the state. She brought together the women most influential in the kindergarten project, but she also worked with many others to promote women's issues. "Strength & [sic] Gentleness. Men have cultivated the one, women the other. Do thou cultivate both."[54] This quote which Severance copied into her notebook reflects her philosophy of the woman's movement. She believed in the special nature of women, but she also wanted to help them "think on their feet, which is still an uncommon accomplishment among us."[55]

Severance was also instrumental in making important connections for the woman's suffrage movement. As early as August 1869, Caroline Severance joined Lucy Stone, Julia Ward Howe, T. W. Higginson, and George H. Vibbert in signing a general letter to promote the American Woman Suffrage Association.[56] She was also an active participant in national, international, inter-West, and state activities for the promotion of woman's suffrage. At one point, the W.C.T.U. tried to locate a Colorado woman to speak on voting rights for women. They turned to Caroline Severance because she was the best source for finding contacts.[57]

Susan Look Avery of Louisville, Kentucky commended Severance's work. "From what I see and hear," she wrote in 1905, "it seems to me that you Los Angeles people are in advance of even Bostonians! You seem to live right under the sun! It delights me to hear of your opportunities, of what you are saying and doing." In concern over the upcoming national election, Avery continued, "Never has there been a time in the history of the world when women's influence was so much needed."[58] Here again was evidence of the moral obligations behind the domestic strategy that prompted women like Caroline Severance to work for woman's suffrage.

Separatist Strategists

While the Domestic Strategists attempted to work within the existing system to fulfill their moral obligations, other separate sphere strategists chose to irritate the status quo, challenge male advantages, and attempt to build new, female-oriented institutions. Radical strategists promoted easier divorce laws, economic equity for women, birth control, "free love," and other revolutionary topics that are still considered controversial. Separatist strategists were a little less obtrusive and merely segregated themselves from the male domain whenever possible.

One of the basic problems that precipitated the woman's movement was what to do with the single women and widows of the East. When home-based spinning and weaving were considered necessary industries, single women and widows had been very useful. Nineteenth-century industrial society, however, had taken away the economic value of women's work in the home. In an industrial economy, the spinster aunt was no longer a welcomed addition to the household. As textile and other domestic productions were moved to factories outside the home, single women became a burden rather than an asset.

Not only were unmarried women losing their economic place in the home, but there was a growing number of these extra women. Emigration during the nineteenth century created a remarkable division in the two sexes. Men, in ever-increasing numbers, migrated West to explore the land and seek their fortunes. They left behind wives and potential wives. Soldiers of the Civil War and Indian wars tipped the balance of men to women even further.

This regional sex differentiation fostered contrasting delineations of a woman's role. The more urban Eastern states tended to follow old world traditions of women's domesticity but added new definitions to the value of that domesticity. A "separate sphere" attitude maintained that women had roles different from men, but their duties were equally important to the public good.

Single women were aware of this problem. In 1846 Catharine Beecher acknowledged that the "excess of female population in the older state from the disproportionate emigration of the other sex" had caused a serious shortage of opportunity in "all branches of female employment in the older states." In contrast, there was a dramatic regional demand in the new western states for "domestics, nurses, seamstresses, mantua-makers [dressmakers], and female teachers."[59]

Beecher's solution was to train intelligent women who were "possessed of missionary zeal and benevolence" to teach in the western states and territories. Women could be sent "to the most ignorant portions of our land, to raise up schools, to instruct in morals and piety, and to teach the domestic arts and virtues." The result would be beneficial for both regions. The West would be educated and more equivalently populated with women, while the women of the East would have less competition for jobs. As a consequence, Beecher argued, "the value of female labor will rise at the East, so that capitalists can no longer use the power of wealth to oppress our sex."[60] She also believed the efforts would lead to a higher respectability for womanly professions.

The unbalanced gender population contributed to the economic necessities for women to seek separate sphere relief, but other American experiences helped construct the design of the separate sphere. One of the strongest influences on the separatist persuasion of the woman's movement was the Quaker tradition. Mary Maples Dunn points out that Quaker women's separate meetings gave them a special status; they could control their own agenda, their own funds, and discipline their own members. Sliding partitions between men and women in meetings provided "women and men with separate spaces for the conduct of their separate business."[61] No women of any other denomination had such control. Dunn contends that this physical control was central to Quaker women's more autonomous spiritual role in the community. Quaker women's experiences in their own communities helped give them more confidence to lead women in national projects. Lucretia Mott and Susan B. Anthony as leaders in the woman's rights movement and M. Carey Thomas as the first female president of Bryn Mawr (a Quaker-inspired university for women) are excellent examples of Quaker women who successfully led the way.

Women's participation in religious reform movements was another important factor in the separatist emphasis on women's moral superiority. Barbara Epstein posits that the rise of these reform movements first of all revealed to women their differences from and antagonism toward men, and secondly, developed a domestic culture that helped form the nineteenth-century "middling classes." Although popular culture's reform converged with the woman's movement by the late nineteenth century, Epstein cautions that they should be clearly distinguished. Women did what they could within the culture that confined and restricted them while feminists challenged male power outright.[62] In other words, radical strategists created a separatist philosophy while the domestic strategists along with non-activist women tried to work *with* the men in their lives.

Estelle Freedman has found separatist strategies in other avocations for women besides religion. She traces the origins of women's reform in regard to separate female prisons. She emphasizes the "separate but equal" political reforms, especially in the earlier period (beginning in the 1830s). Sexual differences led women to become keepers of their own prisons. Quaker women led the way followed by charity workers and then social strategists. Beneath the reform activities was an acknowledgement of women as a separate sexual entity. Freedman points out that women saw themselves as morally superior, thus if the fallen woman was given a chance, she could be redeemed as a true woman. Women reformers demanded separation of female prisoners from male prisons, differentiation of treatment, and female staff and management.[63]

Separatism was a deliberate strategy, according to Freedman, in other areas as well. Women established their own networks to nurture their own culture. Freedman contends that feminism was most successful when women had a physical space of their own. A *public female sphere* was created by the building of female institutions which emerged from the middle-class women's culture of the nineteenth century. This included women's clubs and colleges, women's trade unions, settlement houses, women's buildings (such as those constructed by the Y.W.C.A.), and political organizations.[64] Jane Addams' Hull House is a well-known example. The New Woman that emerged from the separatist ideal was single, highly educated, and economically independent.

The New Women instituted new roles for women and, according to Carroll Smith-Rosenberg "amassed greater political power and visibility than any other group of women in American experience."[65] They sought an education not equal to but identical with the highest male education. They turned to each other for love and companionship and shared their economic necessities and professional inspirations. Their goals to reform American cities gave them power and legitimized their separatist world. That environment also had its setbacks. Smith-Rosenberg attests that "their struggle for autonomy often led to estrangement from their own mother and female kin."[66] By avoiding marriage and motherhood, the New Woman had rejected her mother's world. She therefore had to create alternatives different from the old domestic order or even the newer but poorly paid career of the unmarried schoolteacher. Because of the New Woman's failure to fit into any of the normative choices, Smith-Rosenberg labels her as "a perennially luminal figure" who remains "outside the existing social structures" with "no way of coming in."[67]

The separatist strategy forced women to segregate themselves from mainstream culture. One example is M. Carey Thomas. In order to achieve her dream of a good education, she had to attend an all-male college, Cornell University, and compete with classmates who believed her either intellectually inferior or an inferior woman. She had to put up with the abuse or else accept a lesser education. To combat this problem for other women, she helped establish Bryn Mawr University for women to receive a quality education that would be equal to what men could receive at their male colleges. Co-education did not seem to be a viable option for Eastern culture. Even with the creation of the women's college, Thomas had to settle for a predominately male faculty and administration in order to attain the excellence she demanded.

Being segregated from mainstream culture created new psychological problems for women. The separation was often a painful experience. Independent women were frequently cut off from parents and siblings who found their behavior abnormal and perhaps even threatening. Unmarried women were symbols of family failure and an economic deficit. Women who strayed too far from their assigned domestic duties were accused of being "mannish women, like hens that crow…a class of wild enthusiasts and visionaries—very sincere, but very mad."[68]

Another problem that Smith-Rosenberg identifies with the New Woman was the establishment of homophobia. The New Woman not only rejected the female role of motherhood, she also scorned the male world. In an attempt to understand her behavior, her contemporaries imagined her as "a male soul trapped in a female body" which they labeled as "Mannish Lesbian."[69] Rather than rejecting the man-made, artificial constructions of gender and viewing her ideal of androgyny, however, they saw her as a social and biological deviant.[70]

By the 1920s, fear of lesbianism convinced many college girls to marry and follow more traditional paths of domesticity. It was not uncommon to discredit political, professional, and career-oriented women with charges of lesbianism. Feminist organizations and institutions often suffered from similar charges.[71]

Thus, although the separatist strategy brought a great deal of personal and political power to one generation of independent women, it did so at the expense of their social and psychological well-being. This was a pattern of life that could not afford to regenerate itself.

Radical and Militant Feminists

In the northeastern states where civilization was more advanced, another alternative to a male-dominated society came into use.[72] This alternative which ignored traditional proper social behavior took two different forms. During the settlement of western territories where women's work was still considered economically valuable, men and women would accept alternatives to the Victorian style of proper, gender-divided behavior. People could not afford to maintain strict gender divisions of labor. Where women were scarce, men learned to cook, sew, and wash. Similarly, women were needed to care for animals, help with farming, and run boarding-houses and restaurants. Women did not have to resort to moral superiority to gain respect. In the East, however, dissenters defied the boundaries of the Cult of Domesticity and were considered radical or even militant.

Radical feminists were accused of attacking the very core of civilization: marriage and the family, the church, and the "natural" order of the universe. Many of their demands such as easier divorce laws and birth control were eventually adopted in the twentieth century (although divorce laws were adopted in the West even earlier. See Chapter 5). Initially, however, their revolutionary ideas and antagonistic tactics provoked defensive responses. They were accused of advocating the irresponsibility of "free love" that would completely demolish the institution of the family. It was not until later that calmer arguments were made to convince the public that birth control would improve the quality of family life rather than merely promote promiscuous behavior.

Suffragists' behavior seemed radical at times. When Amelia Bloomer, Elizabeth Cady Stanton, and others adopted the costume of short dress with baggy pants which came to be known as "bloomers," they were forced to tolerate rude and critical behavior whenever they appeared in public. Even small boys would ridicule them.[73] Their contemporaries feared these women were becoming too mannish.

Lucy Stone's refusal to change her name when she married caused confusion. At a time when women were addressed by their marriage status, how should they identify the woman who should be regarded as Mrs. Henry Blackwell? She was no longer attached to her father's identity and thus could not be called Miss Stone. First name basis was out of the question except in extremely close relationships. Even Susan B. Anthony, who was Elizabeth Cady's Stanton's closest friend, still addressed the elder woman as "Mrs. Stanton." Stone was ahead of her time and left her contemporaries uncertain as to how to address her properly but often referred to her as Mrs. Stone.

The biggest problem was not the confusion. Women who refused to give up their birth name symbolically denied the basic principle of marriage that women would leave her father to cleave to her husband. Such assertiveness rejected the social foundation of women's subordinate status, especially when the requirement of women "to obey" their husbands was taken out of the marriage vows. Again Lucy Stone and her husband Henry Blackwell led the way in this radical behavior. Stone and Blackwell, however, are not remembered as radical feminists. Their greater devotion to the abolitionist movement persuaded them to set aside woman's rights until the Fourteenth and Fifteenth Amendments were passed. By that time, Lucy Stone had given up most of her activism in favor of more domestic pursuits, particularly in raising their daughter Alice Stone Blackwell.

Militant activities were minimal in the United States and did not come until the latter part of the movement. Those who pursued such tactics followed European influence. Emmeline and Christabel Pankhurst of the Women's Social and Political Union of England received the greatest publicity. The Pankhursts adopted their militant ideas from the Irish republicans who smashed windows and assaulted guards around government buildings. When they were arrested for the destruction of property, they staged hunger strikes while imprisoned. On the whole, the Women's Social and Political Union was not as violent though they disrupted male politicians' meetings and held mass marches and street demonstrations for which they often clashed with the police.[74]

Militant activities in the United States were more likely to adopt civic disobedience such as refusal to pay property taxes in protest of "taxation without representation." Striking became a common form of protest among women workers in the textile industries between 1905 and 1915. The National Women's Trade Union League which formed in 1903 and the Equality League of Self-Supporting Women led by Harriot Stanton Blatch in 1907 brought working class women into the woman's rights coalition.

After 1907, the woman suffrage campaign "blossomed with techniques planted by the political left." Nancy Cott credits the source of this shift in strategy to the influence of the British suffragettes, women workers on strike, and contributions of socialist women.[75] Many new women's political organizations were formed and leaders took advantage of the sensationalist news media and grass roots participation in mass marches, train campaigns, and outdoor lectures. The early 1900s brought a distinct new look to the woman's rights movement with a new generation of leaders such as Alice Paul who used much stronger political tactics including lobbying, pamphlets, boycotts, petitions, picketing, parades, demonstrations, and hunger strikes.[76]

After women won the right to vote in 1920, the woman's suffrage strategies continued to shape the direction of politics. According to political scientist, Kristi Anderson, the strategies of suffragists through the use of women's clubs, volunteer organizations, social work, League of Women Voters, and lobbying efforts helped transform the political system "from a male ritual to a good citizen's obligation." In particular, voting booths moved out of barrooms and into schools and churches. Women voters also influenced the movement "from the partisan-structured politics of the nineteenth century to the politics of advertising, interest groups, and candidates that characterize the twentieth century." When women became "voters, county treasurers, heads of federal agencies" [which occurred with western women first], they "began to slowly change how [male] politics was conceptualized" through suffragists' "particular experiences, political strategies, and political styles." Specifically, women working through their service clubs used "lobbying practices…to educate leaders and to move public opinion on specific issues through the use of expert testimony, public education campaigns, and grass-roots pressure."[77] Gender distinctions in politics continued even after Amendment Nineteen passed giving women in all states the right to vote.

Beyond Domesticity

The biggest difference between the woman's rights campaign in the East and the attainment of measures of equality in the West during the nineteenth century involves the contrast between the two regions in terms of the social environment and the political strategies of the movement. The woman's rights movement in the East was viewed as much more radical. Activists introduced revolutionary demands that their contemporaries believed would turn the world upside down. Men saw their power directly challenged with the suggestion that old traditions and institutions—marriage, family, and separate gender spheres—be antagonistically uprooted. Radical, militant, and separatist strategies gained the greatest recognition in the East.

In contrast, the West was still developing. States could afford to experiment with new social ideas and incorporate them into new constitutions. Work by both women and men was necessary for settling the new states and territories. Woman's rights advocates sought evolutionary changes and attempted to work within the system. Men as well as women supported the advancement of equal rights for women. Human rights equality and the domestic strategy were the strategies most common and most successful in the West.

A problem with using the separate spheres analysis to describe the experience of women in the West is the centrality of domesticity to this theory. Nineteenth-century women attempted to change their domestic status in two ways. First, they wished to increase their power and authority within the home. If this was to be a woman's assigned domain, then she should have control over it. However, many women, whether by preference or by necessity, chose to go beyond domesticity. Single women, widows, and working-class women could not afford the luxury of limiting their lives to the domestic sphere. Women of intelligence and special talents did not wish to be restricted by only one option of marriage and motherhood. In most cases, the strategy for assertive women was to *expand* women's domestic qualifications and moral superiority to encompass community involvement. For example, it was considered logical in both the East and the West for women to teach younger students because of their assumed natural nurturing abilities as mothers. Women's leadership and participation in community activities could be considered acceptable if based on their moral obligations to society.[78]

While Catharine Beecher and others used the language of women's domestic qualifications and moral superiority to extend women's roles to the public sphere, their true intent was to provide opportunities for women to work *outside* domesticity.[79] This would allow women choices and alternatives outside their traditional role as housewives and mothers or spinster aunts. Nineteenth century women did not wish to expand domesticity so much as they desired to increase women's choices and authority. Domestic terminology was merely the strategy by which they could make their new public roles appear to be more socially acceptable.[80]

This distinction between strategy and intent becomes especially important when analyzing how the experiences of western women compared with their counterparts in the East. Because of economic and environmental differences between the two regions, pioneer women and their daughters procured some semblance of social, political, and economic equality while Eastern women were forced into separatist strategies.[81] Although continuity of the Victorian cult of domesticity was a part of western women's experience, divergence from the separate spheres ideology was also an essential factor.[82]

Studies of specific women suggest that the cultural ideology of the East did not equate to actual experience in the West. Harriette Andreadis in her article "True Womanhood Revisited" contends that "Texas women, like their sisters who stayed home in the East or South, were deeply affected by the prevailing cult of true womanhood." She suggests that because the women of her study attempted to mold themselves after the virtues defined by the Cult of True Womanhood, the western environment for them was "painfully isolated from female friends and kin and the culture that gave them their value."[83]

At the other extreme were women like Lizzie Johnson of Texas who ignored the restrictions of the Cult. Johnson was educated and then taught at her father's co-educational institute, married but also successfully owned and operated her own separate cattle herd, wrote and published extensively under a secret pseudonym, and became a pioneer among women in the field of finance. Biographer Emily Jones Shelton contends that the nature of the western environment allowed Johnson opportunities equal to men and encouraged her toward a high level of achievement.[84]

Although there is evidence to support both extremes, the common experience most likely fell somewhere between complete oppression and outright liberation. The lives of western women were multi-dimensional.

In "Women as Workers, Women as Civilizers: True Womanhood in the American West," Elizabeth Jameson discards not only the one-dimensional labels of gentle tamer and reluctant pioneer, but she also discards other prescriptive concepts such as the liberating frontier thesis and the Cult ideology.[85] Jameson contends that three factors changed and weakened the impact the Cult of True Womanhood in the West. The first problem for the Cult was that "the belief system clashed with daily necessity." Pioneer women could not remain genteel when forced to adapt to collecting and cooking with buffalo chips. Furthermore, that behavior was bound to affect daughters "who appear to have been more receptive to new roles than their mothers were to the western journey."[86]

The second factor to modify the Cult's influence was that "internal inconsistencies within the belief system itself were heightened" by western lifestyles. Jameson points out that "the Cult of True Womanhood contained a widely recognized internal contradiction: women had to leave the domestic sphere for public action to achieve the moral authority they were told they should exercise."[87] In other words, the domestic sphere could not simply be expanded; some women had to be willing and able to work *outside* the domestic sphere and compete in the male-dominated public sphere.

These first two factors of change could not occur immediately. Jameson points out that the Cult's influence had to be weakened "over time through different generations' responses to the West and to larger social and economic changes." Some of those changes included new technology and access to national markets for western farmers. Miners confronted dangerous tasks in order to earn their daily wages. As a result, westerners began to perceive of "common enemies" that began to pull the family together. Jameson suggests that "the interdependence of family members and what women and men shared" became more important "than what separated them." Women frequently joined men in public activities such as "reform and protest groups and partisan politics." Thus, according to Jameson, "outside forces may have helped transform genteel beliefs about appropriate behavior in the West."[88]

It was not outside forces, according to Katherine Harris, so much as "a large measure of mutuality, or sharing, between the sexes" that reduced the power of separate sphere practices for western homesteaders. Harris contends that women in the homesteading areas of Colorado acquired respect and equality in both family and community activities. Gender responsibilities often overlapped, and gender-role distinctions were muted. Geography encouraged isolated homesteading families to meet weekly with neighboring families in religious and community activities where "extensive mingling of the sexes" was promoted during dances, picnics, and literary nights in which the entire family participated. Harris points out that although men and women in general performed different tasks, "the mutuality between the sexes enforced by the needs of homesteading expanded women's power to negotiate and win."[89]

After 47 years of equal suffrage in Wyoming, one of the leading women of the state reported that "[w]e have not turned the world upside down, nor have we intended to do so. We have tried *not to be radical...*" [90] Reports from judges and congressmen of the state also announced that the practice of women voters had not revolutionized the state—except perhaps to make the polling places a little cleaner and the politicians more accountable.

Governor John M. Thayer, the third governor of the Wyoming territory, supported equal suffrage. He reported to the Territorial Legislature: "Elsewhere, objectors persist in calling this honorable statute of ours 'an experiment.' *We know it is not.* Under it we have better laws, better officers, better institutions, better morals, and a higher social condition in general, than could otherwise exist." He pointed out further that this benefit to the political structure had done no harm to the domestic sphere as many opponents believed would occur. "Not one of the predicted evils, such as loss of native delicacy and disturbance of home relations, has followed in its train."[91]

Women were reported to cross party lines if a bad or immoral candidate was running on their ticket. "The women watch the nominating conventions, and if the Republicans put a bad man on their ticket and the Democrats a good one, the Republican women do not hesitate a moment in scratching off the bad and substituting the good." Since this also occurred with women in the Democratic Party, the result was "nearly always...a mixture of office-holders."[92]

Mrs. L. W. Smith, Superintendent of Schools for Carbon County, Wyoming explained that since "[a] woman is more apt to work for the individual than for party," and since "the entire feminine vote" would go against a candidate of incorrect character, it forced political parties to "nominate good men, or their defeat is a foregone conclusion."[93] Judge John W. Kingman, judge of the U. S. Supreme Court of Wyoming observed that reputable women of the state voted and voted independently: "Our best and most cultivated women vote, and vote understandingly and independently, and they cannot be bought with whiskey, or blinded by party prejudice."[94]

As recent work has indicated, to concentrate simply on separate spheres ideology ignores the reality of western society. Jameson points out, women "did not see themselves as passive civilizers or as uniquely oppressed, as wholly private or public. They understood that they performed valuable work for their families and their communities, and that these efforts were intertwined."[95] Therefore, the use of prescriptive theories such as the Cult's public vs. private dichotomy leads to an incomplete and inaccurate picture.

More suitable is an understanding of westerners' inter-relationships and work experiences. Jameson asserts that "the daily details of work, family survival, and relationships dominate [westerners'] words." For example, she describes an old Colorado pioneer, May Wing, who worked hard throughout her life and was proud of her work and variety of community activities. Wing wanted to establish an active community that would encourage closer relationships. Her projects included the promotion of a hot lunch program in the local schools, organization of a boys' choir, the founding of and teaching at a multi-denominational Sunday school, and management of the local museum during her elderly years (age 70 to 90). In addition, Jameson stresses the interconnection between Wing's concern for family, her work, and her community involvement. "May Wing valued her work and *wanted recognition for it*."[96]

It was important to women that they satisfy their basic emotional need for recognition. Jameson, however, minimizes the value of that need for recognition. She suggests that relationships dominate all other psychological needs: "Our fore-mothers may have known that the details of daily survival and human touch dominate our lives, not brief moments of public recognition or a few minutes in a voting booth."[97]

Jameson overlooks part of Wing's motive. Details of daily survival may have accounted for a major portion of Wing's time, but what dominated her mind, her goals, and her inspirations was a need to be recognized, to have her existence acknowledged, and to prove that her life had meaning. For many people, these objectives may be achieved through interpersonal relationships with family and friends, but they may also require recognition of a person's work in the larger world.[98] Wing did not want people of her community to forget her nor the work she did to make the town a better place to live. Her work had given her life meaning, and she desired public recognition of that fact.

The need for recognition was a significant factor according to Harriette Andreadis's analysis of Mary Maverick, a Texas pioneer. Lack of recognition was more a source of Maverick's depression than was her failure to live up to the feminine ideals of the Cult: "…and oh I sigh ever more for some one to believe in me, to think well of me, to call me good—I say if some one thot [sic] me so, I might succeed in getting to be some what so…" Maverick wanted to be loved, by both her husband and her slaves. She was crying out for recognition that she existed and that her life had meaning.[99]

Recognition and meaning came in several different forms. Moynihan, Armitage, and Dichamp, editors of an anthology of narratives entitled *So Much Work to Be Done* about "women settlers on the mining and ranching frontier," claim that women were involved "in every aspect of the frontier settlement process." Women who migrated West with their husbands found culturally acceptable alternatives to the limitations of Eastern domesticity. Women who emigrated "chose instead to assert that their marriages were egalitarian units." They chose to endure the same hardships as their husbands and were "eager and willing to work." Women settlers proved to have a great deal of control over their own lives and maintained their own hopes. They provided for the family welfare in whatever manner was best suited to their abilities and environment. They also discovered "entrepreneurial and creative ingenuity" which helped to enhance their lives.[100]

Whether recognition came from acknowledgement of public activities and work performed or from mutual sharing and caring from family members or women's support networks, women wanted their lives to have meaning. The Cult and separate spheres ideology did not work well during the settlement periods of the West because women's lives, especially the lives of non-traditional daughters, centered on interdependencies and activities with men. This meant they often found meaning for their lives and mentors outside of domesticity.

The experiences of the non-traditional daughters compose an important area of study. Their lives were unique. They were the first generation to fully adapt to the conditions of a new region. They shared similar hopes, disappointments, and a common disillusionment with their mothers' domestic ideology. Because their mothers did not experience the unique conditions of the western environment in their own youths, they were unable to provide the model by which their daughters could learn to adapt. The non-traditional generation was forced to develop new styles based on their own experience and to discover new role models suitable for their unique situation.[101]

When culture came into conflict with the frontier environment, westerners, particularly the more assertive and open-minded emigrants and the younger generation who developed their own model of behavior, modified Victorian notions of feminine behavior. Because domestic ideology and strict gender division of labor were impractical on the frontier, men and women frequently exchanged chores and responsibilities, and boys and girls commonly worked, played, and studied together. Old, restrictive conventions were set aside as non-traditional daughters began to reject their mothers' model of domesticity in favor of more adaptive alternatives and stronger role models.

Chapter Two

New Role of Fathers

Fathers have an enormously important role to play in the socialization of "liberated" daughters...If the fathers of the future communicate a belief that career commitment is not incompatible with femininity, we shall see many fewer women experiencing doubt about the compatibility of their social and occupational aspirations.

~Michael E. Lamb
Paternal Influences and the Father's Role

Helen (Fiske) Hunt Jackson is remembered by her friends as being "the most brilliant, impetuous and thoroughly independent woman of her time."[1] This, however, was not necessarily complimentary to a Victorian woman. Even though she openly criticized woman's rights advocates for overstating their cause, she argued publicly and passionately for Indian rights. In her book *A Century of Dishonor*, she cited cases of "cheating, robbing and broken promises" against one tribe after another.[2] In order to be heard, she sent a copy to every member of Congress in 1881. Her emotion-packed appeal drew sympathy from senators, and she was the first woman to be appointed Special Commissioner of Indian Affairs.

As Commissioner, Jackson spent a great deal of time and personal funds to travel through her appointed territory of southern California. She carefully observed tribal conditions and discovered poverty and negligence. When her report to Congress was virtually ignored, she turned to other means of making the public aware of the ongoing injustice. In order to reach this larger audience, Helen Hunt Jackson wrote a fictionalized history, entitled *Ramona*. It gained wide-spread recognition and has endured as an important historical story of Southern California.[3]

Born in New England on October 14, 1830, Helen Maria Fiske's parents, Nathan Wiley and Deborah (Vinal) Fiske, had hoped she would be a boy to replace their infant son who had died shortly before Helen's birth. In spite of their disappointment, they expected her to act like a sweet, innocent child. Instead, Helen proved to be wild, adventuresome, and totally independent. She seemed to have inherited the characteristics of her worldly, indulging maternal grandfather rather than the conservative, Puritan nature of her parents.[4]

In contrast to her younger sister Ann, Helen was a spirited child. Mrs. Fiske wrote despairingly of her oldest daughter: "I cannot play with Helen so well as with Ann. Helen is so wild—jumping rope, dressing up in odd things, jumping out behind doors." Ann was the perfect daughter, "honest, artless, and affectionate," and could tell everyone "how well she loves them," whereas "Miss Helen has no idea of 'liking all those folks' nor of telling the whole of everything."[5]

Helen hardly seemed like a little girl. She once took off unchaperoned into the forest with a neighbor girl so they could "see live snails with horns."[6] After she was found and returned to her parents, she felt no remorse for this misconduct. Because of her unrepentant spirit, she was confined to the attic for a week. Helen was an intelligent child full of curiosity and adventure—characteristics which she later learned to control but never outgrew. She was exceptional only in that she was a girl. Had she been a boy as her parents had originally hoped, her activities would have seemed more normal. Her excursion to the forest would have been cultivated rather than condemned. However, since she was raised in a conservative household, she was expected to follow the special rules of conduct for women.

After both her parents died while Helen was a young adolescent, legal guardianship fell to her Grandfather Vinal who allowed her much more freedom. Still, she was forced to learn feminine control in order to earn the popularity of her friends and schoolmates. Later she learned to become the submissive wife after she married the handsome Lieutenant Edward Hunt. To her two sons, she was the loving, attendant mother who gave them her full devotion. Unfortunately, separate accidents and illnesses caused early death to her husband and both sons.

Widowed and childless, Helen Hunt at age thirty-five could no longer adhere to the feminine role she had adopted for her family. She was forced to look for alternatives. Her first pursuit was writing poetry, an accepted role for women. Under the mentorship of Thomas Wentworth Higginson, she became a prolific writer of poetry, articles, and novels.[7] Her curiosity and adventurous nature also led her to pursue her dream of travel. In 1872, she set out for a trip to California with her friend Sarah Woolsey. She loved the natural beauty of California and was intrigued by the people. She returned to the East and began to plan for another trip to the Pacific coast; however, respiratory ailments caused by damp climate interfered with her plans. Her doctor advised her to move to the healthier climate of Colorado where Hunt made her home in Colorado Springs. There she met and married a prominent gentleman, Mr. William S. Jackson.

Helen Hunt Jackson, circa 1875
Source: William S. Jackson Photograph Collection,
Photographed by Marshall, Boston.
Courtesy of Tutt Library Special Collections, Colorado College

In October 1879, Helen Hunt Jackson became a social activist. She attended a reception in which two Indians, Standing Bear and his niece Bright Eyes, made a public appeal to stop the government's systematic extermination of the Ponca Indians of Nebraska. Jackson was incensed by the injustices they described. She realized that something must be done in their behalf. Suddenly, she became a woman with a cause—which was something she had formerly criticized in woman activists but could finally understand.

For the next six years until her death in 1885, Jackson dedicated her time, travels, and writing to advance the rights of Indians. Her work inspired the formation of an Indian Rights Association in every major city in the U.S. The popularity of her book *Ramona* motivated the Dawes Act of 1887 which allotted sixty acres of land to each head of Indian households. Jackson's leadership was important even if short-lived. At her death, she felt no remorse for her social impropriety. She only wished that she had not had such a late start at such a worthy cause.

Psychosomatic Disorders

One indirect form of protest against the Cult of Domesticity (or Cult of True Womanhood) was psychosomatic disorders. Women who could not live up to the ideal nor be restricted by its limitations were usually weak, frequently ill or depressed, and often died young. Nineteenth century women were renowned for hypochondria, fainting spells, and even suicide.[8] It was not uncommon for female protagonists in the fiction of that period to become hysterical, neurotic, or suicidal. Two of the most famous are Kate Chopin's *The Awakening* and Charlotte Perkins Gilman's *The Yellow Wallpaper*.[9]

Alice James is an excellent example of a nineteenth century woman whose talents and intelligence were stifled by the Cult of Domesticity. As a child, Alice shared some of her older brothers' education and tutors. Her father and brothers teased her to be their sweet little darling at times, while stimulating her intellect more frequently. However, as an adult she was expected to follow the model of her mother.

Her mother Mary was the model of true womanhood; she shared her husband's piety but was always willing to subordinate her will to his. She accepted responsibility for running the household, she nursed the family whenever they were ill, and she dedicated herself selflessly to the good of the family. This was a role Alice was unable to follow.

James suffered a lifetime of neurosis. Born eight years before Freud, she did not have the benefits of psychoanalytic understanding or treatments. She vaguely knew her somatic problems were somehow associated with her nerves. Unfortunately, nervous disorders in the nineteenth century were misunderstood;

and patients, including James, were usually treated unsuccessfully for their physical symptoms. Realizing this, she wrote to her brother William at one point in regard to the hopelessness of her life, "When I am gone, pray don't think of me simply as a creature who might have been something else, had neurotic science been born." In her biography, Jean Strouse describes James as a helpless victim of the time and a misunderstood child of her family and society.[10]

Alice was born in 1848 to Henry and Mary James, the youngest of five children and the only girl. Her two oldest brothers were to become famous— William for his scientific advancements in philosophy and psychology and Henry Jr. for his novels of estranged Americans, especially female characters, living or traveling in Europe.[11] Her father, Henry James, Sr., was eccentric. In reaction to his strict Calvinist upbringing, he became wild and rebellious. On one reckless occasion, he badly burned his leg and had to have it amputated. During his recovery, his own father had become much more caring and affectionate. From this experience Henry Senior decided to adopt a more nurturing fatherly image for his own children. He had no specific occupation but considered himself a student of his own version of theology and philosophy. He encouraged his children to develop their internal selves and their intellect rather than limiting themselves to any specific vocation.

One of central experiments of Henry's fatherly role was to provide the best possible education for his children. At first, he believed this would be found in Europe, so the family wandered all over Switzerland, France, and England. Each time, the father was disappointed. He finally decided that tutorship was a better choice than all the expensive schools in Europe. The family could finally settle down to a home in the United States.

Unfortunately, Henry's emphasis on quality education for his children was limited to his sons. He assumed that his daughter, though quick witted and obviously intelligent, would not live a life of the mind. Instead, he believed in the feminine domestic virtues of the Cult. He saw women as "personifications of virtue, innocent purity, holy self-sacrifice." Boys, on the other hand, "had to learn to be good, through suffering and the interesting uses of perception." Thus, boys needed an education while "girls were good by nature and could dispense with interesting ideas."[12] In her father's eyes, Alice was to remain his "sweet little girl" all her life.

The problem for Alice James was that she was intelligent. Her father did not allow her to compete intellectually with the male members of her family, and she continually tried to please him. At the other extreme, however, she could not match the self-sacrificing purity of her mother and the maiden aunt who lived with the family. Nor could she reduce herself to their lower intellectual level. Since the only acceptable occupation her Victorian society offered her was marriage and she had no prospects, she found no healthy purpose for her life. Her only alternative was to resort to illness. Nervous disorders gave her the air of fragility and delicacy which were feminine charms of the period. Here was the one feminine virtue she could adopt.

Illness was profitable for Alice James. Whenever she fell ill, her family lavished her with extra attention and love. In a family where all members (except the mother and aunt, neither of whom were of "true James' blood") suffered psychological break-downs that resulted in painful physical symptoms, they were particularly sympathetic to each other's suffering. Strouse contends that the James' family believed each suffered poor health so the rest could be well. Since Alice was overcome by ill health more than any other member of the family, her sacrifices were the greatest. She was praised for her patience in suffering. She rarely complained and bounced back optimistically after each bout. In this way she was seen as morally superior, and thus, ill health became her symbol of moral good.

Although science was gaining ground during the nineteenth century and her own brother was the leading American psychologist, Alice James was born too soon. Doctors knew no permanent cure for neuroses (nor even how to identify them as such). James tried all the trendy cures. The general belief of the time, led by S. Weir Mitchell, was that women could not physically control the over-stimulation of their intelligence. He believed that absolute rest, special massages, and limited physical exercise would help them develop control over their bodies. It is probably true that women had difficulty managing over-stimulation of their intellect, but it was not because of an innate physiological inferiority. Rather, these women lacked an acceptable outlet to develop and display their intelligence.

Perhaps if Alice James had been born to another generation or another family, she may have left an important intellectual contribution to humanity. According to Jean Strouse, James' diary reveals an intellect that could possibly have surpassed even the fame of her two older brothers, William and Henry. However, Alice James could provide only limited insights during her life of repressed intelligence. Her parents' belief in the feminine virtues of the Cult denied her a healthy self-identity and the opportunity for self-fulfillment. James needed a social environment that appreciated special talents of women as well as men, one that would have allowed her to be a social equal to her brothers.

Alice James's predicament was not especially unusual. Other women with special talents and high intelligence struggled to find alternatives to the restrictive social role defined for them by the Cult of True Womanhood. Helen Hunt Jackson was also raised and limited by the Cult. Unlike Alice James, however, she was able to defy the social limitations placed on women (although this was not activated until she became a childless widow at age 35). The important difference is that James resigned herself to nervous disorders while Jackson could escape from the restrictive environment. Jackson found alternatives by asserting her talents and pursuing her dreams of travel to the West. Her domineering parents died when she was young enough to still be able to develop a strong self-identity under her grandfather's guidance. James's father, as her idealizing selfobject, refused to allow her to emulate him in her adult life. She remained frustrated and confused. The only continuity she could discover in herself was the role of the delicate, self-sacrificing, little darling of her father and brothers.

While many of the male physicians of the period believed that women's brains were too small and their constitutions too delicate to handle intellectual or professional pursuits, Catharine Beecher reported that an enlightened few recognized that the nervous instability of women came from their *"inactivity of intellect and feeling."* Those who were most likely to fall victim to "melancholy, hysteria hypochondriasis, and other varieties of mental distress" were women of the middle and upper classes who were "of a nervous constitution and of *good natural abilities.*" The source of the problem was "a state of *irritability to the brain occasioned by imperfect exercise."*[13] Women needed more exercise—both physical and intellectual—than they were receiving in the confinement of their "proper sphere" of domesticity.

Fathers and Daughters' Non-Domestic Relationships

During the mid-nineteenth to early twentieth centuries, a new generation of women emerged in the American West who promoted a new standard of female behavior. Part of this group was composed of exceptional pioneer women, but most of these women were daughters of emigrants to the trans-Mississippi West. What made them remarkable were the ways in which they rejected their mothers' Victorian tradition of the domestic mothering pattern. They tended to adopt what was then considered more masculine behavior, particularly in regard to interests in outdoor activities, male mentors, and career alternatives. This behavior distinguished the non-domestic western generation from their mothers and demonstrated the possibilities of gender equality.

This new standard of behavior emerged as a result of a distinguishable pattern of development in non-traditional women of the West. It was the second stage in the evolutionary process toward equality. When the old domestic model was rejected, new role models became necessary to make the change. Western daughters developed an early and significant relationship with fathers or father substitutes (i.e., grandfather, other male mentor, or unusually strong, non-domestic female relative). Much of the time spent between the daughter and father or father substitute was involved in outdoor activities or in developing more masculine-oriented skills. The non-domestic abilities and interests of the daughter became a strong part of her identity.

Elliott West, a historian of childhood on the western frontier, has observed that much of the labor, leisure time, and play of frontier girls were carried out "alongside boys and men in the fields, countryside, and boomtown streets." He contends that much of the girls' "feelings of accomplishment came largely from helping with men's work—those transforming tasks and celebrated changes linked to a grand national purpose."[14]

On the trail westward, fathers were compelled to have greater contact with their children. Young girls and boys alike were expected to help herd the animals, fetch firewood or buffalo chips for the evening fires, and otherwise help either parent whenever needed. Fathers helped supervise the chores of both daughters and sons, but men's concerns often contrasted with their wives. For example, on one occasion, a young girl who was helping to drive the wagons learned to crack the whip over the oxen's heads. Her father admired her new skill and believed it could prove to be useful. Her mother, however, was indignant that her daughter should display such masculine behavior, especially in the presence of others.[15]

Fathers' influence on non-traditional behavior in daughters continued into the settlement period. Men sensed that their daughters should be prepared to take care of themselves, if necessary, because the untamed environment offered only minimal domestic security. Mothers, on the other hand, were trained to believe that conventional domestic patterns of marriage and motherhood should remain a young girl's primary concern.

The Cunningham family is a case in point. Imogen Cunningham, born in 1883, took advantage of her father's encouragement that she extend her career interests beyond domesticity even though she did so to her mother's chagrin. Cunningham's father, Isaac, was a free thinker in religion, politics, health practices, and his daughters' future. Not wanting his children to go through life struggling from one odd job to another as he had done, he encouraged all twelve of his children to train for a profession. His sons became printers and his daughters became nurses, except his favorite child Imogen. He hoped that she would become a schoolteacher. However, when she stubbornly pushed for a career in art and photography, he grumbled about her choice but supported her by enrolling her in art classes, building her a functional dark room, and paying for her college chemistry courses.[16]

Isaac Cunningham's conviction that daughters as well as sons should be educated and trained for a professional career, although not the typical national view, was more prevalent in the American West. His attitude allowed Imogen

Cunningham, though a woman, to compete against men to become one of the pioneers and leaders of photographic art.

Cunningham's mother, Susan, was not as liberal. She was disappointed to see her daughter competing in a male profession and longed for the day when her daughter would settle down to domesticity and motherhood. The younger woman, however, was too independent and her work meant too much to her to merely abide by a domestic routine. Even after her marriage and the birth of her three sons, Cunningham found ways to continue her photographic art career in or near their home.[17]

There were many families like the Cunninghams during the western frontier period. Their internal family relationships suggest that a different pattern of fathering was emerging in the West. Fathers were not limited to an Oedipal role in recreating heterosexuality and distinct gender divisions of labor. Instead, fathers and father substitutes were more directly involved in the raising of their children, became essential role models, and provided recognition for and approval of the talents and abilities of their daughters as well as sons.

Esther Pariseau (1823–1902), who was later recognized as the Pacific Northwest's first non-native architect (a posthumous title conferred on her by the American Institute of Architecture in 1953), grew up under her father's influence. As a child, she spent many hours with him as he worked in his carriage shop. She learned to identify his tools and distinguish the variety of wood with which he worked. As she grew older and started playing with his tools, he taught her how to use them. He allowed her to imitate his work and design some of her own projects.[18]

Esther Pariseau was the oldest of several daughters. Perhaps because she had no brothers, an inquisitive nature, and exceptional talent in handcrafts, her father took particular interest in her development. The western daughter, however, did not have to be the eldest child nor did she have to be brotherless to win her father's attention. An only daughter who preferred the companionship of her father and brothers might also spend more time outdoors than in the house with her mother. In one such case, Esther Clayson Lovejoy (1869–1967) grew up in Oregon back country with no companions other than her father and brothers. She played games with her brothers and followed her father around to various logging camps serving as his assistant.[19]

Strong orientation toward non-traditional goals was a common characteristic of assertive women. These women believed they could achieve valuable careers and were confident they could overcome traditional obstacles. For example, Agnes Wright Spring, born in 1894 and raised in rural Colorado, pursued dreams in which she had no fear of competing with men. She once remarked that there was no generation gap when she was growing up. Her father and the old timers who frequented her father's stage line and post office seemed to have plenty of time and patience for her. As a result, she was more apt to behave like her father than her mother. Her mother was an active, hard-working woman, who sold meals to passengers on the stage line for thirty-five cents and served as postmistress for twenty-five years. Young Agnes was not interested in domestic pursuits, even for pay, and spent most of her time working, playing, and fishing with her father. She was the tomboy of the family and always tried to climb trees higher than anyone else. She recalled that she "always wanted to be the best at everything" she did, "from working the bellows at the blacksmith shop to fishing for trout."

When she was old enough to set out on her own, her goal was to become a mapmaker. She signed up for civil engineering classes at the University of Wyoming, but her corsets interfered with the compass and earned her the nickname of "Old Ironsides." She eventually discovered she had a preference and natural talent for history and writing. She chose a career in journalism and served as state historian in two states over the course of her lifetime.[20]

Theodore Schrader's family's first Christmas on homesteading claim, Montana 1910
Young girl, center front is Teresa Neal's grandmother, Edith Schrader

Children of frontier regions rarely had the security of a normal family pattern where father was the sole breadwinner and mother the primary caretaker. One homesteader's daughter in Montana recalls how her father took over when her mother died. "Mama had hated Montana so that she didn't want to be buried here…Daddy tried to hire women to take care of us little ones, but finally gave up and did it himself and hired men to do the farming until we got large enough to take care of ourselves…Many were the nights Daddy would be baking bread or washing clothes after we children had gone to bed."[21]

Death and desertion were common. May Arkwright Hutton (1860–1915) was an illegitimate child whose mother left her in the care of her father. Her father accepted the roles of both mother and father during his daughter's early childhood. He taught her domestic duties including his special skill in cooking and baking. This proved to be a valuable asset when Arkwright moved to frontier Idaho and worked among the silver miners where she became famous for her pies.[22]

Although Arkwright had a good relationship with her father, her idealized role model came into her life at age nine when he took her out of school to care for her blind grandfather. The girl and her grandfather became close companions. Arkwright accompanied the older man to all the political lectures that passed through town and joined him in lively discussions with his cronies. The interest in politics she developed during these early years inspired her to become politically active as an adult. She ran for office in Idaho where women already had the vote. Later, after she and her husband, Al Hutton, moved to Washington, she campaigned for woman's suffrage in that state. She was very active in the Democratic Party and was chosen as one of the nominating delegates to the National Convention in 1912.[23]

Fathers, grandparents, and other father substitutes were not always available to raise their daughters or support and encourage them as they matured. This was especially true with the high mortality rate of the frontier West. Nevertheless, many daughters were able to achieve confidence and self-fulfillment in spite of the loss of their fathers. This was achieved during a two part process. First, the daughter had idealized her father as her role model while he was still alive. Secondly, she was able to absorb some of his strength and confidence into her own self-perception. In order to maintain this identity, the girl would often direct her energies toward some symbolic object or experience that would connect her with memories of her father.[24]

Studies have indicated that even if the father or father substitute is absent or fails to reciprocate the child's identificatory love, the daughter will seek a fantasy object to help her through the individuation stage.[25] After the death of her father, Phoebe Ann Moses (born in 1860 and professionally known as Annie Oakley) was completely dependent upon her mother who was unable to provide for the family. The five-year-old child began to focus her attention on her father's rifle which hung over the mantle. She longed for her father but settled for his rifle which served as a reminder of his ability to control the outside world. Because her mother was unable to provide adequately for the family, young Annie sought the help of her father through the use of the rifle to provide meat for the table.[26]

According to Jessica Benjamin's investigation of the psychology of father-daughter relationships, the difficulty for a daughter at the separation stage is ambivalence between a desire for independence and fear of losing the security of her dependency on her mother.[27] This fear of separation for Annie Moses was compensated for by her association of the rifle with the dependency needs (i.e., finding something to eat) that she and her mother both shared. Even later, when Annie Oakley used rifles for competition rather than for hunting, she always sent the money she won back home to provide for her mother's comfort.[28]

Phoebe Ann Moses was only five when her father died, but her life was shaped by that loss. Phoebe Ann, later to become the world-renowned "Little Miss Sure Shot," was born in a log cabin in the backwoods of Ohio on August 13, 1860. As a small child, Annie tagged along with her father to hunt, trap, and work with the farm animals. She watched with intense interest as her father loaded the rifle, and he probably allowed her to assist him occasionally. She was fascinated by the weapon's power and was pleased with the meat it supplied for the family table.

The winter of 1866 was especially hard for this frontier family who grew low on supplies, and wild game and birds were scarce. When a break in the weather finally came in March, Jacob Moses rode into town. It was a dangerous time of year to travel, but the young family was without food. Tragically, Jacob was caught in a snow storm on the way home. His horse found its way home with the supplies, but the man was nearly frozen. He hung on for a few days but died before the family could get through the storm to send for a doctor. Annie was deeply touched by her father's death. Her mother taught her that her father had gone away to heaven. Annie believed that her father had died a heroic death to bring food and supplies home to his family, and he became a family legend.[29]

During the months following, the family learned more about hardships after losing their provider. Hunger was a constant threat. Mrs. Moses went to work, but she made little money and was gone a good deal of the time. Annie's older sister found employment with neighbors from whom she caught tuberculosis. In August she became the second member of the family to die while trying to provide for the family.

Little six-year-old Annie decided to do her share. She began to trap quail and longed for the day she could hunt rabbits with her father's rifle. She became quite skillful in supplementing the family diet. One day when her mother was out, Annie could no longer resist the temptation to bring down the rifle off the mantle. She practiced loading the powder and shot into the barrel and then quietly put the instrument back on the shelf. That night her mother discovered Annie's secret. After she swept off the mantle and tossed the powder and dust into the fireplace, Annie confessed what she had done. She insisted that she could "shoot rabbits they could eat" if her mother would just let her.[30] That was the beginning of Annie's shooting career.

Annie became an excellent markswoman and provided the table with a good supply of meat. Annie Moses had developed her skill for one purpose only: to provide food for her family. She felt a special obligation to take over her father's role in providing for her mother. To Annie, the rifle symbolized a special connection to her father especially since it became an important means for family survival.

After Susan married Dan Brumbaugh, life became a little easier for Annie and the rest of the family, and their happiness increased when a new baby was born. Little Emily became Annie's favorite, but she was not to enjoy her little companion for long. Brumbaugh died, and the family was again without a provider and short on supplies. Susan sent baby Emily to be raised by an aunt and uncle. Annie was then hired out to work at Mrs. Eddington's orphanage. Annie loved to sew clothes for all the orphans and was proud to put away a little cash for her mother.

Just when things were looking hopeful, Annie's life made another turn for the worse. A family came to Mrs. Eddington looking for a young girl to help them with work on their farm. They promised to allow her a good education and light chores. They wanted someone who could help look after their small children. Mrs. Eddington recommended Annie, and Susan agreed to the arrangement. Unfortunately, the family whom Annie later referred to as the "Wolves" lived a good distance from Annie's home, so she would not be able to visit her mother often.

In the Wolves' home she became a virtual slave. She was required not only to look after the children, but to work from early in the morning until late at night doing household and farm chores. Both Mr. and Mrs. "Wolf" were ill-natured and prone to beat Annie at the slightest provocation. Annie continued to work for the Wolves because she believed them when they deceitfully told her that her mother was still overburdened and could not care for her. They intercepted all correspondence between the young girl and her mother and sent letters of their own telling Susan how much Annie enjoyed her work and wished to stay longer.

After two years of their abuse and lies, Annie managed to escape. When she arrived home, she found that her mother had remarried, was living in a comfortable home. Susan had only left her daughter at the Wolves because she had naively believed the letters telling her Annie was very happy and preferred to stay another season to finish school. She was appalled at the bruises on the child's back and resolved never to send her children away again. The elderly gentleman her mother had married was good to Annie and all the children. Nevertheless, Annie still considered herself responsible for her mother's care. She continued to hunt birds and wild game and sold extra meat to a hotel in a nearby town.

It was from the hotel connection that her professional shooting career began. The hotel owner and Annie's brother-in-law set her up to challenge a famous competitor. The winner's pot was $50 and Annie always looked for extra cash to make her mother's life a little more comfortable and secure. The other contestant was Frank Butler. The family legend reports that Frank and Annie were tied shot after shot until Frank heard why Annie wished to win. Frank took a liking to the girl and figured she needed the money more than he. He missed the next shot, and Annie won.

Frank, who was ten years her senior, became Annie's mentor and close friend. Two months before Annie turned sixteen, she and Frank were married. They started out as a team of trick shooters that entertained audiences around the area. At that point, she chose her stage name of Annie Oakley.[31] After they joined Buffalo Bill Cody's Wild West show, however, Frank decided to become Annie's full time manager. He designed new stunts for her to perform, and her popularity confirmed the success of her career.

During all her fame, Oakley never forgot her childhood. Orphans held a special soft spot in her heart. Whenever she heard of an orphanage in towns where they performed, she persuaded Cody to let the children in free. Following the show, she would then treat them to ice cream. Another memory she never forgot was her self-assigned responsibility to her mother. Money won in every shooting competition was sent to her mother. Because of her daughter's concern, Susan was able to live a comfortable elderly life. In this manner, Oakley was able to maintain a dependent relationship with her mother, although the roles were reversed. The daughter was the provider while her mother accepted the role of the dependent.

Elyce Wakerman, author of *Father Loss*, has found this role reversal common among women whose fathers have died while they were still relatively young. Wakerman contends that the more passively accepting a mother is, the more she will expect to continue to be taken care after her husband's death. The daughter fears the loss of the second parent and is urgently willing to fulfill her mother's expectations. Therefore, both mother and daughter, "for her respective reasons, requires that the daughter assume the behavior of an adult." The result is that the "daughter's little-grown-up behavior comes to reflect a deeper determination: *not to be like mother.*"[32]

Girls who have lost their fathers tend to take on a new relationship with their mothers. On the one hand, the daughter will reject her mother for her powerlessness. If the girl experiences a close relationship with her father before his departure, she will often cling to the love and sense of achievement he may have instilled in her. Like Annie Oakley and her father's rifle, the daughter may seek to follow her father's example of power and accomplishment. It permits her to feel confident and be in control.

On the other hand, she also strives to please her mother, to behave, to be helpful. She does not want her second parent to leave her too. A young daughter in this situation adopts adult patterns of behavior. She feels the need to be mature and take control. After interviewing a large number of fatherless daughters, Elyce Wakerman concludes: "Particularly if she is an only child or the eldest sibling, the daughter of a single mother appoints herself…'the little man of the house.'"[33] This was the case with Phoebe Ann Moses and it was true for other western daughters as well, such as Kate Shelley.

Kate Shelley became the "man" of the family after her father died in 1878. She was "her mother's most dependable helper and guide to the younger children." Though only twelve years old, Kate took over the care of the animals and farm. She had learned from her father the skills and confidence to maintain the family homestead and provide for the family's needs. Although Kate Shelley did not have the advantage of a secure life with a living father, her father's special attention to her while he was still alive plus her mother's dependence on her gave her the self-confidence to carry on successfully as the family provider.[34]

When Kate was 15, she proved how brave and dependable she could be. One night, Kate and her mother observed a train wreck as the bridge in front of their house on Honey Creek, Iowa, collapsed during a flood. The young girl rushed to help the engineer and trainmen. She recognized them as friends of her father, but she was helpless to save them. Two of them were holding onto branches, but she could not reach them. She crossed the swollen, flooding river in the dark and rain on a narrow railroad bridge. Kate ran over a mile for help and to warn the agent to stop the midnight train before it reached the bridge.

When she arrived at the station drenched and winded, one gentlemen questioned the word of a child. Fortunately, the station manager recognized her and insisted that "Mike Shelley's kid would know."[35] The midnight train was contacted in time, and Kate Shelley was recognized as a hero.

For a long time, Shelley mourned the deaths of Engineer Pat Donahue and Fireman Olmstead. The men had been her friends and reminded her of special childhood days with her father. It was not easy for her to forget the tragedy, but there were chores to do, fuel to be cut and hauled, and potatoes to be harvested. The family looked to her for leadership and strength, and she gradually recovered from the trauma by concentrating on the chores and looking out "across the sunny valley."[36]

After her heroic night, several organizations, including the Chicago *Tribune* and C&NW Railroad raised money to help pay for the mortgage on the farm. Shelley also managed to earn a little money from speaking at various meetings. Her bravery had become a local legend, and in 1901 a new bridge was named for her. Rural schools hired Shelley to teach until she became the railroad station agent at Moingona in 1903. She felt at home in the "railroad world of timetables and tickets, lanterns and keys and train orders" that had made up her earliest and happiest childhood memories.[37]

Kate Shelley chose to become the "man" of the house because she had the memory of a strong role model. As the daughter's idealizing selfobject, Mike Shelley had helped her develop the self confidence she needed to be successful. She adopted his strong characteristics and achieved self-reliance. Through sheer bravery and determination, Shelley was able to save a train load of people and earn the respect of her community. More importantly, her every day leadership and dependability allowed the family to secure their home.

Loss of economic support from the traditional source of father and husband was a physical and emotional loss, but it did not translate into total devastation. In fact, in cases where women had the legal and economic opportunity to provide for themselves, death of a father or husband led to stronger self-reliance, confidence, and community participation. In spite of tragedy, the frontier West provided both Phoebe "Annie Oakley" Moses and Kate Shelley with opportunities to develop successful careers and maintain a sense of continuity with the self identity they had developed in early childhood under the guidance of loving, empathic fathers. These women are remembered not for their loss, but for their ability to rebound, make a success of their lives, and serve as strong role models for future generations.

Opposing the Victorian Role in Parenting Daughters

Women of the nineteenth century generally found it easier to accept their domestic role of dependency based on the ideals of the Cult of Domesticity rather than risk social ostracism by asserting their independence. This created a repetitive psycho-social pattern that represented the Victorian norm. Women were defined by their domestic dependency and reproductive roles while men were recognized as more autonomous and public-oriented. Men were expected to go outside the home to work and to provide income for the family. Children would follow this gender division of behavior.

Observations of men and women of the Victorian era led Sigmund Freud to describe the influence of parents on childhood development in terms of the Oedipus Complex.[38] During the Oedipal stage of development, boys and girls respond more readily to the parent of the opposite sex. Figuratively, the boy desires to "kill" his father to get him out of the way so that the boy may receive more of the mother's attention. The girl learns to be "daddy's girl" to experience his autonomy and receive his special attention. This theory was biased on the social norms of the era. Freud's theories about women, therefore, reflected the prevailing definitions of women's physical and intellectual inferiority. Victorian women were generally domestic and submissive and doomed to psychological instability if they did not follow the norm. Fathers of this period represented autonomy and love but accepted the social convention that their daughters would remain life-long dependents longing to love and be loved. Since there were few acceptable autonomous goals for women, the father's symbolic identity as an autonomous being was generally viewed as a fearful, exterior image rather than an idealized model.

Not all families, however, fell into this pattern. At times fathers needed or wanted daughters who were not strictly passive and domestic. In these cases the choice of independence overpowered the more socially acceptable role of submissive dependence. Social life for these women would not be comfortable, though, if their communities were not prepared to accept deviation from the Victorian norm. Assertive women of the East were generally ostracized and often suffered from psychosomatic disorders such as headaches and depression when they tried to pursue non-domestic goals. Such was the case with Margaret Fuller.

Margaret's father, Timothy Fuller, believed strongly in education and wished for a son. Disappointed that his first child born in 1810 was a girl, he nevertheless broke the traditions of female education and tutored her with the strongest classical education possible. At age six, instead of learning needlepoint like other girls her age, Margaret learned Latin and read only classic literature. Her father gave her the same rigid education that boys had received a century earlier. Timothy wanted an educated daughter. As a result, Margaret indeed became very knowledgeable and independent; however, she had difficulty finding an acceptable social niche.[39] As a well-educated young woman, Fuller stood out in sharp contrast to her refined and conformist classmates. She initially rebelled at her unusual upbringing because she wanted to be popular with the other girls at the young ladies school she attended during her teens. However, her self-will was too strong to be like them.

The lives of other women fascinated her. Besides observing their dress and behavior, the affection-starved woman often spent hours listening to the emotional and marital problems of others. Fuller believed in both the heart and the intellect of women and encouraged them to do whatever they wanted even if they wanted to be sea captains. With some of her closest friends—both male and female—she would exchange letters in which both she and they searched for self-knowledge and self-realization. With men, she could hold profound, intellectual discussions. She had a long list of brotherly companions with whom she never advanced beyond a platonic friendship.

Fuller became a respected member of several male-dominated intellectual groups but struggled with what path her life should take. She tried writing fiction but received disapproval from the friends she wrote about. This led to a period of migraine headaches, spinal weaknesses, and depression. Then her father paid her a subtle but much needed compliment. He told her that he did not believe she had any faults—defects of course, but no real faults. She recovered shortly thereafter.

She suffered another transitional period after her religious conversion when she accepted her duty to submit to the domestic duties of caring for and tutoring her younger brothers and sisters. For the first time in her life, she experienced the joy of conformity: "I saw there was no self; that selfishness was all folly, and the result of circumstance; that it was only because I thought self real that I suffered, that I had only to live in the idea of the All…"[40] The joy, though short-lived and self-destructive, was important to the family survival at this point in her life.

Fuller found few socially acceptable options to achieve self-realization when she pursued intellectual interests. One potential position, however, became available when she served as her father's secretary and companion. Timothy was proud of his daughter's education and wanted to put it to use. For Margaret, this occupation was ideal. She could use her intellect but contain it within the acceptable parameters of True Womanhood. In terms of proper social behavior, she was serving her father. Unfortunately, Timothy died in 1835 before this new relationship had a chance to make a substantial impact on her professional career.

After her father died, Fuller searched for a mentor and a lover. Potential lovers rejected her, and she began to accept celibacy as a higher order of life. Mentors were easier to find than lovers. Bronson Alcott believed her to be an excellent teacher and encouraged her to begin a career as an educator. Horace Greeley promoted her ability to write critical reviews and hired her to work for his paper in New York. In these reviews, she was just as demanding and unmerciful on American writers as her father had been toward her educational performance. Like her father, she insisted that only the highest standards for literature were acceptable.

Following her journalistic career, Margaret Fuller began working with women and set up lecture and discussion sessions. During these "Conversations," she encouraged women to do whatever they wanted with their lives. This included anything as common as marriage to something as risky and daring as teaching school in the West. As a literary critic, she had insisted that American writers treat women realistically and intelligently. In her book *Woman in the Nineteenth*

Century, published in 1845, Fuller emphasized that women had the same intellectual abilities and will as men. She stressed that women should also have the same opportunities for self-realization and achievement.[41] This book provided rationalization for the demands that woman's rights activists would use during the Seneca Falls Convention of 1848.

The relationship between Margaret Fuller and her father was intellectually stimulating but socially devastating because of the traditions and restrictions of her environment. The Cult of True Womanhood confined women of Fuller's society to a life of domesticity. Had her culture been less gender divided, she may have appreciated her upbringing more and found herself less of a social misfit. Instead she had to limit her talents while living on the margin of acceptability.

Fuller's book *Woman in Nineteenth Century* had a strong impact on future woman's rights leaders. However, the ideas she advocated were considered radical and dangerous to the general good. Victorian society did not know how to cope with women who refused to submit to their domestic duties. Nevertheless, change began to take place once adventurous pioneers to the unsettled American West adopted radical ideas and evolved them into a practical way of living acceptable to both women and men.

Timothy Fuller was ahead of his time. He believed his daughter capable of intellectual pursuits, and she proved him correct. Fuller represents a role of fatherhood that is important to the development of daughters as well as sons. This role has been documented in certain situations where social or political conditions required more endeavor-oriented relations between fathers and daughters instead of the traditional dependency relationship. Daughters worked with or for their fathers in non-domestic activities that did not automatically give way to the feminine tradition. There is evidence that this occurred in exceptional cases and during traumatic events even before the trans-Mississippi crossing. During the colonial period, Eliza Lucas believed her commitment to running her father's plantation took precedence over her domestic role as wife and mother.[42] During the Civil War, many young southern women quite ably took over the operation of the farms and plantations when their fathers and husbands enlisted.[43] No occasion, however, had the scope or duration of the new standards of female behavior that was established by the non-traditional generation of western women. They grew up with fathers who served a role in their development that did not fit the Victorian pattern, nor did the Oedipus complex apply. A different role of fatherhood emerged in the American West.

Fathers' Historical Roles

The role of fatherhood has been relatively ignored, and very little historical or theoretical material on father-daughter relationships is available.[44] In a 1986 essay on fatherhood, John Demos argues that "fatherhood has a very long history, but virtually no historians."[45] It is generally accepted that female bonding between young girls and their mothers, aunts, and grandmothers during the Victorian period was a common principle.[46] The patriarchal role of fathers which was practiced in earlier centuries had lost much of its influence.

Recent interest in this subject has initiated exploration into the dimensions of fatherhood beyond the role of the patriarch. Work in the field of family history has indicated that the role of the father in England and the United States changed significantly from the sixteenth and seventeenth centuries to the nineteenth and twentieth centuries with the late eighteenth and nineteenth centuries as the transitional period. Before the 1800s, fathers were considered patriarchal and the ultimate authority in child-rearing practices, but by the end of the century, mothers were clearly seen as the primary caretakers of children.[47]

In his book *At Odds: Women and Family in America from the Revolution to the Present*, Carl Degler identifies three logical and interrelated reasons why this shift from fathers to mothers occurred. One was a changing philosophy in regard to children; a second was the separation of gender spheres which increasingly restricted women to domesticity; and a third was the industrial revolution.[48]

According to family historians, children in the sixteenth to eighteenth centuries were viewed as miniature adults. They were given tasks and responsibilities as soon as they were able to perform them and were treated as inferior adults.[49] This practice, based on the old Christian philosophy that children were born into sin and the will of the child must be broken, was gradually replaced with the notion of *tabula rasa*, that a child was innocent at birth, a blank slate that must be shaped and molded. The childhood innocence philosophy was made popular by Jean Jacques Rousseau's renowned book *Emile* (1762). Rousseau believed that in the natural order of life children should be children before they become adults.[50]

The second and third reasons for the shift from patriarchal fatherhood to mother love are closely interrelated: industrialization and women's domesticity. The increasingly specialized role of women's domesticity and separation of spheres came about primarily as a result of industrialization. When productivity was taken out of the home and moved to centralized locations, the distinctions between gender spheres of influence were intensified. Men spent most of their work and social life outside the home while women were increasingly confined within domestic boundaries. In addition, industrialization, according to Degler, began "removing or simplifying some of women's traditional duties in the home."

This allowed her more time to specialize in "the proper rearing of offspring." Degler saw this as a positive, enlightened change: "Exalting the child went hand in hand with exalting the domestic role of woman; each reinforced the other while together they raised domesticity within the family to a new and higher level of respectability." He concludes that it was not "accidental" that "the century of the child is also the century of the Cult of True Womanhood."[51]

Mary Ryan essentially concurs with Degler's conclusions, but she discovered that the transition did not occur in New York until the nineteenth century. This was soon after the Second Great Awakening of religious fervor but before industrialization took over frontier communities. Ryan contends that the result of the new specialization in childhood and mothering set a "new direction and pace to the course of the human life cycle." She suggests that the "idea of fatherhood" began to "wither away" as it was replaced by the mother-child bond. "Mother love" became the new "linchpin" whereby children were socialized. It meant that the old "patriarchal will-breaking" would be replaced with "mother's tender ministrations" and the innocent male child could be guided gradually from the "maternal cocoon" into "the wider, more masculine and grueling universe."[52]

This pattern was carried over into community affairs and a variety of new social organizations. Ryan contends that a reorganization of social reproduction occurred whereby new associations—such as the Young Men's Association, the Maternal Association, the Republican Club, and the Female Moral Reform Society—"could act as a substitute for the family." In almost every case, Ryan found that the organization "contradicted patriarchal notions of family order and honored a new set of social values." One such change was that "stern reverence to elders" was replaced with "affectionate bonds between peers."[53] These organizations tended to promote separate spheres between men and women.

When patriarchal authority gave way to a new family and social orientation based on the influence of mother love, the role of the father was redefined and new behavior was expected. John Demos claims that the "wrenching apart of work and home-life is one of the great themes in social history." The roles of father shifted from "father as pedagogue," "father as moral overseer," and "father as companion," to part-time roles such as "father as playmate," "father as psychologist," and "father as example." The father's role as provider was his central role, and his "product" or income became more important and better known to family members than what he did in his shop or office. What father did outside the home was "mysterious and wonderful" because the details were unknown, but the results (i.e. the income) allowed for family needs and wants. His "mysterious" mastery of the outside world and his "intrinsic connection to all that lay outside home gave him a special status within it." His "sacrifices," "experience," "risks," and "recognition" in the outside world "made his opinions especially worthy to be heard (and accepted), his orders to be followed." On the other hand, his mysteriousness and unique relationship with the outer world could lead to misunderstandings, fear, and distrust in family members who were left behind in the home.[54]

While some measures of patriarchal authority were preserved, particularly in certain religious households, nineteenth-century mothers emerged as the primary parent responsible for child-rearing. Fathers were assumed to be out of the home, and therefore, out of control of their children for the majority of the day. Still, fathers were expected to gradually take over the molding of boys into manhood and to help their sons settle into worthy occupations. Degler indicates that mother's role was central to the child's early years, at least until puberty, after which the father's role expanded "especially on the farm" and "especially with his sons." Daughters, on the other hand, continued to be guided by their mothers toward their proper gender role. Degler concludes that while father's role became "relatively democratic," it also played a smaller part as men's work led to their absence from the home.[55]

Psychology and the Role of Fathers

Both Carl Degler and John Demos have suggested that fathers served only part-time roles as parents and that fathers had little impact on children until their sons reached puberty.[56] The corollary to this is that fathers had little influence over daughters. In *The Reproductions of Mothering* Nancy Chodorow concurs with the notion of the relative insignificance of fathers, especially for daughters. However, she acknowledges that fathers play a secondary role during the Oedipal stage of development for both boys and girls. It is believed that at this stage fathers help the child establish a new relationship with the mother that is less dependent upon her. The child also begins to learn behavior necessary for the regeneration of heterosexual relationships. Chodorow believes this Oedipal phase to be a socially reproduced pattern rather than a biological drive as defined by Freud. [57]

The central theory Chodorow sets forth in *The Reproduction of Mothering* is that the female personality is based on the cyclical pattern of mothering. She contends that women produce daughters who will become mothers and sons who will not "mother." Because mothers are the primary caretakers, a division of psychological capacities occur and are reproduced with each generation. This, Chodorow emphasizes, is a socially-induced, structured, psychological process. As a result, cultural practice has created a female personality based on retention and continuity of external relationships. Boys, on the other hand, define themselves as more separate and distinct, with a greater sense of rigid ego boundaries and differentiation. Chodorow suggests that the positive side to this social reproductive cycle is that women have learned to accept and to be fulfilled by the mothering role. The negative side is the creation of "a psychology of male dominance and fear of women in men." As a result, the "social world" is divided into "unequally valued domestic and public spheres, each the providence of people of a different gender."[58]

Chodorow's observations of the feminine cycle, based on Freud's Oedipal Complex, fails to account for the developmental pattern of all women, particularly the non-traditional generation of western women. First, it assumes the mother to be the primary caretaker and role model. Second, it fails to consider environmental factors that modify parental roles.

The Oedipal pattern of social control and feminine adherence to a domestic identity which has been associated with the first generation of frontier women proved to be less typical for their daughters.[59] Women who adhered to the Oedipal or Victorian model of womanhood did not excel in the western environment. Since non-traditional western women were not surrounded by the rigid social conventions of their mothers' upbringing, they could more easily reject the Victorian norm and go beyond the limitations of submission and domesticity. Thus, the reproduction of mothering and the ideology of domesticity were not automatically passed down from mother to daughter during the westering experience.

When the Victorian pattern failed to shape the lives of the non-traditional generation, an alternative pattern of development emerged which focused more on fathers, father substitutes, and male mentors. Men played a more important role for this generation than was prescribed by the Victorian formula. Fathers treated their daughters more like sons and provided them with the skills and motivation to go beyond domesticity. This was a result of the development of the inner "self" and the environmental factors and relationships that shaped that development.

That inner self has been described by Heinz Kohut in *Self Psychology*[60] and Ernest S. Wolf in *Treating the Self*. Self psychologists contend that an individual needs to organize an inner psychological self into a "cohesive" identity. This self learns to deal with the environment by establishing "self-sustaining relationships"[61] In other words, all the components that give a person a sense of his or her separate existence are the factors that compose that individual's *self*. These include influential people, especially parents, and are called *self-objects* because they are viewed in reference to the development of the *inner self*.

For the first generation of western women, the self-objects were usually mothers, aunts, or grandmothers. Their self identities tended to emerge in a domestic-oriented behavior with feminine-defined goals, thus maintaining the reproduction of mothering as described by Chodorow. For the non-traditional daughters, however, mothers were often sick, disturbed, and unable to adapt to the new environment. Aunts and grandmothers were unavailable and neighbors were often several miles away and predominantly male. Therefore, the mirroring self-objects were frequently fathers or father substitutes, and idealizing figures included strong influences of fathers, older brothers, uncles, male mentors, and public-oriented women.

As a result of the stronger male influence on non-traditional daughters at a young age, western women were better prepared for more public-oriented lives and what formerly had been considered men's work. Lora Heims Tessman, a psychoanalyst who has researched father-daughter relationships, identifies the father-influenced phase as *endeavor excitement* and contends that it signifies an important stage in the daughter's development.[62] Tessman contends that around age two, both boys and girls begin a process of separation from the mothering symbiosis. This is where the father or father substitute becomes particularly important. A healthy relationship with the father figure at this stage in a girl's development helps her individuate from her mother and begin asserting her independent identity. In a healthy environment, the father works and plays with the child. He teaches her that her new mobility and simple acts of independence are valuable, and he tries to instill in her a sense of confidence. This first role of the father, then, affects the autonomy and success (or failure) in the daughter's work life and achievements.

In Victorian society, the father's endeavor role with daughters was considered insignificant. In cases where fathers did instill an achievement orientation in their daughters that went beyond domestic pursuits, the daughter often faced a reversal during her adolescent years as in the case of Margaret Fuller. Fathers usually expected their favorite daughters to adapt normal feminine behavior once they reached puberty as in the case of Catharine Beecher (introduced in Chapter One). Daughters who continued to be encouraged by fathers to follow professional endeavors were faced with a maladaptive environment. "Decent" women were not allowed to compete with men. The daughter's social and mental stability was shaken if she did not adapt.[63] Thus, the Oedipal Conflict seemed to be the appropriate role of fathers in Victorian culture.

Daughters in the West, on the other hand, could translate their *endeavor excitement* into feminine models that went beyond the old domestic patterns and opened up new avenues formerly reserved for men. The effectiveness of their endeavor excitement and the father-daughter relationship is revealed in what Tessman describes as the young woman's *intentionality*. "Intentionality," is the ability for an individual to "experience and transform excitement into vitality of involvement." Low intentionality occurs when the father is uninvolved and uninterested or shows pride in the daughter's developmental activities but does not participate.[64] In contrast, high intentionality toward non-traditional goals was a common characteristic of non-traditional western women. These women believed they could achieve valuable careers and were confident that they could overcome traditional obstacles.

What Tessman has introduced as *endeavor excitement,* Jessica Benjamin calls *identificatory love.* Benjamin's ground-breaking interpretation of father-daughter relationships focuses on the importance of the role of the father when children are torn between their fear of separation from mother and their desire to be independent. The conflict rages between their dependency and security *needs* represented by the mother and their independency *wants and desires* and adventure which are represented by the father. Benjamin contends that "identification with the father is a vehicle for avoiding conflict as well as for separation, for denying helplessness and the loss of practicing grandiosity." [65]

The daughter's dependency vs. independency conflict can be alleviated, according to Benjamin, if the father fulfills a twofold duty. First, he must accept his role as the idealized model. He symbolizes the child's longing for autonomy and the excitement of the outside world. Secondly, he must provide direct recognition through approval and confirmation of the child's efforts to separate from the attachment figure of the mothering symbiosis. The father's response is critical at this point if the process of identification is to be reciprocated. The father at this stage in the child's life becomes "the mirror of desire." Assuming that environmental situations allow the father's availability and willingness to be idealized, and assuming that the identification process is reciprocated, the gains the child receives from identifying with the father are twofold. First, through *"direct recognition,"* the child receives approval and confirmation (which is similar to Tessman's theory of endeavor excitement). Secondly and indirectly, the child also receives "recognition through *symbolic identification*"; that is, the father provides a model the child wishes to imitate. In this manner, the father figure becomes the powerful object that the child idealizes.[66]

Whether or not this modeling pattern occurs between fathers and daughters depends a great deal on whether or not the father reciprocates the daughter's need for identificatory love.[67] In general, fathers are more likely to identify with their sons, and boys usually spend more time with their fathers than do daughters. When, however, a father figure takes a special interest in the development of a young girl's intellect, talent, or skills (as opposed to limiting his interest to her normal heterosexual development as defined by Freud's Oedipal theory), he serves as the autonomous role model that girls as well as boys need in order to separate from the dependency role they have maintained with their mothers. This occurred frequently with the assertive daughters of the West.

Once identificatory love was established between the non-traditional daughter and her father or father figure in the westering experience, the social situation allowed a healthy self-identity to emerge from the idealized relationship. Social, economic, and physical factors in the West allowed the father or father substitute time to spend with his daughter and serve as her role model.[68]

The difference for the non-traditional daughters from their Victorian counterparts was the role of the environment in allowing the necessary role of the father. First, the environment determined what role models and idealized models were available to the young girl. Second, the environment affected how well and how often the idealized person could serve as a model. Third, the environmental situation determined how long that particular person could continue to serve as the role model. Fourth, grandparents, as representatives of social tradition, were a symbolic factor in the modeling pattern. When grandparents and others of the older generation are not available as in the West, traditional ideals and behavior were less likely to be reinforced.

The social and economic environment of the frontier West where gender divisions of labor were not strictly enforced allowed daughters to have a more equal relationship with fathers. Since a greater majority of time was spent outdoors, fathers had a stronger influence over the daily behavior of their children. Daughters were neither confined to household duties nor restricted to female-centered activities.[69]

The environment of the frontier West represented a *configurative culture*. This is Margaret Mead's classification for new environmental conditions in which children and adolescents are placed in situations (through migration or domination by another culture) where they must learn to adapt to new circumstances. Because their own parents did not experience the new environment in their youth (and which they never expect to fully adapt to), they cannot provide the model by which the children learn to adapt. Children, therefore, must be taught by their peers. Grandparents are generally absent, or if present, their old ways of life are no longer applicable to the new conditions.[70]

Margaret Mead has determined that the availability of grandparents in traditional, gender-divided societies helps the new generation to accept their predetermined roles and gender-defined place in that society. Parents provide the working models while grandparents confirm the continuity of the culture. Mead classifies this as a *postfigurative culture*. In this setting, change is rare and gradual and is absorbed into the culture smoothly by being transformed into older forms that people accept as the continuing order of life.[71]

The Victorian culture of the eastern United States could be considered a postfigurative culture in terms of gender orientation. Although civilization was going through rapid change in terms of industrialization and urbanization, people attempted to transform the new into older forms of organization. In particular, gender roles, based on earlier patterns of gender orientation in which women were characteristically responsible for small children and household duties, became even more distinct. In such a gender-divided society, the father was customarily away from home most of the day. If he found time to interact with his daughter, he was generally expected to teach her to be dependent and submissive. Departures from this prescribed pattern caused the daughter to suffer social disapproval. She learned either to conform to established social standards, to accept herself as a social deviant, or suffer the psychological consequences.[72]

Mead contends that "conflict between generations" when cultural and environmental conditions change "arises when the new methods of rearing the children are found to be insufficient or inappropriate for the formation of a style of adulthood" [e.g., one based on old cultural ideals and values] "to which the first generation, the pioneers, had hoped their children would follow."[73]

In a configuration culture such as the frontier West, new forms of role models became necessary. Because girls spent more time in the outdoors, fathers and other male mentors were readily available role models. Female teachers, women missionaries, and other working women also had potential as idealizable objects who presented alternatives, especially when the domestic model (i.e., mothers) appeared to be too weak, fragile, or otherwise restricted.

The effectiveness of male and unusually autonomous female models depended upon the level to which the new frontier settlement had become "civilized." Did Victorian culture have the time and organizational factors necessary to dominate the more natural conditions? For example, was it important that the daughter herd and watch the livestock, or was it more important that she stay inside to protect her delicate face from freckles while she sewed linens for her future household? If the livestock were more important, then the father would have more influence over his daughter's time. If, however, preparations for a domestic future took precedence, then the mother would captivate most of the daughter's time and talents.

Father Influence in the West

How long role models would serve for daughters depended upon the environment and social conditions. Many fathers and father substitutes had an early impact on daughters' lives even in the East. Many young girls found that their fathers or grandfathers encouraged them to be autonomous and assertive and to explore their abilities outside the domestic tradition. The father influence on character development of daughters was less stressful for girls in the American

West because gender divisions of labor were not strictly upheld. Of course, some girls stayed in the house and helped their mothers, but others spent more time with their fathers. Barbara Davis, a Colorado ranch woman recalls: "I went with my father right from the start. My older sister would help in the house, but I tagged along with Dad."[74] Later, she and a younger sister helped with the ranch work.

The western girl did not have to be brotherless to get her father's attention. Carole Horn was the only girl in a family of boys, but she spent more time with her father than her mother. She believed herself to be "the apple of Dad's eye," and she loved to be outdoors with him. Horn's father took her everywhere with him. "When I was tiny, he'd set me up on one of the workhorses and we'd scrape out a ditch..." Father and daughter shared ranch chores with enthusiasm: "I think Dad took a lot more time teaching me things than he did with the boys because I was enthusiastic about it."[75]

It was not always easy to break feminine traditions. Westerners were occasionally reminded of the more rigid gender lines drawn by their eastern relatives. Marie Bell, a Wyoming rancher, learned of the regional differences as a young girl. Her mother was new to the land and adapted her domestic training to her new home. She cooked for the family and the ranch hands and raised flowers, but she refused to ride horses. The daughter, however, was not confined to the household. As a girl, Bell helped her mother with the domestic chores but preferred to "work out" helping her father run the ranch. Her mother, who had been raised in the East, thought her daughter should be helping out more in the house, but "she never objected to me riding so much and helping my dad." The big objection came from Bell's visiting grandmother from the East. Grandma scolded her own daughter because her granddaughter spent so much time riding with the boys. "She thought Mama should keep me in and make me a lady." Grandma went so far as to charge her son-in-law with "making a boy" out of her granddaughter. She insisted it was not proper. Bell's father replied that Marie "was his daughter and he would raise [her] the way he saw fit." That was the end of the discussion.[76]

These examples illustrate that western society was more tolerant of females who participated in a variety of roles. Once encouraged, the western woman could find her niche in the public sphere. There were still ties to old, eastern social customs, but these were not strongly enforced. For example, pioneer women would insist that their daughters wear sunbonnets to protect their fair complexions. The young girls, though, preferred to run across the prairie with the wind blowing through their hair and the bonnet flopping on their back. Children were not worried about freckles and had no formal society where they would be on display. As far as they were concerned, bonnets were just a nuisance. Such displays of female independence frequently outweighed submissive domesticity in the "uncivilized" society of the West.

One important difference between eastern and western women was the matter of career choice. Western women could remain completely domestic, but if they chose to compete in male-dominated occupations, they simply had to prove themselves capable. For example, two ranch sisters recalled the episode that proved they were respected in the male-dominated occupation they had chosen for their career. They were such good cow hands that a neighbor asked for their help in a cattle roundup. They were in the middle of helping their father shuck grain, but the neighbor promised to send a couple of his men over in exchange for the girls' help. Elsie and Amy Cooksley were pleased because they preferred riding to all other chores. They felt honored, too, because the cowboys treated them as equals—or maybe with just a little more respect because the cowboys never swore around them or told dirty stories. The ultimate proof of the cowboys' acceptance of them, Amy recalls, was when the cowboys refused to eat with two refined ladies that came to the ranch for dinner. The cowboys felt uncomfortable around prim and proper behavior. One of them said, "I don't mind Amy and Elsie and the rest of the boys. But I'm not going in with those women."[77]

Ranching was not the only career choice for western women. A famous early photographer from the West achieved her fame because her father was willing to support her ambition. Imogen Cunningham (introduced earlier) was born in Portland, Oregon in 1883. Her "mild, passive" mother wanted Cunningham to get married and settle down to domestic life. Her father wanted her to have the economic security of a teaching career. Cunningham, however, had enough self-will to pursue her interests in art and photography. Her father did not always approve of her career decisions, but he never failed to supply her with the materials and education she needed to improve her talents.[78]

While still quite young, she convinced her father to buy her watercolors. Later, because he was pleased with her ability, he enrolled her in a private art class. When she turned to photography (after viewing one of Alfred Stieglitz's student's work in a trade magazine), her father built her a special hut for her dark room. Her interest in photographic development led to college chemistry. This thrilled her father because he believed she would receive a strong education to help her toward a teaching job. Cunningham, on the other hand, only wished to pursue her fascination with photography.[79]

Emily Swett Parkhurst was another western woman who succeeded because of her father's interest in her development. Her father, John Swett, was a strong role model. An emigrant from the East to California during the gold rush, he tried to make money in mining but found greater satisfaction in helping build the California school system. He served as State Superintendent of Public Instruction from 1863–1868 and promoted a state-supported normal school for teacher training. Swett believed that "one great cause of the evident superiority of our American Common schools over the primary schools of Europe is the employment of female teachers."[80] But he also believed that even college graduates needed special training in order to become better teachers. The purpose of this deliberate emphasis on methodology was to elevate educational careers. "Higher professional training," he argued, "would raise the business of teaching to the rank of a noble profession."[81]

It was in this setting that Swett's daughter Emily attended the normal school in San Francisco and hoped to be a teacher. She graduated valedictorian of her class in 1881. However, even with this high achievement and the political clout of her father in the education system, there were no teaching jobs available.

Like her father, she had the strength and confidence to adapt to the circumstances and called on other personal abilities and ambitions. She nurtured her writing talent and promoted publication as an important vocation for women. She established a literary bureau and organized the Pacific Coast Women's Press Association to help not only her own career but to advance the profession of other women as well. Emily Parkhurst helped many west coast women become self-supporting who, previous to her efforts, received little to no recognition for their literary work. Her support network of writers "encourage[d] women to make a fight for themselves."[82]

These are examples of women who excelled in their independence to pursue their talents. The difference between them and those who remained predominantly submissive and domestic is based primarily in who (or what) they idealized as they went through the stages of development of their self-identity. Emily Swett and Imogen Cunningham received the support of their fathers who encouraged them to cultivate their talents and pursue professional careers. Another important consideration was to what degree the social environment allowed women to advance their independent identity. Margaret Fuller also had the support and encouragement of her father to seek her independence, but her environment provided no respectable career opportunities for women outside of marriage and family.

Career-minded women such as Emily Parkhurst, Imogen Cunningham, and Catherine Beecher had a greater opportunity for self-fulfillment in the West. Evidence of their experiences indicates that the well-balanced, cohesive self-identity of the independent woman began with a strong "mirroring" relationship with her mother. This supportive reflection would help her to gain awareness of her independent existence and gradual separation from her mother. If this early stage with her female parent failed, however, she had a second chance to develop a cohesive self with a caring, empathic relationship with her father. In this stage of the daughter's development, the father served as an idealizing parent imago. In other words, he provided the model of strength and confidence that the daughter could gradually build into her own individual identity. Only the less restrictive social environment of the frontier West would permit this type of father-daughter relationship to develop into a socially acceptable adult pattern of a non-domestic career orientation.

In contrast to nineteenth century eastern civilization, the social conditions of the American West prompted a different but important developmental pattern for women. The difference in the two patterns was not only induced by but also had a significant effect on the community. Environmental and social conditions, to a large degree, determined how parents raised their children (i.e., whether they would serve as empathic, "mirroring" and idealizing self-objects; and whether or not they would allow the child to develop smoothly through the separation/individuation stage.)

In the East, most parents followed the Victorian pattern, and children went through the Oedipal phase in much the manner that Freud observed. However, in households where unusual patterns occurred—such as in families where no healthy and intelligent sons lived through infancy, or one daughter proved to be exceptional and a special favorite of her father for one reason or another—then another pattern often occurred. In this case, the daughter might grow up with an unusual degree of autonomy. If her social environment adhered to Victorian principles, she, like Margaret Fuller, would discover during adolescence or early adulthood that there was no acceptable place for her to practice her special abilities beyond the domestic, feminine realm. If, on the other hand, she lived in an area during a time when her exceptionality was needed and thus acceptable as did Emily Swett Parkhurst, then her self-development and talents would be a fortunate asset.

The West, with its long continuing frontier, was the symbolic haven for independent individuals. The independent, male pioneers and adventurers have been widely documented, but the West promoted the independent female as well. Much of the pattern of female independence can be attributed to fathers and male mentors who took a special interest in the development of young girls. They hoped to prepare them for a future in which men and husbands were not always present or dependable. In cases where a woman was particularly strong and determined, she could either force her way into a niche or create a new one to specifically fit her needs. Clearly, women of the West had more legal freedom and career opportunities than did eastern women. A large proportion of western women managed to develop their personal talents and skills and enter the public world on an equal footing to men. However, some of the credit goes to their fathers. In an era when social custom made it necessary for women to be predominantly domestic and submissive, fathers (rather than mothers) served as a girl's role model to go beyond the restricted sphere of domesticity.

Chapter Three

New Directions for Assertive Women

You younger women will have a harder task than ours. You will want equality in business and it will be even harder to get than the vote, for you will have to fight for it as individuals and that will not get you far. Women will not unite, since they will be competitors with each other. As soon as a woman has it for herself she will have entered the man's world and cease to fight as a woman for other women.

~Dr. Anna Shaw, 1920

The unique environment of Utah Territory was exceptionally conducive to the development of much needed women professionals, especially in the medical field. Brigham Young frequently and publicly encouraged women of the Mormon church to educate and improve themselves. In one of his sermons in October 1873, he announced that it was time for women doctors. He was probably influenced by Eliza R. Snow, a leading woman of the church, who had argued that women should be trained as doctors so that male doctors would not have to be called in for problem cases in birthing.[1]

The declaration came at a particularly impressionable time for a former member of the Young household. Ellis Reynolds Shipp had just lost her young daughter Anna, the namesake of her own mother who had died when she was fourteen. Shipp reflected on the needless deaths of her mother years ago and now her daughter. She believed that such tragedies could be alleviated if more trained medical care was available.

Ellis Reynolds migrated to Salt Lake with her parents in 1852 when she was only five years old. They came with a group of Mormons to find refuge in the Mormon capital. Her mother died nine years later from a lack of adequate medical care. Poems written many years later describe Anna as a frail, loving, and domestic mother.[2] After her father remarried, Ellis moved in with her grandparents at Battle Creek south of Salt Lake. Grandfather William Hawley was her childhood hero. She was fascinated by his ability to help care for the injured. He had gone to medical school for only a few months but knew how to set bones. She later confessed: "I learned more from Grandfather about setting bones than I did in college."[3]

Ellis Shipp did not answer her medical calling immediately after Brigham Young's sermon. Instead, it was decided that Maggie, her sister-wife (i.e., one of the other wives of her polygamous marriage), would go as soon as she weaned her baby. Ellis, as the first wife of a polygamous marriage, had to consider what was best for the extended family. She had married Milford Shipp in 1866 even though Brigham Young, her guardian at the time, did not approve. Milford was eleven years her senior and twice divorced. At age nineteen, however, she was enchanted by his ambition and energy and was fascinated by his power of language. He gradually married other wives and they lived together in one household. Fortunately, the wives were able to care for each other and view each other as "sisters."

There were advantages and disadvantages to the marriage. One of the first disappointments Ellis faced within a year after her wedding was the move away from Salt Lake and her contact with the "Beehive House." Brigham Young had invited her to live in his household and attend school after she turned seventeen. She loved her lessons and the social life of his home, but gave it up to spend her life with Milford Shipp. When they moved to Fillmore, Ellis felt isolated until three sister-wives were added to the family.

With the other women sharing her home and responsibilities, she found it a little easier to carry out Brigham Young's recommendation that women within the mountain refuge improve themselves and work together with the resources that were available. In order to continue her self-education, however, Shipp arose early to begin her daily reading schedule from 4:00 to 7:00 a.m. She became particularly close to her sister-wife Maggie who shared her interest in accumulating every tidbit of medical advice they could to alleviate the pain and misery of the sick and injured.[4]

Maggie was chosen first to attend medical school in Philadelphia in the winter of 1874, but she became so homesick within a month that she returned home. Ellis immediately left by train to take Maggie's place since the tuition was already paid. Although she, too, missed her children, she did not worry about them since they remained in the protective care of her sister-wives. This was the second advantage of her polygamous marriage.

Ellis Shipp graduated with honors from the Woman's Medical College of Pennsylvania in 1878. When she returned home after graduation, she moved into a separate home for herself, three sons, and one daughter where she could open an office. Dr. E. R. Shipp advertised in local papers as a physician and surgeon with "Special attention given to Obstetrics, diseases of women and minor surgery."[5] Dr. Shipp was extremely dedicated to her profession, and private practice proved to be only the beginning. She opened her own School of Obstetrics and Nursing in Salt Lake City. Her students came from Mormon settlements throughout the West.

In 1893, she spent a year of postgraduate work at the University of Michigan Medical School. Shipp was soon recognized as one of the best-educated physicians in the state, and male doctors did not hesitate to consult with her. She traveled throughout Mormon communities in Utah, Idaho, Arizona, Canada, and Mexico to conduct classes where little professional medicine was available. She was also devoted to breaking down some of the Victorian barriers that caused women to distrust male doctors. Male physicians were invited into her classes to convince her students that modesty could be dangerous when it interfered with the health of a woman or her children.[6]

Shipp continuously agonized over the deaths of women and children, including her own. Of the ten children she bore, only five survived. She knew her work alone was not enough and influenced her husband and a sister-wife to become physicians. She taught anyone who showed an interest how to alleviate suffering. During more than fifty years of medical service, she attended around 5,000 births and trained several hundred midwives who attended thousands of other births. Her two sons were inspired by her dedication, and completed degrees in medicine and law. Her three daughters also followed her professional model by completing their educations at the Universities of Utah and Michigan, and one earned a master's degree from Columbia.[7]

Ellis Shipp was intelligent, energetic, and inquisitive by nature, but it was her family and environment that encouraged her to excel in a profession that was traditionally reserved for men. She grew up with loving parents who gave her a strong sense of confidence and well-being. Her mother's tragic death when Ellis was only fourteen began to set the stage for her future career. First, she became sadly concerned with suffering and death and then learned from her grandfather how to care for the sick and injured. During her youth, she was recognized by her church leader, Brigham Young, as an exceptionally bright young woman. She once confessed that after leaving the Young household, she "began to realize most fully the blessings of work and mental activities."[8]

Young's concern for her was reinforced by his general attitude that encouraged the advancement of women. Because there was a shortage of qualified doctors, Shipp and other women were encouraged to attend medical school and found a busy practice awaiting them following their graduation. The western environment and the Mormon community made it easy, even desirable, for Ellis Shipp to go beyond the traditional limitations of domesticity and become actively involved in a male-dominated career. She had an internal child care service with her sister-wives to help raise her children while she attended school and a church-supported practice once she graduated.

Moving toward the Public Sphere

The third stage in the evolution toward equality was the blending of gender roles. While the first generation was raised by women and was taught domestic chores and feminine culture that was clearly separate from men's work, the second generation found a larger choice of role models and career opportunities. First of all, a small but visible group of pioneer women had already begun to expand the sphere of domestic ideology. Some served as missionaries and teachers to the West. Others earned income from domestic work done for others, especially western bachelors.[9] These models of expanded feminine roles replaced aunts, grandmothers, and ministers' wives (who were still living in the east) as young girls' idealized role models.[10] It was more difficult, therefore, for frontier mothers to enforce strict adherence to a submissive, domestic behavior upon their daughters.

During the earlier part of the century, the idealized role model was often a missionary or religious woman. Esther Pariseau chose to emulate women of earlier times who had been "heroines," or women who had done something noteworthy. She particularly admired nuns who were remembered for their "good works."[11] Narcissa Whitman, the first white woman to make the trans-Mississippi crossing to Oregon Territory, decided during her adolescent years that she would become a missionary after she read a history of Harriette Boardman, a missionary to India. Whitman had already begun to model herself after her father who was a leader of their church.[12]

Women teachers could also be projected as idealized models. Mary Atkins, an 1845 graduate of Oberlin College, was an important administrator in early female education in California. She modeled her career after an early educator, Mary Lyon, the founder of Mount Holyoke Seminary.[13]

If the non-traditional daughter had the added advantage of mothers who migrated West as missionaries, teachers, or other working professionals, and fathers who took an interest in her development, she was even more likely to strive for positions of equality regardless of the challenges that were imposed upon her. In these cases, education was a significant factor. Parents wanted their daughters to receive good educations, often teaching the children themselves and then supporting them financially, emotionally, and intellectually when they went away for higher education. Although most mothers gave up their careers for marriage and motherhood, they introduced the idea that there were alternatives and choices for their daughters. The father or grandfather presented additional options when he taught his daughter special, male-oriented skills and allowed her to tag along to watch him at work. He projected a level of ability and confidence with which the daughter began to identify. She was also encouraged to pursue her own abilities and talents outside the domestic sphere.

In the case of the Hebard family, the mother served as a model of the expanding domestic sphere by becoming a missionary to the West. However, after the children were born, she settled for a more traditional role as wife and mother. Both of her daughters chose careers over marriage and motherhood. Reverend and Mrs. Hebard devoted a great deal of time and money to make sure all four of their children, daughters as well as sons, received a solid education and a chance for higher education. Mrs. Hebard taught the children at home while they were young and when they were sick. The older daughter, Alice, chose to teach younger children—a career which fell inside the proper feminine sphere. This was a less domestic and more career-oriented version of her mother's model. The younger daughter, Grace, chose a non-traditional career in engineering that placed her at work side by side with men at the University of Wyoming. While her inspiration came from her missionary father and church designer, she became one of the few female professors and department chairs in the nation.[14]

As a former teacher, Olive Pickering Rankin set an example for her daughter. Drawn by the opportunity to teach in the West, Pickering arrived in the Montana Territory from New Hampshire in 1878. She met and married John Rankin, a lumberjack farmer who had emigrated from Canada in search of gold. As Mrs. John Rankin, she gave up her teaching career in favor of her role as wife and mother. Her daughter Jeannette, however, chose career and political activism over marriage and domesticity. Encouraged by both parents, Jeannette Rankin completed a high school education and a degree from the University of Montana in 1902. Rankin believed that the ideas and experience she learned from working with her father on the ranch were more valuable than anything she learned in school. Inspired by the virtues and political ideals of her parents, especially her father, Rankin became actively involved in settlement house projects and suffrage campaigns in the states of Washington and Montana. As the first woman to be elected to the U.S. House of Representatives, Rankin's career path was an obvious departure from her mother's domestic model.[15]

As women became more involved in public occupations and careers, young girls had a wider range of female role models to choose from. Imogen Cunningham took up a career in photographic art after coming across the work of Gertrude Kasebier, a student of Alfred Stieglitz. While still in high school in Oregon, Cunningham discovered the New York artist's photographs in the *Craftsman* magazine.[16] In another case, Esther Clayson Lovejoy decided upon a medical career after a woman doctor in Portland, Oregon made a house call to take care of her mother.[17]

The idealized figure, however, was not necessarily a woman. Because of a lack of variety and quantity of female role models, male mentors and models were the only other logical choice. In the West where co-education was common, young women were used to working, playing, and competing with boys. Finding a male mentor, therefore, was a reasonable response. For example, Julia Morgan, a famous woman architect from California, admired the work of her mother's cousin, Pierre LeBrun of New York City. Before Morgan became acquainted with his architectural career, she and her sister had pondered careers in art, music, or medicine. During her education at the University of California, Morgan also acquired another strong male mentor, Bernard Maybeck, who inspired her to attend the renowned French school, the *Ecoles des Beaux Arts*. There she challenged the administration to allow her to be the first woman to graduate from that architectural institution. Maybeck and LeBrun gave her the confidence to believe she had the talent to compete.[18]

In another example, Georgia Arbuckle Fix (1852–1918), a woman homesteader and country doctor, found a foster parent to be her role model. Her unwed mother, who raised her alone for nine years, was often sick with consumption and the young girl spent many hours caring for her. Dr. Dinsmore, the local doctor, observed the daughter's natural medical skill and took a special interest in her education. When her mother decided to marry a man who would take her farther west where the climate was better for her respiratory illness, Arbuckle remained behind under the care of Dinsmore and his family. She admired the doctor's work and soon became an enthusiastic student. Later Arbuckle moved with the Dinsmores to Omaha, Nebraska and enrolled in the state university's medical school. Since she had exceptional medical experience with Dinsmore, she was able to complete the degree a year early.[19]

Strong role models, even if seen only from a distance or read about in books, helped the young girl realize that she had options for her future other than her mother's domestic model. The idealized person served as a projection of the girl's own desires and was often only a distant figure the girl read about, heard about in community talk, or met during a special occasion. The significance of this person was that he or she was someone such as a missionary, doctor, or respected lecturer whom the young girl could look up to as an idealized role model. The daughter would associate this person with her own motivation to aspire to achievements outside the domestic realm. The idealized figure, therefore, represented a public version of the confidence and interests that the father or father substitute had already begun to instill in the daughter as a child.

Professional Advancement

The American West during the nineteenth century provided women with an unprecedented opportunity for independence, self-realization, and professional advancement. Isolated from the social conveniences and conventions of urban civilization, the frontier West offered freedom from traditional restrictions. The first professional opportunities for women were missionary work, teaching, and writing. These professions were considered respectable because they allowed women to expand their sphere of influence into community affairs without departing excessively from Victorian standards. In the West, women in these professions had greater opportunities to assert a positive image as strong, public-oriented women. They were later joined by other western women who challenged the gender division of labor more directly—women who developed advanced administrative or medical skills, women with a desire to own their own property and run their own businesses, women who were not afraid to work side by side with men and compete for the most prestigious and dynamic occupations.

Women of the West were the first to be appointed and elected to public office, including the first women justices of the peace, superintendents of public education, legislators, congresswomen, and state governors. (These will be discussed in a later chapter.) In the professions, women doctors, lawyers, professors, architects, artists, and businesswomen were more apt to find positions in the West at an earlier period than in the East. T. A. Larson's analysis of the 1890 census indicates that the West supported a highly disproportionate number of women workers in the professions: fourteen percent compared to only eight percent in the East, although the West had only four percent of the national female adult population.[20]

Economic circumstances were often the most obvious reason for women's advancement. Westerners simply needed more people to fill all professions. When there was a shortage of teachers, doctors, or ministers, communities could not afford to reject a qualified professional just because she was a woman. Conversely, in the East where most careers were already filled by men, women had difficulty competing. Social bias in the more "civilized" regions favored male doctors, lawyers, and administrators. Alice Kessler-Harris has observed in her study of working women in the United States that "the freer environment of the western states" provided more compensation for the working woman.[21]

Barbara Mayer Wertheimer has also pointed out that because "western women found themselves unhampered by many of the restrictions placed on their eastern sisters," they were able to turn "their traditional homemaking talents into successful businesses." Wertheimer notes that unlike the East, westerners accepted women "in a wide range of jobs and careers."[22]

Along with economic factors of change, a new psychology developed in the West which involved the social relationships of women and men. In addition to the advancement of professional careers for women and placing a high economic value on women's domestic work, the frontier West also weakened the stigmatism that associated working women with the lower classes. In the homestead environment and early mining communities, it was necessary for everyone to work: men, women, and children. Interdependency was honored as a necessity. There were very few people, at least during the early years of settlement, who could enjoy the luxuries of a leisured elite. Wealth could be made and lost overnight. As the editors of one collection of women's diaries and letters has pointed out: "Neither wealth nor status nor sexual 'delicacy' could command creature comforts that were not yet available." Because of the "newness" of the yet untamed physical environment, "familiarity and some egalitarianism among both men and women, and the need to 'do for yourself' encouraged independent decision making and entrepreneurial experiments." In this kind of environment, "[f]ew women could be passive or dependent."[23]

Mary Austin, a California author who grew up on the western frontier, proposed that "the contempt in which woman's talent was held, from the professional and economic handicaps to a woman's career," varied depending upon the region. The women who grew up "at the *western edge* of American culture, *suffered less than* might have been the case *farther East* from the repressive conventions hedging femininity on every side."[24] Austin believed that life in the West focused on different priorities from the culture of the East. Therefore, westerners could either ignore or modify old traditions that were inappropriate to western life. The result was expansion of economic and professional opportunities for western women.

Working Women in a Gender Divided Work Force

Although Victorian culture in the United States emphasized that women's proper place was in the home, women, by necessity, worked in the paid labor force. Alice Kessler-Harris has pointed out that initially women preferred to supplement the family income by adding to their domestic duties by taking in boarders or selling extra butter, eggs, and garden products. Widows, single women, and wives and daughters of the lower classes, however, often found it necessary to work outside the home in order to earn survival wages for the family. Working women were an obvious symbol of lower class standing, and jobs were limited. Therefore, urban women worked only when absolutely necessary, and children were frequently sent into the labor force before wives. Many farmers' daughters worked for up to five years in order to help provide for the family and fund their dowry but quit working when they married.[25]

Before the Civil War, jobs for women were limited to factory work or domestic service. According to Kessler-Harris, household servants were poorly paid, and as technology increasingly replaced the servants' tasks within the household, this job fell to the bottom of the hierarchy. Factory work remained gender divided, and employers capitalized on this distinction to keep wages low. The only positions open to women in the professions were teaching and writing. These fields were also gender divided. When women teachers began to take over the former male occupation, men retained the higher paid, more prestigious positions in higher education and administration. This was true also in library work; women accepted positions doing the routine work of small community libraries while men worked with the more important books and documents in larger, more academic libraries. In the writing profession, women were basically limited to sentimental topics in which they advocated the proper, domestic sphere of women.[26]

After the Civil War, new opportunities opened up for women in nursing and clerical jobs. Kessler-Harris contends that these occupations again supported gender divisions of labor. Working women continued to represent a lower class standing, and the separation between middle and lower class women grew more intense. While working women demanded higher pay and struggled for union recognition, middle and upper class women of the woman's movement fought for suffrage and property rights. Middle class women began to expand their "proper" domestic sphere to include "social housekeeping." They justified their involvement in public matters by utilizing their reputation for moral superiority and used volunteer organizations to improve the social environment. In so doing, they opened new professions, still gender divided, in social work and home economics where women dominated the field.

These professions encouraged women to obtain college educations. However, once women completed their degrees, there were few professional jobs available to them. According to conventional standards, they had discredited themselves from marriage and had to look elsewhere for financial support and self-fulfillment. Between 1890 and 1920, a new sort of woman emerged who looked for jobs, not out of economic necessity, but out of a desire to occupy her time. These women sought better paying, more professional jobs—such as clerical work in offices and retail stores, or in social work or home economics—that could be considered suitable for decent, respectable, middle-class women. At the same time, men remained in control of the higher professions and administrative positions. The professions, therefore, remained gender divided.[27]

By the time the Nineteenth Amendment to the United States Constitution was ratified in 1920 giving women the right to vote, women had already begun to penetrate the male sphere to participate in business and professional careers. However, they had done so only on a small scale. Barbara Harris points out in *Beyond Her Sphere* that "despite discrimination, isolation, and ridicule," women "proved that females could compete and succeed," but as Harris observes, "these brave spirits" remained only "a tiny minority" in their field. Most American women were not willing "to endure the personal sacrifices and practical difficulties involved" in following the example of women who worked within the male world. They found it easier to maintain the familial pattern outlined by the Cult of Domesticity. Harris concludes that following the passage of the Nineteenth Amendment, "feminists faced the monumental task of turning these initial gains into more genuine economic equality between the sexes."[28]

Most professional occupations open to women in the East during the late nineteenth and early twentieth century were limited to female academies or other female-dominated institutions. Women who entered male-dominated occupations in older states had difficulty fitting into the mainstream. As Carroll Smith-Rosenberg has pointed out in "The New Woman as Androgyne," women's professions generally forced them to segregate from mainstream culture and set up homes in all-female environments such as settlement houses or women's universities. Well-known examples are Jane Addams and her Chicago settlement house and M. Carey Thomas who became President of Bryn Mawr.[29]

Interdependent Work Roles in the West

In contrast, gender differences were alleviated somewhat during the settlement period of the West. New social relationships were created, and new formulations of power were considered. Part of this change can be credited to the nineteenth century woman's movement in the East which attempted to establish stronger economic and political power for women. Because these ideas were advanced at the same time the West was being settled, the modified gender roles that evolved in the West were influenced by and influential to the woman's movement in the East. In this way, the West acted as an experimental social laboratory for women's rights. Without this frontier experience, it is unlikely that the equality movement for women would have made as much progress in the time frame that it did. The new patterns of male-female relationships in the West, therefore, had a direct bearing on the actual implementation of equality laws for women.

Eastern women's tendency to segregate themselves from male domination by creating separate social and political organizations was not imitated by western women. Women of the frontier West were more likely to integrate with male organizations and find a place for themselves within the existing structures. In her essay, "Women as Workers, Women as Civilizers: True Womanhood in the

American West", Elizabeth Jameson asserts that "we need to stop assuming that all westerners believed in the Cult of True Womanhood." She contends that western women believed their lives to be shaped by family responsibilities and hard work. Rather than defining their lives along private or public divisions, these women recognized the value of their work and that family and community concerns were intertwined.

Jameson further maintains that while the Cult was created to describe the "changing realities of an elite who did not perform productive labor and who were valued for their very economic uselessness," the ideals of the Cult were "far from the reality for homesteaders or for working-class women in mining towns or urban areas." The reality of western life emphasized interdependency. Under normal conditions, work was divided along gender lines. On the homestead, men plowed, planted, and cared for the animals. Women were responsible for raising and preparing food for the table, making clothing, and maintaining the household. However, these traditional conditions were often disrupted. Men were frequently absent, and women learned to take over field work and wage income. Jameson concludes that "family survival depended on flexibility and interdependence in work roles." Men shared women's responsibilities of cooking, housework, and caring for the sick. On the occasion that no women were available, they were even known to help deliver babies. Jameson suggests that the ultimate value of this cross-gendered experiment with work roles was the creation of new respect and better understanding of the work load of others.[30]

Similarly, Katherine Harris has observed from her research of Colorado homesteaders that mutuality of obligations caused men and women to work together, share each other's traditional responsibilities, and intermingle during leisure activities. Harris contends that an "extensive mingling of the sexes" was the result of isolation. Because distances between homesteads made daily communication impossible, families looked forward to the social activities of religious and community gatherings. Female networking was "relatively weak" because it was common for husbands and children to participate in the activities of women's clubs and organizations. Harris points out that "dances, picnics, box suppers, spelling bees, baseball games, card parties, 'literaries,' and other events involved the whole family." It was also common for girls to perform the same type of chores as boys because, as Harris points out, work on the homestead "was in such demand that the gender of the laborer was relatively unimportant." The result was that daughters "had a greater scope for their behavior than married women."[31]

Domestic Work as a Financial Opportunity

The first generation of emigrant women generally remained domestic-oriented but discovered they could easily supplement the family income. Because of the scarcity of women, their domestic skills were in high demand, and although the work was often strenuous, women were well paid for their work. Prostitution is probably the best known and most infamous service that a small group of western women provided.[32] However, most women did other kinds of work and, as Sandra Myres points out, "were justifiably proud of their skills and their contributions to the family economy."[33]

Some farm women sold eggs and butter for needed goods or extra cash.[34] In mining towns, women commonly took in boarders or laundry. Luzena Stanley Wilson, a `49er recalled that women were a rarity among the rough miners and were given special consideration. She found that she could acquire credit where none was given to men. Miners were willing to pay a high price for "woman-cooked meals." Wilson opened a boarding house, earned a good stash of money, and as the business expanded, took in her husband as a partner.[35] In South Dakota in 1880, Cora Babcock and a neighbor were earning $14.00 a week in the winter by taking in washing and ironing while their household expenses averaged only $2.00 per week.[36]

Theodore Shrader Homestead, Montana

A report from the Helena, Montana Board of Trade in 1878 revealed that farm labor averaged $50.00 per month and "female labor, cooks and general house work" averaged from $30.00 to $40.00 per month.[37] Although this suggests that male employment was paid higher wages than was female labor, it is interesting to note that payment for domestic work was common enough to be noted in official records. In the East, such duties were commonly performed by female members of the household without pay unless the family was wealthy enough to afford servants. Eastern servants, however, generally worked for much lower wages—often not much more than room and board—and could not expect to earn three- to four-fifths the wages of male labor.[38]

Western Women Move into the Public Sphere

The uncultured settlements of the West were much more receptive of non-domestic achievements of women than were the urban centers of the East. Eastern society was already established and controlled by social traditions. A woman's proper place was in the home. Catharine Beecher, Eliza Farnham, and others tried to change this pattern and were given just enough attention to peak their confidence, but eventually they switched to other projects to alleviate the social pressure ignited by their supposedly deviant ideas.

When Catharine Beecher started a school for girls in Hartford, Connecticut in 1823, it was such a success that she transformed it into a seminary in 1827. This, too, was well received until Miss Beecher decided to add a woman associate principal who would be in charge of the moral development of her students. This plan did not get off the ground for two basic reasons. First of all, Beecher's choice of candidates, Miss Zilpah Grant refused the position because she did not care for Beecher's attraction to the leadership of the elite. Secondly, the Hartford community did not care for the idea that a single, unmarried woman should be in charge of the philosophical development of their daughters. Parents did not want overeducated daughters who were so intellectually inclined that they would become old maids.[39]

Catharine Beecher's next idea to turn the seminary into a teacher training school was also a failure. Hartford refused to support the idea that women take over the teaching field. However, when Catharine proposed the plan to western communities—Cincinnati, Ohio, Milwaukee, Wisconsin, Burlington, Iowa and other towns in Illinois and Mississippi—they not only supported her plan but the first two gave her the initiative to begin the Western Female Academy of Cincinnati (1830s) and the Milwaukee Female Academy (1850s). The major aim of both of these schools was to train women to teach in the West.

Westerners supported any opportunity that brought women to their towns, camps, and ranches. When Eliza Farnham advertised in 1849 for women to travel to California with her, she had in mind women of quality. She required women at least 25 years of age and of good "education, character, capacity."[40] Even though her campaign was supported by such prominent leaders as Horace Greeley, William Cullen Bryant, Henry Ward Beecher, and Catharine M. Sedgwick, rumor soon spread that she was promoting an elaborate prostitution scheme. Easterners, on the whole, were not supportive of her efforts.

Men in the Far West, on the other hand, were quite enthusiastic. One forty-niner reported on June 10, 1849: "Went to church 3 times to day. [A] few ladies present. [D]oes my eye good to see a woman once more. [H]ope Mrs. Farnham will bring 10,000."[41] When word came to San Francisco that Eliza Farnham had given up the project, the opposite effect occurred. An observer of the disappointed male crowd wrote: "I verily believe there was more drunkenness, more gambling, more fighting, and more of everything that was bad that night, than ever before occurred in San Francisco within any similar space of time."[42]

Territorial legislators and town councils believed that women were essential to a stable and civil population. In 1869 one of the arguments that convinced Wyoming men to include woman suffrage in their territorial legislation was the hope that they could lure more women into the area. The logic was that if women migrated to Wyoming, then men would be more willing to settle down, have families, and thereby increase the population enough to meet the requirements for statehood.

Women were also believed to have a civilizing influence that would make men more responsible for their actions. Where women were scarce, men were reputed to have been starved for even the sight of a woman. Migration of women meant potential wives; real, home-cooked meals; clean homes, bodies, and minds; kind hearts and nurturing hands.

Opportunities were greater for the more assertive women who emigrated west on their own initiative, particularly in homesteading and professional careers. Although there were few professional occupations available for women during the early nineteenth century, these careers were more likely to be advanced in the West. Missionary work, teaching, and writing allowed women to expand their sphere of influence into the public sector. Women in these professions did not appear to be too threatening to the social order because their work in these fields generally complied with the gender divisions of labor and supported women's domesticity, submissiveness, and moral superiority.

As they moved to the West with these careers, however, women began to assert their right to expand their involvement to unprecedented levels. For example, because of the restrictions place on single women, Narcissa Prentiss married Dr. Marcus Whitman in 1836 primarily so she could serve as a missionary to the Oregon Territory.[43] In 1871 Abigail Scott Duniway began publishing a radical newspaper in the Pacific Northwest demanding more rights for women, particularly the right to her own property and the right to elective franchise.[44]

All three vocations—writing, teaching, and missionary work—were promoted as appropriate careers for enterprising women of the East. However, the East did not need missionaries; the West did. As for teaching careers, there were only limited possibilities for female teachers in the settled areas of the older, established states. In the East, women basically taught only the primary grades in public schools or girls in female academies. Competition for positions was heavy.[45] Women had a better chance of finding a position in the West.[46] As for the third profession, a vocation in writing did not necessarily require women to travel to the West, but if they did, they could depart from feminine conventions and limitations when writing about the more adventurous and uncivilized topics and settings of the West.

Missionary work was one of the most honorable professions for women. Volunteer work for the church was viewed as a reasonable extension of feminine virtues, and it was one of the earliest acceptable forms of women's participation in community affairs. Because of woman's special domestic skills and assumed moral superiority, she was particularly suited for charity work and benevolent societies. Providing food and clothing for the needy was a good excuse for women to become more involved in public affairs. It also gave women a chance to spend more time with other women, so it served as a secondary social purpose as well.[47]

Not all women's benevolence, however, kept them within the security of their own communities. Missionary work to Christianize Native Americans generated another alternative to volunteer church work, but it required a special kind of woman. Female missionaries had to be strong enough to endure the isolation and dangers of missions located hundreds to thousands of miles from eastern culture and conveniences, and they had to be hardy enough to adapt to the new environment.

Regardless of their dedication and stamina, the evangelical role for female missionaries was limited in scope. First of all, women could not travel as missionaries during the first half of the nineteenth century unless accompanied by husbands or supported by a convent. Among the first to volunteer to go to the Oregon Territory as a missionary, Narcissa Prentiss was rejected by the American Board of Commissioners for Foreign Missions. After she was told she would not be sent without the protection of a husband, Prentiss sought out and married Dr. Marcus Whitman who had already been approved to establish a mission among the

Flathead tribe of Oregon.[48] Similarly, Mary Augusta Dix married W. H. Gray in 1838 because he was seeking not merely a wife, but "a co-laborer in this missionary field." Dix accepted Gray's offer of marriage because she believed it to be "the voice of the Master [God] calling her to his Service."[49]

In the Catholic Church, concern for the protection of women also restricted nuns from serving in frontier missions. Since husbands were not the solution, a nun could only emigrate with a sisterhood of other nuns. Mother Joseph (born Esther Pariseu) waited seven years after deciding she wanted to serve at a Pacific Northwest mission before a new order of the Sacred Heart was established in 1855 and she was allowed to go.[50]

The second limitation placed on missionary women was the kinds of work they were expected to perform. Only on rare occasions did women become ordained ministers, yet a woman-organized Sunday school was sometimes the only religious service available to westerners.[51] In *Born for Liberty*, Sara Evans contends that those women who chose to follow their God rather than merely submitting to a husband found a greater opportunity for independence and self-worth than did the traditional wife. Evans also points out that "the role of missionary presented one of the few opportunities for middle-class women to escape the confines of domesticity." Ironically, however, it was the duty of these women to teach women of other cultures "how to be properly domestic."[52]

While this may have been the official role of missionary women, it is, nevertheless, a stereotype and oversimplifies what female missionaries did. Their value should not be measured merely by the domestic model they felt obligated to portray. Their duties were essential to the success of the mission and generally included teaching women and children, operating orphanages and Sunday schools, feeding the poor, and nursing the sick. Sarah Deutsch has noted that 19 of the 21 missions in New Mexico in 1900 were run by women.[53]

Missionary women contributed a wide variety of skills and services including some of a rather unusual or more masculine nature. Perhaps the most unusual and outstanding service was performed by Mother Joseph. After arriving at the Vancouver mission in 1855 and finding the locality lacking in adequate facilities, Mother Joseph used the architectural and construction skills she had learned from her father during childhood. She built eleven hospitals, seven academies, five schools for native children, and two orphanages. Her best work was the House of Providence in Vancouver which was reputed to be the largest building north of San Francisco. It was built in the shape of a cross, three stories high, and of brick on a stone foundation. It covered two acres. Mother Joseph began collecting contributions for the building in 1873, which had a floor by 1888 and was completed in 1892. The settlement of Vancouver, Washington would not have physically advanced so quickly or successfully without the talent and ingenuity of Mother Joseph.[54]

Female missionaries refused to be restricted by the limitations of domesticity. They proved themselves capable of duties and talents outside the immediate care of home and family. They modified feminine virtues in order to expand the dimensions of woman's sphere and participate more vitally in the traditionally male-dominated public sphere. Because of environmental conditions, this was easier to achieve in the new settlements of the West. Sometimes, as in the case of Mother Joseph, the scarcity of human resources required these women to accept roles and duties that were otherwise reserved strictly for men. In these cases, rigid gender divisions of labor made little sense and alternatives were accepted. Thus, women missionaries used the skills they had learned not only from their mothers, but also from their fathers to provide the services needed for western settlement.

Teaching Profession for Women

Another area of early departure of women from traditional boundaries of domesticity was the teaching profession. Similar to women missionaries, teachers who volunteered to go West found a unique strength in their religious associations. Nancy Cott contends that women who were sent to the West by the National Board of Popular Education answered a religious calling to serve God. One of the requirements of the Board was that applicants must prove membership in an evangelical church and describe their conversion experience. By transferring their submissiveness from fathers and husbands to God, they were able to achieve a sense of self-reliance and self-dependency. In order to serve God, these women had to establish confidence in their own abilities and independence.[55]

Early female educators such as Mary Lyon, Frances Wright, and Catharine Beecher countered the historical limitations to women's education by establishing female schools. They hoped to overcome women's intellectual disadvantages while at the same time protecting feminine virtues and special needs. Initially, these female educators were not necessarily interested in providing women with an education equal to men's. They did not believe women needed the same kind of skills as men and should be provided a different system of education. Despite this difference, they hoped to pull women up from their inferior intellectual status. The teaching profession, they believed, could be a vehicle for women to establish prestige within their communities.[56]

Catharine Beecher was particularly concerned with the improved status of women and initiated several enduring projects. Her first goal was to achieve more public prestige for women by encouraging young women to go into the teaching profession for a few years prior to marriage. For a second goal, she attempted to recast domestic duties into a respectable science and wrote a book on domestic science to publicize this need.[57] These first two goals were important to the progression of female professions in the East. The third goal was more relevant to the West. Beecher popularized the notion of sending female teachers to the West at a time when education was just beginning to be feminized. (This idea was also supported by Margaret Fuller who encouraged women to teach in the West as a means of achieving self-fulfillment and escaping a sacrificial, self-effacing domestic life.[58]) Beecher put this objective into action by establishing several female academies on the frontier where women could be trained as teachers.[59]

The trials, failures, and successes of some of the six hundred teachers who were sent out by the National Board of Popular Education is discussed in Polly Welts Kaufman's book, *Women Teachers on the Frontier*. Kaufman's research indicates that of the women who were sent by the Board to teach in the antebellum frontier (e.g., in Illinois, Nebraska, Oregon), at least half of them were orphans or women who were already attempting to support themselves. The West provided them a reasonable opportunity to do so.[60]

Kaufman also notes that the mythic western schoolmarm and her heroic cowboy lover actually existed. However, popular eastern-based literature exaggerated and thereby mythologized the schoolmarm's purpose and character. Kaufman contends that the portrait of the "eastern schoolmistress in the West...is, of course, a stereotype based on the prescriptive literature of the time." The authors of such literature based the image of the schoolmarm on the ideal virtues of womanhood; they describe her as "moral, self-sacrificing, discreet, dedicated to the welfare of children, and capable of bringing out the best in man." The myth suggests that the schoolmarm was "unconcerned with personal goals or needs." This was the eastern perception, but western reality was more practical. Kaufman's study of letters and diaries reveal that teachers who went to the West had personal motives and economic concerns more basic than Victorian ideals; they expected to find self-fulfillment and financial opportunity.[61]

Women Involved in the Development of Education in the West

Women who taught or helped promote education during the half century after California became a state in 1849 confirm Kaufman's contention. A study of the development of female education in California provides insight into both the personal and economic issues that prompted women to pursue a career in a previously male-dominated sphere. The western experience, as represented in the following discussion of the development of California education, provides an example of the ways in which revolutionary eastern ideas about women's rights were given practical application in the evolving settlements of the West.

Mary Lyon, a New Englander and an early proponent and teacher of female education, believed in combining Christian virtue and domestic training to mold the ideal woman. After teaching for several years in Ipswich, Massachusetts, Lyon founded Mount Holyoke Seminary in 1837. Her intent was to design a school where women could prepare for their moral and civic responsibility to teach their children to become good citizens of the Republic. She had a strong influence on the women who left her seminary as teachers and mothers. Like Catharine Beecher, Mary Lyon encouraged young ladies to realize that teaching was an acceptable profession.[62]

Lyon's graduates helped establish additional schools for young women throughout the country. One group of her graduates was specifically responsible for convincing Oberlin College in Ohio to develop a female department in 1836 and thus establish the first institution of co-education in the United States.[63] The Midwest, under the ideals of frontier experimentation, was the leader in other new educational ideas as well, such as state-supported public education, state superintendents of public instruction, and kindergartens using the Froebel methods of play.[64] Women played a significant role in advancing these ideas in states farther West.

The leadership of Catharine Beecher, Mary Lyon, and Oberlin College significantly affected the education of women who went West. Several of their students became dedicated teachers, helped establish schools and kindergartens, and served in administrative positions. They also became role models for a new generation of women who would dominate public education and expand women's influence in administration, school boards, and county and state superintendencies.

One such example was Mary Atkins, an 1845 graduate of Oberlin, who became an important early administrator of female education in California. A few years after her graduation, Atkins left to join her fiancé in California. On her way through Panama, she received unfortunate news that her husband-to-be had died. Atkins completed the trip and found California to be in desperate need of educators. Shortly after her arrival, a group of gentlemen in the San Francisco Bay area heard of her exceptional education and asked her to become president of their school for girls. Parents in Benecia had established the Young Ladies Seminary in 1852 hoping they could provide suitable training and education for their daughters without the expense and loneliness of sending them back East. The stability of the school was in jeopardy, however, because the first two women to run the school resigned shortly after being hired, each accepting marriage proposals. During her administration, Atkins provided the needed stability and developed a good reputation for both the school and herself.[65]

After thirteen years of dedicated service, Atkins turned the school over to Dr. and Mrs. Cyrus Mills. Susan Tolman Mills, one of Mary Lyon's graduates, had begun her career as a teacher at Mount Holyoke. She married Dr. Mills, and they served as missionaries to Ceylon for six years. On their return trip to America via Hawaii in 1863, they met Mary Atkins and decided to purchase the Benecia school in 1865.

In 1871 they moved the school to Oakland where they were able to expand both the enrollment and the curriculum of the school. Their intention was to improve the educational opportunity at Mills Seminary to the Pacific Coast equivalent of Mount Holyoke. The community had always believed the institution should be more than simply a finishing school. By 1885 the Seminary qualified for a charter to become Mills College. The school offered an unusually rigorous classical curriculum while maintaining a Christian atmosphere.

Susan Mills, who had served from the beginning as Associate Principal, accepted a temporary presidency after the death of her husband in 1884. Later, after losing two male interim presidents to other schools, the trustees unanimously voted to return the highest office to Mills. As college president from 1890 to 1909, Mills became one of the first women in the U.S. to achieve this high administrative position.[66]

One interesting aspect of the school's success was its emphasis on physical exercise. Many eastern educators were still in conflict over what was proper for young ladies' health and whether they were capable of sustained learning.[67] One state educator remarked of Mills school that "the health standard of scholars and graduates has been so high as to disabuse the public mind of prejudice on account of the early breaking down of educated women."[68]

Although the curriculum included many courses required at male colleges, Mills College maintained a conservative philosophy. State Superintendent Carr commended the private school which he said "ranks with the best modern college for the higher education of women." He pointed out, "Like Vassar or Smith College...it unites the features of home and school life, and, with increasing means, offers enlarged facilities for high scholarship and accomplishments in the practical duties as well as refined pursuits of womanhood."[69] The faculty encouraged students to serve the community as teachers for a few years before they married and settled into long-term roles as wives and mothers.[70]

Benecia families wanted their children to be educated and somewhat self-reliant, but they did not wish their daughters to be forced to compete with men. They avoided the state's co-ed university because it was considered more appropriate for the "few who are to contest for the prizes of the bar, or the healing art."[71] Parents who sent daughters to Mills College expected their daughters to adapt to a more traditional domestic life. However, in view of the frequency of death and abandonment in the West, the school also taught their students skills with which they could support themselves, especially as teachers or in cases of emergency such as when husbands died. Harriet Russell Strong, a Benecia graduate, for example, turned her ranch into a thriving business after the death of her husband in 1883. She invented a method to control flooding problems in the area and was asked to become the first woman to join the Los Angeles Chamber of Commerce. Women's organizations invited her to speak nationally on the career needs of women. Strong became an important representative of business-women's potential.[72]

While most nineteenth-century women chose neither to go into the professions nor to study at the college level, California did provide the opportunity. In the constitution of 1849, California legislators agreed to finance a state university "made free and open to both sexes on equal terms." When the school first opened in Oakland in 1869, both women and men attended classes.[73]

In the rest of the country, there was a great deal of debate and tension over the admission of women students. The Morrill Act of 1862, which required state support for college education, did not specifically include the rights of women, but women were often included. The earliest state-supported universities to admit women between 1855 and 1870 were all from the West: Iowa, Wisconsin, Kansas, Indiana, Minnesota, Missouri, Michigan, and California. Southern universities and the elite private institutes of the North such as Harvard and Yale kept the doors closed to women. Separate institutes were established for women such as the Mississippi State College for Women in 1885 and Radcliffe which began as an unofficial "Harvard Annex" during the mid 1870s and 1880s.[74]

The idea of co-education at the university level in California was well received by the public, according to President Ezra Carr. After traveling through the state to promote the university in 1870, Dr. Carr was able to report to UC Regents, "In many places the people have pledged themselves enthusiastically to its support." He added that "by bringing its instruction into direct contact with the people…the admission of young ladies…meets with universal approval."[75]

Actual attendance by women at the university varied. Carr taught chemistry classes to "twenty young men and about the same number of young women, which numbers are daily increasing."[76] Overall, the numbers were not so even. In 1879 there were 210 men and only 53 women registered.[77] Whether women students took certain classes at UC depended not so much upon their age or marital status as upon their individual interests and their communities' special needs. Law was considered a male occupation and no women appeared on the UC list of law students in 1879. In contrast, not only young, single women but also married and widowed women enrolled in the college of medicine. Since women had had a long tradition in informal medicine, it seemed logical that they should extend their experience to formal training as well. Many pioneer mothers had served as midwives while other mothers had to do the best they could with home remedies when doctors were scarce. Once the universities were open to women, they could then enroll in medical courses to fill the shortage in qualified medical care. In this manner, the University of California reflected the needs of the frontier West.

Teaching was the most popular career choice for educated California women, and the California education system encouraged this trend. The 1849 constitution promoted two progressive ideas in public education which affected women. The first was state responsibility for public education of boys and girls at both the grammar school and university levels. Although co-education was fairly common at the elementary level, state financing was still a relatively new concept. Most eastern schools were still locally or privately funded. The second progressive idea was the establishment of the position of state superintendent of public instruction. Following the lead of Midwestern states, California was only the fourth state to include this position. Both these provisions for state responsibility for education passed without debate during the constitutional convention.[78]

Californians found few problems with co-education at the primary level. John Swett, a former New England educator who moved to California and became a leading administrator wrote, "Coeducation of the sexes was a necessity, not a theory."[79] Superintendent Swett did not expand upon the reasons; to him co-education was simply a matter of economy. Swett's successor, Superintendent Ezra Carr hoped to relieve any lingering doubt about the value of educating both sexes when he reported, "The progeny of a single illiterate and depraved woman of the State of New York has cost more in taxes than the education of a hundred thousand children."[80] In this manner, the environment of the West had successfully moved issues of eastern debate and theory into practical western implementation.

Along with co-education, California state superintendents of public instruction were avid supporters of women teachers. Andrew Moulder, state superintendent from 1856 to 1862, believed women teachers had a particular skill in working with small children. "It is...indisputable, that many females...are admirably adapted, by tact, disposition, habit, and acquirement, to the instruction of early childhood on the first elements of knowledge."[81] Superintendent Swett (1863–1868) was even more emphatic: "I am of the opinion that one great cause of the evident superiority of our American common schools over the primary schools of Europe is the employment of female teachers."[82]

Unfortunately, many frontier teachers did not have a chance for proper education themselves. The lack of teacher training was a problem for the state, and the burden fell upon the superintendent. To advance the level of state education and increase the competency of teachers, California passed legislation in 1855 to create a state school board and provide for a state convention of teachers. State Superintendent Andrew Moulder realized that more than occasional conventions would be necessary to improve instruction. In 1861 he supervised the state's first Normal School in San Francisco. Ahira Holmes, a Midwesterner, became the first principal of this teacher training school. Helen M. Clark of California and Kate Sullivan, another educator from the Midwest, served as instructors.[83]

State Superintendent John Swett continued to support the Normal School as a means of improving quality education. He contended that even college graduates need special training to teach. The purpose of this "higher professional training," was to "raise the business of teaching to the rank of a noble profession."[84] This was especially important to women who were new to public occupations.

Eventually women also began to serve as administrators in the public schools. For example, Clara Kate Wittenmyer, an 1874 graduate of Mills College, served on the Contra Costa County Board of Education from 1881–1891 and officiated as president from 1885 to 1891. She was also a teacher, principal, and dean of women.[85] Kate Sullivan, who taught for a while at the San Francisco Normal School, was a principal at Lincoln Primary School.[86] Kate Smith Wiggin managed kindergartens in Los Angeles after her appointment to the position by Emma Marwedel who had been brought into California as a specialist to set up kindergartens in both the Los Angeles and San Francisco areas.[87]

As early as 1867 the California Educational Society included women. Mrs. C. L. Atwood, who taught in San Francisco, became the first woman to hold an elective office in this organization. In 1874 California legislators passed an act to make women eligible for educational offices. This included appointments to county boards of education, membership in state school boards, and candidacy for county superintendents. Three women became county superintendents in 1876: Alice Walker of Mono County (1876), Mrs. D. M. Coleman of Shasta County (1876–79), and Rose R. Morgan of Tuolumne County (1876–77).[88]

Perhaps the most significant symbol of women's advancement in educational management in California was the appointment of Mrs. Jeanne C. Carr as Deputy Superintendent of Public Instruction. She served under her husband from 1875–79 and received state-wide publicity. She was asked to address the state teachers' association in 1878 where she stressed that both women and minorities merited a good education. She believed that the "hereditary progressive culture" of California was linked to the duties of womankind. "Not only the nurture of the race in infancy is confided to her, but she is intrusted [*sic*] here in America with a large part of the work of the schools."[89]

Deputy Superintendent Carr recognized the moral virtues of women in educating the races, but she also realized that women could not achieve such a responsibility without a public voice and the right to vote. In her address to teachers, Carr suggested that woman's suffrage had become a moral necessity. "It is doubtful whether woman will ever take her place as educator of the race," Carr stated, "until she ceases to be a ward of the States, ceases to share its guardianship with idiots and criminals." Her goal was the same as the women activists of the East, but her tone appealed to the idea of evolutionary change rather than revolutionary uprooting.[90]

As a result of the inclusion of women in key administrative positions, women's empowerment became a growing issue. In 1890 the Prohibition Party nominated Sarah M. Severance to run for State Superintendent of Public Instruction. A life member of the Woman's Christian Temperance Union, Severance ran for office even though she and all other California women were denied the right to vote. Despite this, she received over 6,000 votes.[91] Her campaign encouraged the Prohibition, Socialist, and Republican Parties to run female candidates in elections for the next two decades even though California women did not win full suffrage until 1911.[92]

The practice of co-education in primary and secondary schools at the university level in California was a trend that was followed in other western states and territories. Women taught not only at the primary level, but were also hired at high schools and universities. Primary teachers needed little education to receive a temporary certificate to teach, especially in the more isolated areas. This level of teaching, therefore, was a popular job for women who planned to teach for only a few years before marriage or to earn enough money to establish their own homesteads or run their own businesses.[93]

Teaching at the upper levels required more education and was generally pursued only by women who intended to make teaching a permanent career. At the secondary and university levels, women began to compete with and work more directly with men. Higher salaries and prestige were the reward. How successful women were at being hired depended upon the competition. Although Emily Swett, daughter of the state superintendent of education graduated valedictorian of the San Francisco Normal School in 1881, she could find no positions open in the area for either women or men.[94]

In contrast, the less populated regions of the West advertised for educated women. Matilde Wergeland, a Norwegian who had immigrated to the United States after being offered a scholarship at Bryn Mawr in 1890, was hired at the University of Wyoming in 1902 after failing to be hired at Bryn Mawr (where a male faculty dominated the woman's college) or at the University of Chicago (where again because of her sex she found only part-time employment).[95] Wergeland shared a house with another female professor, Dr. Grace Hebard, who had been drawn away in the early 1890s from her high-paying job with the Survey General's office in Cheyenne to teach history and political economy at the university.[96] In addition to their professorships, both Wergeland and Hebard became published writers. Hebard's history books and school texts were used by Wyoming and surrounding states well into the twentieth century.

Chapter Four

Environment Creates Expanding Career Opportunities

Every gentlewoman…make herself familiar with business methods, papers, etc.; to prepare herself for any and all emergencies; so that if the head of the house be removed, the home that he has established may be kept intact.
~Harriet Russell Strong

Grace Raymond Hebard was a highly talented woman who found success and self-fulfillment in Wyoming during its early years of statehood. She had experiences and a personality similar to other independent women of the American West and serves as an excellent example of how women connected to something larger than themselves in the western environment which helped advance equality for women.

Hebard's parents had been missionaries to Iowa during early settlement. She was born in Clinton, Iowa in 1861, but her family moved to Iowa City shortly after where her father designed and built a church for a new Presbyterian congregation in 1869. Hebard was a fragile child, and for many years her mother taught her at home rather than sending her to public schools. In spite of her weak condition, the child loved to watch her father and the builders as they constructed the new church. She admired her father's strength and confidence. When Hebard was nine years old, her mother's failing health persuaded Reverend Hebard to take a trip to the West to find a better climate. He stopped in Wyoming and California, both of which had potential to become his family's new home. Unfortunately, he caught pneumonia and died of complications soon after his return to Iowa.

Grace Hebard never forgot her father. The beautiful church stood as a memorial to his faith, and her education was dedicated to his memory. Her mother, though, now a struggling missionary's widow with four children, upheld the father's wish that all his children—daughters included—be educated. Hebard attended the University of Iowa, which was noted for becoming the second coeducational university in the nation. She was the first woman to graduate with a Bachelor of Science degree from that institute.[1] Her fascination with construction and engineering inspired by her father led her to enroll in civil engineering and become the first woman to graduate from the University of Iowa with a science degree.

Six days after graduation in 1882 she accepted a job with the Surveyor General's office in Wyoming. She still carried the memory of her father's goals. Cheyenne was the place he had wanted the family to move before his death in 1870. She took her mother, older sister, and two brothers with her and established a home in Cheyenne. Grace Hebard was thrilled with her job that paid a large salary for a six hour day. She was proud that she could be the "man" of the family in supplying financial support for her mother. She later confided to friends that "her aim in life was to make up, in some degree, for the hard work and privations that her mother had suffered, as the wife of a self-sacrificing Home Missionary."[2] In essence, she had honorably taken over the responsibilities of her dead father.

As a resident of Wyoming, Hebard had full voting rights. This was a privilege allowed no other group of women at the time except in the Territory of Wyoming.[3] During Wyoming's constitutional convention for statehood, Hebard was one of three women asked to write the woman's suffrage clause.

In 1891, three years after the founding of the University of Wyoming, Grace Hebard was appointed to serve as a Trustee. She was also hired as librarian. In 1893 she completed her Ph.D. from Illinois Wesleyan University. In 1898 she was the first woman to be admitted to the Wyoming Bar. Still working at the University, she became a professor of political economy and history. In 1906 she was promoted to associate professor. She attained full professorship and became head of the department of political economy in 1908.

Hebard combined her surveying skills with her love of history. She traveled throughout her adopted state and was one of the first professionals to record Wyoming history. Memorials to famous western women were erected because of her efforts. These include Sacajawea who died in Wyoming (though her fame came as guide for Lewis and Clark through Montana and the Pacific Northwest); Narcissa Whitman and Eliza Spalding who spent Independence Day at South Pass, Wyoming during their trip as the first white women to cross the continent in covered wagons; and Esther Hobart Morris who is credited with the inspiration behind the introduction of woman's suffrage to the first Wyoming Territorial Congress in 1869. In addition, Hebard wrote twelve books and many articles and continued to write textbooks after her semi-retirement. These were used in the public schools for many decadess.

Grace Hebard

*From the Collections of American Heritage Center
University of Wyoming.*

Through all her energy and achievement, Grace Hebard sought political equality for women and attempted "to make the West woman's place."[4] She was given equal opportunity and equal pay for every job she undertook, and she was respected and appreciated for the work she accomplished. Although the Hebard name is relatively forgotten (there is a storage room in the University library that carries her name), the early history of the state that she so carefully and thoroughly recorded is still a lasting reminder of her diligence and dedication. Grace Hebard did not receive the national recognition of Susan B. Anthony. Instead, she built a great many memorials to others and did much for the advancement of equality.

The success of Grace Hebard and many women like her came about in part because of an early relationship with her father that inspired confidence. These early developmental patterns, however, could only be maintained in a social environment conducive to equality. The strict social traditions of the Victorian era that was prevalent in the East denied women a smooth transition into social equality. Intelligent and talented women of the eastern seaboard either had to ignore their abilities, steer them into domestic energy, appear as radical "unsexed Amazons," or move to the less populated and less restrictive areas of the West.

Many independent women discovered the different social climate and physical environment of the West offered them opportunities to become part of something much larger than the restrictions of the domestic world. They frequently preferred outdoor adventure to the restrictive domestic activities of their mothers. They were attracted to the physical freedom of male activities, and often adopted tomboyish behavior. Julia Morgan (1872–1957) loved to sneak out to the stables to swing on the rafters or steal away into the back yard to play on her brothers' gymnasium even though her mother had strictly forbidden her from such unladylike behavior. As an adult, she continued to defy proper feminine behavior by climbing around on scaffolding used for the construction of her architectural projects.[5]

Girls who grew up on ranches were particularly accustomed to outdoor life. Jeannette Rankin (1880–1973), for example, spent more of her time outdoors on the ranch than she did indoors with domestic duties or school studies. It was not uncommon to see her working beside her father and the ranch hands. She and her father discussed everything together, and she debated politics with her younger brother as well.[6]

A common characteristic among the second generation was that as young girls they participated in activities with brothers, fathers, and other males. They typically spent more time in the outdoors than their mothers had. Elliott West concludes that the daughters of the frontier West worked and played "mostly out-of-doors, away from the houses that were their mothers' domain."[7] When girls spent more time involved in traditional male activities, they were more naturally inclined to be influenced by the behavioral patterns of the men and boys with whom they worked and played. Because the western frontier was not a "frontier" to the children nor had they grown up with eastern standards, they did not tend to compare the West to life in the East. Their responses to their environment were usually quite different from the early experiences of their parents. Thus, West points out, "a distinctive generation was born" that "began when they looked at the land."[8]

An only daughter who preferred the companionship of her brothers might also spend more time outdoors than in the house with her mother. Esther Clayson Lovejoy, born in 1869, grew up in the back country of Oregon. Her only companions were her brothers and her father. Her brothers included her in games, and she accompanied her father as his assistant when he worked at various logging camps. A baby sister was born when Esther was twelve, but she still spent most of her time with the male members of the family.[9]

Martha Maxwell (1831–1881), famous for her display of Rocky Mountain wildlife at the 1876 Centennial Exposition in Philadelphia, credited her grandmother for her interest in nature and animals. She replied to an interviewer that "those rambles in the woods with Grandmother among the rocks, birds and squirrels had perhapse [sic] something to do with fixing my natural tastes." Maxwell spent many of her early years with her grandmother, because her father died when she was two and her mother was an invalid suffering from symptoms of hysteria. Later, Maxwell's stepfather was largely responsible for helping her to receive the education and training she needed to pursue her career.[10]

Georgia O'Keeffe (1887–1986), famous for her western paintings using animal skulls, flowers, and colorful canyons, was shaped by her environment. One biographer, Laurie Lisle, contends that the open prairies and the freedom of the West inspired O'Keeffe in ways that cities, especially New York, never could. Lisle points out that O'Keeffe tended to adopt her father's "love of the land" in preference to her mother's aloof, cultured "world of learning."[11] O'Keeffe once stated, in reference to one of her paintings of a red Wisconsin barn, that "the barn is a very healthy part of me…It is my childhood."[12]

As a child, O'Keeffe loved to run wild on the farm, and in the school yard she beat most of the boys at games of running and jumping. Her sophisticated, aloof mother was often displeased and tried to teach the girl to behave like a young lady. Although her mother did not condone O'Keeffe's tomboyish behavior, her own life instilled a contrary message. Mrs. O'Keeffe was somewhat embittered that she had obediently chosen marriage and motherhood over her dream of becoming a doctor. Though she did not discuss this openly, the young O'Keeffe and her sisters learned to regard careers as preferable to marriage and domesticity.[13]

Often the development of assertive behavior in girls was a matter of survival. When her environment denied a girl the chance to grow up in a protective, domestic residence, she had to learn to fend for herself. Although it was a difficult task for a young girl, Elinore Pruitt Stewart learned to run a farm mowing machine after she was orphaned. In order for her and her five brothers and sisters to stay together, they had to take care of all chores on their grandmother's farm. The young girl's farming skills became a valuable asset in her adult life when she decided to homestead.[14]

Some women acquired their assertive behavior simply because the environment required it. Born in Birmingham, England, Mary (Banner) Garrett (1863–1925) adapted quickly to her new home in the American West. She became skilled at horseback riding and shooting and could "hold her own in any situation." Her ability to render aid in a variety of emergencies was highly respected. Because of her strong and reliable personality, she was appointed postmaster of a small town in Wyoming and later was the first woman to be elected justice of the peace.[15]

Many western women found inspiration in the unique physical beauty of the West. The outdoors provided them with a sense of identity and purpose. Although girls were generally associated primarily with indoor activities,[16] independent women of the West clearly associated with outdoor spaces which provided them with personal freedom for exploration and self-realization. It also promoted the blending of gender roles.

Elaine Goodale (1863–1953), following her father's curiosity and love of the West, established a day school in 1885 on a Sioux reservation in South Dakota. A few years later she was appointed to a new position, created especially for her, as Supervisor of Education in the two Dakotas. During the year preceding the massacre at Wounded Knee, Goodale traveled throughout the area setting up new day schools for tribal families and inspecting those already in existence. She had inherited her father's sense of adventure and was unafraid of the privations and roughness of the native style of living. She lived with the Sioux, traveled with them, learned their language, and adopted many of their customs including simple manners of dress.[17]

Growing up in frontier Illinois, Eliza Farnham (1815–1863) loved the freedom of prairie life and the spaciousness of the frontier. In 1846 while living an unhappy life in New York, she reflected on her old sense of freedom and memorialized it in a book entitled *Life in Prairie Land.* She wrote: "I have lived again in the land of my heart. I have seen the grasses wave, and felt the winds…and exulted in something of the old sense of freedom which these conferred upon me."[18] She connected the environment to the possibility of freedom.

Adventure and freedom became more important to Clarice Richards than material comforts. In 1900 she married and moved to her husband's ranch in

Colorado. She observed that "life in any primitive, sparsely settled country is fraught with adventure." She viewed adventure as "the element which gives zest to everyday affairs and which lifts existence above the commonplace." The vitality of the West, according to Richards, was not without its price of danger and "annoying circumstances." Nevertheless, Mr. and Mrs. Richards were willing to sacrifice comfort and convenience for the "abounding health and freedom" with which they soon became accustomed.[19]

Richards described her life on the ranch as "fascinating, full of incident, rich in experience which money could not buy." Although she often went for weeks without the company of other women, she appreciated the unexpected surprises of the land. It gave her a broader view of life: "Living so close to the great heart of nature during those years on the plains, the vision of life partook of their breadth and a new sense of values replaced old, artificial standards." Her reward was "a new sense of proportion, freedom from hampering trivialities and a broader vision of life and its responsibilities."[20]

Freedom was the most striking sensation the West inspired in those who chose to live there. Georgia O'Keeffe spoke of the plains as her spiritual home: "That was my country—terrible winds and a wonderful emptiness."[21] Her biographer asserts the "unleashed forces of nature seemed to meet, and free, some similar emotional energy in O'Keeffe, and, instead of intimidating her, their wildness and unpredictability made her euphoric and repeatedly she enthusiastically described them as 'beautiful.'"[22]

Sometimes the physical beauty and freedom became intertwined with the friendliness and free hospitality of the people. Elinore Pruitt Stewart loved her new life in frontier Wyoming. She believed women of the cities would be happier if they could experience life in the openness of homesteading the "bracing mountain air, glimpses of the scenery, a smell of the pines and the sage…[and] the free, ready sympathy and hospitality of these frontier people."[23]

Stewart had grown up an orphan, but she and her brothers and sisters had learned how to work in order to survive. She married and lived in Denver with her first husband until he passed away. In order to support herself and daughter, she was forced to open a business in her home washing other people's laundry. When she heard of an opportunity to homestead in Wyoming in 1909, she quickly made arrangements to stake a claim. She later decided that her homesteading years in Wyoming were the happiest, most fulfilling years of her life.[24]

Stewart found homesteading to be liberating for a working woman and "the solution of all poverty's problems." She realized, however, that it took a special type of personality to take on the coyotes, hard work, and loneliness that were also a part of ranch life. A traditional, domestic woman might not find such a life appealing. Nevertheless, Stewart reported that "any woman who can stand her own company, can see the beauty of a sunset, loves growing things, and is willing to put in as much time at careful labor as she does over the washtub, will certainly succeed." The most important components of her success, according to Stewart, were freedom: "independence, plenty to eat all the time, and a home of her own in the end."[25]

Carrie Lingwood Lenz, Wyoming Homesteader, 1914
Photo Compliments of Valerie Schreibeis

If the routine of daily life became too stressful, western women often turned to nature for a fresh source of inspiration. When business became overwhelming, Laura Scudder (1881–1959), the potato chip queen of California, would drive out of the city and regain her strength and faith by viewing the vastness of the canyons of California. She believed that in "God's mighty canyons" a person would forget herself and learn to serve."[26] Scudder's favorite vacation spot was in the Sierras. The timeliness of the mountains gave her a sense of peace.[27]

The very ruggedness of the West inspired strong women to turn inward for personal strength. In doing so, they not only renewed faith in their own abilities, but they also recognized their role in a broader, more enduring world.

Women's Writing from Causes to Environmental Focus

The environment often inspired women to write. A writing career was another area, along with missionary work and teaching, in which American women sought to break into the professions. Nineteenth-century women writers from the eastern states were expected to espouse the virtues of the Cult of Domesticity. Society accepted women writers because they could physically remain in their domestic sphere while supporting the societal restrictions of the Cult. Parlor topics, fashion news, domestic interests, and sentimental novels earned them the reputation of "scribbling women" by their male contemporaries.[28] Women in the West, however, could more easily pursue a journalistic or professional career outside the feminine domain. This is not to suggest that all eastern writers adhered to themes that were strictly domestic, but they did try to maintain a feminine composure.

Margaret Fuller, for one, took advantage of her writing career to communicate her dissatisfaction with the subordinate status of women. Her book *Nineteenth Century Woman* (1845) made the public aware of philosophical and economic injustices inherent in the traditional inferior status of women that disallowed them a proper education and a legitimate choice of occupation. One of the opportunities she encouraged for her female acquaintances was to teach in the West.[29]

Other women writers who agreed with certain aspects of the Cult sought to extend the boundaries of woman's sphere. In publishing *Uncle Tom's Cabin* (1852), Harriet Beecher Stowe used popular literature as a forum for her anti-slavery views.[30] She intimated by this action that women were justified in taking a public and political stance on issues of morality. Similarly, her sister Catharine Beecher wrote copiously about teaching careers as a logical extension of woman's sphere. She believed that legitimizing the teaching profession for women would serve a dual purpose. First, it would alleviate the boredom, idle time, and incomplete education of middle- and upper-class women. Secondly, and of more importance, women could fill the shortage of educators who were needed for the illiterate children growing up in the uncultured West.

The West seemed to be the key, or at least the symbol, to more freedom for career advancement for women. While *Godey's* and *Goodhousekeeping* were publishing fashion news and printing serials of sentimental novels,[31] Abigail Scott Duniway of Oregon published a western newspaper that combined articles of interest to women with news and politics of the Pacific Northwest. The central purpose of Duniway's printing career was to expose injustices to women and inequitable laws. Duniway was also a strong advocate of woman's suffrage and used her paper to advance women's right to vote and control her own property in Oregon.[32]

Women writers who found domestic sphere limitations too restrictive in the East could pursue more freedom in the West. One New England writer who chose to move west for a new home and career was Helen Fiske Hunt (a.k.a. Helen Hunt Jackson). She had inherited enough money to lead a private, domestic life, but unlike her childhood friend Emily Dickinson, she had no introverted tendencies. After the death of her husband and both sons, Hunt turned to writing poetry to help ease her period of mourning.

Eventually, Hunt began to share her writings with other grieving widows and mothers, and discovered that her poetry communicated a message to these women that helped alleviate their sorrow. Their response gave Hunt confidence to pursue a career in the writing profession. Eventually, she used her talent as an excuse for travel, particularly to report on life in California. She moved her home to Colorado on the advice of her doctor. Her excursions through the West helped Helen Hunt Jackson find a moral purpose for her work. After it was brought to her attention that the poverty of the Indian tribes was the result of a continuous history of broken treaties on the part of the United States government, she devoted the rest of her life to making the public aware of the many injustices committed against native tribes. She wrote a report entitled *A Century of Dishonor* (1881) which she paid to have published and a copy sent to every member of Congress. This report led to her appointment in 1882 as the first woman commissioner of Indian Affairs for Southern California. Her stirring novel *Ramona* which defends native Indian and Mexican cultures was her greatest work and remains on the list of important Southern California historic literature.[33]

Women writers of the West commonly found some form of injustice to expose or some cause to advance, but more importantly, they discovered they had the right and the freedom to write on controversial topics. Polly Pry, born Leonel "Nell" Ross Campbell in 1857 in antebellum Kentucky, found the freedom she desired for her journalistic career when she moved to Colorado and went to work for the *Denver Post*. She had already experimented with marriage at age 15 and had dazzled Mexican diplomats who worked with her husband, but she grew bored with the limitations imposed on her by social customs and walked out on the marriage. Campbell then took up a writing career. When her first attempts at a writing career were unsatisfactory, she convinced her father's friend, John Cockerill, to hire her to write for the New York *World*. At first, he refused because of her sex and youth, but she was persistent. She was especially attracted to assignments that included violence and horror. When she discovered that competition was too high and wages too low, she began writing weekly romances which proved to be a lucrative profession for her.[34]

Still unsatisfied, but financially independent, Campbell moved to Colorado to join her parents and ailing brother and help with their accumulating debts. While en route to see her family, she met Frederic Bonfils and was inspired to go to work for the *Denver Post*. She found the excitement of the West well suited to her spirited nature.

Cambell, who had adopted the pen name of Polly Pry back in New York where journalism had not been considered a proper career for women, wrote her first piece for the *Denver Post* entitled "Our Insane Treatment of the Insane." Her research brought her in contact with Alfred Packer, the incarcerated Colorado man-eater. After interviewing him, she realized he had suffered enough and worked to get him clemency from the governor in 1899. As she became more involved in the case, she ended up saving two of her bosses' lives when a crazed lawyer shot at them with the intent to kill. "Plug Hat" Anderson had been hired by the *Post* to handle the legal end of Packer's case. Anderson, however, double-crossed them and demanded money from Packer also. When Polly Pry heard about it, she insisted that "Plug Hat" be fired. In revenge, he attempted to shoot two of her bosses. Fortunately, with her quick reflexes, she managed to protect both men with her skirts while wrestling away the gun from Anderson. The drunken man had not expected a woman to react so boldly.[35]

In 1910 she married her second husband, Denver attorney Harry O'Bryan, but this did not slow up her fast-paced career. "For a time, she presided as hostess at their Gaylord Avenue home, but the printer's ink would never drain from her veins, and she was soon back on the front page with the fires, the murders, the unfortunate juveniles."[36] Polly Pry was always looking for more adventure and more stories with a humanitarian angle. Even the death of her husband while she was en route to Mexico in 1914 did not prevent her from continuing her journey to interview Pancho Villa and report on the Mexican rebellion.

When Polly Pry turned sixty, she was still as active as ever and still anxious to write stories about the unfortunate. Because the United States entered World War I that same year, she found an excuse to travel to Europe with the Red Cross in order to report on the war. When she retired in the 1920s to write her autobiography, college girls interested in a career in journalism were already seeking her out as their female role model.

While emigrant women writers represented the strong, public-oriented woman who fought for the rights of the unfortunate, second generation western women were less concerned with reporting causes and more likely to describe the natural landscape and native cultures. They portrayed female characters as strong-minded westerners who were usually career-oriented and publicly involved. Mary Austin's *Land of Little Rain* provides detailed description of desert life and the indigenous cultures that adapted to the environment more efficiently than the newly arriving Anglo-American people.[37] Austin's novel *A Woman of Genius* illustrates the difficulties women of talent confront when faced with social biases. The protagonist attempts to apply her natural talent as an actress to overcome the period of depression following the death of her child and the failures of her husband. While she is respected for her talent, her social status falls dramatically and old eastern friends no longer associate with her. Her career, however, does not affect her social status among her western acquaintances.[38]

Another writer of the second generation western women was B.M. Bower, famed for her realistic settings of the West. She chose to publish under her initials rather than her name, Bertha Muzzy, because she feared her work would not be respected by eastern readers if they knew she was a woman. The ploy worked, and she sold nearly two million volumes of her 68 novels before her death in 1940. Most of her books were reviewed by eastern critics who assumed her to be male.[39]

Bertha Muzzy, born in a log cabin near Cleveland, Minnesota in 1871, moved with her family to Montana when she was nineteen to try ranching instead of farming. Muzzy received only sporadic education from traveling school teachers, but she was an avid reader of fiction and later developed a taste for opera and drama. After an eleven year marriage ended in divorce, Bower published her first works in 1904, including her first and most popular novel, *Chip of the Flying U* which was published as a serial in Street and Smith's *Popular Magazine*. Four film versions of the story were eventually released. One researcher suggests that "what she put into her writings must have come from observation, if not direct experience." She built her characters on the people she met, and her descriptions were so vivid "that people would talk about cowboys as if they were Bower characters—or even claim to be the model upon which a certain character was drawn."[40]

Bower loved the rugged western ranges and had "a tough, cowboy's sense of humor."[41] The settings of her novels are ranches where her heroes and heroines develop honesty, strength, and sense of identity while adapting to the natural environment. While the outdoors environment provides the impetus for her characters to excel, it also serves as an obstruction for villains who try to destroy or exploit the land and people.

Bower's novels frequently include women school teachers, and most of her female characters either have a career or acquire a professional occupation. Her biographer, Orrin Engen, suggests the reason Bower wrote of the schoolmarm so frequently was "because it was one of the few roles in western society which gave independence and responsibility to a woman."[42] The strong women in her novels were self-portraits of Bower as a small but intelligent and sturdy woman who was an appreciative observer of western life and landscape.

The non-villainous male characters in her novels are usually honest and good natured but are naive and easily taken advantage of. This is especially true of her father characters. The generous father in *Jean of the Lazy A* allows himself to be accused of a crime he did not commit. The guilty party is his brother, but Jean's father is too honest and naive to understand the trickery of his own brother. Instead, he is forced to leave his daughter to fend for herself. She takes care of the ranch but must also take on another career in order to pay for a lawyer to appeal her father's case. She also plays detective to find out the truth about the crime. In the end, she is the good daughter who sets her father free, becomes an independent woman happily confident in her new career, and wins the love and devotion of a good, honest man.[43]

Instead of quietly accepting the limitations of domesticity, spirited and independent women such as Polly Pry, Helen Hunt Jackson, and B.M. Bower were able to excel at highly visible careers. In order to write about public topics, however, these women found it necessary to leave the home, to travel, to experience life outside domestic boundaries. They found that the settlement periods of the ever-changing West provided especially interesting material about humanity and unusual lifestyles. Indians, outlaws, cowboys, and blizzard conditions that forced humans into cannibalism—these were subjects which refined ladies politely avoided. For pioneer women, though, and women motivated to write about such topics, these characters were a part of life.

Because of the lack of traditional restrictions and the unusual nature of the environment, the West provided assertive women with the freedom to write about political, non-domestic, and non-feminine topics. For this reason, then, western women were successful in expanding women's role in non-domestic literary fields. While western women writers tended to depart forcefully from Victorian ideals, the other two early, respectable professions—missionary work and teaching—did not. Women in these careers attempted to stay within acceptable parameters of their feminine sphere while, at the same time, trying to expand the boundaries of that sphere. Nevertheless, their efforts and the unique requirements of the frontier environment encouraged these professional women to assert non-domestic skills and interests and to become more actively involved in community development and administration.

Expanding Career Opportunities for the Western Daughters

Emigrant women sought professional careers first in writing, missions, and education to provide them with alternatives to domesticity; however, assertive western daughters began to look for additional career opportunities and were unafraid to compete directly with men or to be educated side by side with them. These women were dedicated to working in a variety of occupations ranging from homesteading and ranching to medicine and business to art and architecture. Part of the second generation's advancement can be attributed to their isolation from eastern culture which restricted women's choices. However, the reality of the western frontier experience also meant isolation and a shortage of companions. It was not unusual for westerners to adopt animals as their closest and most loyal companions.[44] Human associates were often composed of heterogeneous mixtures of cultures, classes, ethnicity, and races. Without the traditional network of female companionship, western women often based their self-identity more fully on their work.

The isolation of the West often worked as an advantage. Anthony Storr addresses how environment impacts individual development, especially for gifted and creative people. In his book, *Solitude: A Return to the Self,* Storr asserts that what a person does when alone is just as important as interactions with others. In cases of genius and exceptionally talented individuals, Storr suggests that solitude is often more valuable than implacable relationships that interfere with creativity.[45]

Storr points out that "[t]wo opposing drives operate throughout life." One is the need for companionship, love, and interpersonal relationships. The second is "the drive toward being independent, separate, and autonomous." The latter drive is common to most people but is the special concern of great thinkers, writers, composers, and musicians. "The creative person is constantly seeking to discover himself, to remodel his own identity, and to find meaning in the universe through what he creates." Storr further contends that the creative person's "most significant moments" when new insights or discoveries are made occur "chiefly, if not invariably" when that person is alone.[46]

The isolation and loneliness of westerners did not necessarily lead to negative experiences. Because the first generation of migrant women to the West had already established their identity based on interaction with extended family, neighbors, and a variety of women friends, their self-identity suffered when they moved miles away from this structure of interpersonal relationships. For the daughters, however, the same structure was not established. The young girl who grew up on the frontier did not find her home isolated and desolate; her self-awareness was based on the natural environment and whatever people and animals were available for companionship. She was motivated by her situation, therefore, to be imaginative and resourceful.

One example is Ellis Reynolds Shipp who migrated to Utah with her parents when she was five and adjusted quickly to her new, sparsely populated community. When she decided she could make a difference by becoming a doctor, her family supported her decision. Shipp's profession often took precedence over her personal relationships. She sacrificed months away from her children while working on a medical degree. Once she had completed her training, she was not satisfied with a local practice. Shipp traveled throughout the West, leaving children and friends at home while she conducted classes on nursing and obstetrics in distant settlements where there was little or no professional medical care.[47]

Shipp's energetic restlessness and driving motivation to work was a common characteristic among assertive second generation women. A well-known example is Julia Morgan, a California architect who "found immediate interest in her career." Her relatives accused her of "pursu[ing] it twenty-four hours a day thoroughly." They described her as "a very disciplined person" who could "tackle whatever it is that comes along."[48] One of Morgan's biographers describes her as creative, efficient, and directed, with a special emphasis on education. "She ran an efficient office," biographer Sara Holmes Boutelle summarizes. "No time was wasted, no nonsense was tolerated, and an enormous amount of work was accomplished. At the same time, an ongoing process of education was encouraged."[49]

One of Morgan's goals was to establish other women in her profession. However, it was a commitment that most women were unable or unwilling to make because of family obligations. Still, there were a few women such as Charlotte "Kid" Knapp, C. Julian Mesic, and Elizabeth Boyter who did drafting in Morgan's office and went on to do their own architectural designs. Two other southern California women architects were Hazel Wood Waterman (1865–1948) and Lillian Rice (1888–1938). Because Morgan owned and controlled her own business, she was able to advance the artistic careers of several women such as Maxine Albro, Marion Simpson, and Margaret Herrick whom she hired to do frescos, murals, and stained glass work for her buildings.[50]

Morgan's own work is a study in dedicated creativity. She used the native redwood and natural surroundings to enhance the beauty of the homes and community buildings she designed. Boutelle contends that Morgan's "affection for the California landscape infused her work, influencing her choice of styles, material, and colors." Although she had studied stately classicism at the *Ecole des Beaux-Arts* in Paris, Morgan was more inclined toward the more natural styles of the Arts and Crafts movement.[51]

The western landscape was especially instrumental in advancing the careers of women in art. Easterners were fascinated with the spectacular scenery of the West and were willing to pay for stories, paintings, and photographs of this region. The railroads commissioned Abby Williams Hill (1861–1943), an Iowa native who lived in the Pacific Northwest, to paint pictures of the beautiful though rugged terrain in order to attract travelers to the West. Hill loved the freedom and beauty of the wilderness where she found the peace and inspiration she needed to paint.

She spent months away from her husband though she would take her son and adopted children to camp in the back country where they would not be disturbed. Hill came to fame when her commissioned works were displayed at the Chicago World's Fair of 1893, the Louisiana Purchase Exposition in St. Louis in 1904, the Lewis and Clark Exposition in Portland, Oregon in 1905, and the Alaska-Yukon-Pacific Exposition in Seattle in 1909.[52]

New art forms attracted other women of the West who wished to add the emotional dimensions of western scenery into their art. Emily Carr, a daughter of emigrants to British Columbia, loved her wilderness environment. She felt more freedom and security from trees and open country than she did from cities and crowds of people. Carr painted realistic paintings of western Canada in her early career which earned her respect in her community and brought students to her studio. However, she felt the emotional dimensions of her art could only be expressed in a new art form, and she gave up her popularity when she took up a more abstract style in her paintings of the natural environment and native cultures.[53]

Georgia O'Keeffe (1887–1986), a Wisconsin frontier native, earned fame for her paintings of flowers, but her favorite work was her art of Southwest landscapes. She was intrigued by the variety of natural colors and felt the hills and canyons to be more alive to her than people. Her unique artistic penchant for color began when she lived in Texas during her early years as an art teacher. She began to express her intense feelings for the beauty of daybreak and the uncluttered landscape by reducing her pictures to simple shapes and colors. In 1929, she visited the artists' colony in Taos, New Mexico and spent her summers thereafter in New Mexico, apart from her New York husband, Alfred Stieglitz. After Stieglitz died, O'Keeffe claimed New Mexico as her permanent residence.[54]

In business, women operated hotels, general stores, millinery shops, but they also owned printing presses, food industries, and mining shares.[55] One of the most prestigious professional businesses for western women was medical practice. After the Civil War many nineteenth-century women worked toward medical careers but were usually confined to careers as midwives or nurses in the East. The status of doctor was still considered a male domain in the older communities. Medical schools at first refused to admit women. However, Elizabeth Blackwell forced her way into Geneva College Medical School in 1847 and founded a medical school for women as a separate part of her infirmary in New York in the 1850s. This opened the door for women to earn medical degrees. In order to practice, however, female doctors were usually forced to work in the slums or move to west where there was a shortage of professionals.[56] In this manner, the environment of the West again provided opportunities for women.

Westerners often encouraged women to attend institutions to become professional leaders. When Brigham Young encouraged the women of the Mormon church to educate and improve themselves, Ellis Reynolds Shipp responded to his call. After Shipp completed her degree, she not only set up a local practice but established medical training centers throughout Mormon communities in Utah and other Rocky Mountain states. She also trained her husband and a sister-wife and convinced them to earn medical degrees.[57]

Other western women entered the medical profession because of personal interest, but they also observed a community need for qualified doctors. In Portland, Oregon, Dr. Esther Pohl Lovejoy (1869–1967) distinguished herself in the politics of community health. She began her practice with her first husband in Alaska during the gold rush, but after the death of her child, she returned to Portland. She was the first woman to serve on the health board of a large city, and she campaigned particularly for legislation to inspect dairies and insure sanitary milk distribution for children.[58] In Nebraska, Dr. Georgia Arbuckle Fix (1852–1918) established a respected practice where she also took up homesteading and was recognized as a community leader.

The land itself provided new opportunities for women to own their own property and achieve financial independence. Women homesteaders were a common part of the West after the passage of the Homestead Act in 1862 which offered 160 acres to citizens over twenty-one years if they lived on the claim for five years and made improvements. The offer became even more enticing in 1904 when the Kinkaid Act increased the claim to 640 acres. Previously to the Homestead Act, the Oregon Donation Land Law of 1852 allowed wives of settlers to claim 320 acres in their own right.

Single women and widows with children sought the independence and investment opportunities that came with owning and working their own land. Two of the best known women homesteaders, remembered for the vivid and enthusiastic letters they left behind, were Elinore Pruitt Stewart, a widow who took up a claim in Wyoming in 1909, and Elizabeth "Bachelor Bess" Corey, an Iowa native who saved up money by teaching in the Dakota Territory so she could buy a homestead in South Dakota. Both of them wanted to own their own land and found it more rewarding than the labors of domestic chores.[59]

Historian Glenda Riley (1988) has pointed out that women homesteaders took up claims for a variety of reasons including "a chance to look for husbands, to seek investments, to earn money for additional education, to find a way to support their children after being widowed or divorced." Others took advantage of the government's offer in order to add acreage to a husband's farm or ranch or "to homestead as a part of a family or companionship group."[60]

Some women such as Mary Culbertson and Helen Howell of northern Wyoming became partners by building a cabin on the corner of their adjoining claims where they could share the costs and safety of living together.[61] To meet the requirements of the law, their individual rooms were built on their own property.[62] Groups of women were known to form all-female companies, file claims, and develop the land in the newly opened Oklahoma Territory in 1893 and 1894.[63] One historical source estimates that as many as one-third of the Dakota Territory homesteads were held by women in 1877.[64] Another source reveals that 11.9 to 18.2 percent of the claims filed in Wyoming and Colorado were staked by women. These women met the legal requirements at a higher percentage than did men: 42.4 percent of the women "proved up" as compared to only 37 percent of the men.[65]

Ranching opened new opportunities for women. Many women were attracted to the open spaces and love of horses associated with ranch life. Cowgirls and ranch women worked side by side with men or did the work themselves with a sense of independence and equality.[66]

One woman who became a self-reliant rancher grew up as a protected daughter. Harriet Williams Russell was educated at Mary Atkin's Young Ladies Seminary at Benecia, California from 1858 to 1860. She married Charles Lyman Strong, a business associate and friend of her banker father, and they had four daughters. In addition to the usual domestic responsibilities, Harriet supervised the ranch that she and Charles purchased near Whittier, California. This was necessary because Charles and her brother were constantly moving around from one mining adventure to another.

Following heavy losses from a mining fraud, Charles committed suicide. Harriet was left with debts, a ranch, and four young daughters. At the time of Charles' death, Harriet was in Philadelphia receiving treatments from the famous doctor, Silas Weir Mitchell, for her chronic back problems and bouts of depression. She had been pining away with the lack of purpose and prestige, but these physical and mental ailments mysteriously ended after her husband's death. Perhaps she had acquired too many new worries to occupy her time.

Strong realized she was on her own to use her talents and intellect in order to support herself and her daughters. She drew upon her inner strength and determined to make a success of her life alone. Her first challenge was to ward off her husband's creditors. She went to court, presented a strong case to keep the ranch in her own name, and won. After she obtained complete control of the ranch, she began to experiment in plant growth and flood control. Her efforts were richly rewarded. She was even able to pay off the old debts. In addition, her new horticultural ideas received much public recognition, and she became active in her community. She was a member of Madame Severance's Friday Afternoon Club, became the first woman member of the Los Angeles Chamber of Commerce, and founded the Ebell Club of Los Angeles in 1894.[67]

Strong cultivated a lifetime of influence with female community leaders such as Mary Atkins of Benecia and Caroline Severance of Los Angeles. This networking, along with California laws which granted property rights to married women and widows, allowed her to become a successful landowner and an active community leader. She was a popular speaker promoting women in business. Her mission was to prepare the cultured lady for financial emergencies like those she had experienced: "If the necessity never arises for use" of women's technical and theoretical study in business matters, then "individually such knowledge [causes] no harm." On the other hand, Strong argued, "if through adverse circumstances the burden of business or self-support falls upon one to carry, the emergency can be met with fair prospects of saving one's property or independence."[68]

Harriet Strong opposed women who were bound to the obsolete virtues of the Cult of Domesticity. "I found that where there is opposition among women of position," she pointed out during one of her speeches in reference to the woman suffrage debate, "it is due to the presence of personal predjudice [sic] in favor of the old way of doing things." To Strong's dismay, she had discovered that women who had difficulty understanding the need for women's rights were "those who are in sheltered homes, with fathers, brothers, husbands and sons to stand guard chivalrously, to do everything for them even to the expression of opinions in great and grave matter."[69] These were women she had observed on her trips to the East.

In stark contrast to these dependent women, Strong represented the expanded roles of western women. While fathers, husbands, and brothers were off trying to make their fortunes, women often found traditional men's work added to their own domestic duties. This was especially true with the frequency of male death in the harsh western environment. Western women realized they could not remain isolated and alone, nor could they always depend upon fathers and husbands.

Harriet Strong recognized not only the financial value, but also the emotional and intellectual value of being educated and prepared even if a woman submitted to a traditional domestic life. In an address to the Ebell Club, an intellectual organization for women, Strong acknowledged that the home was "the highest ideal of the human heart, is the central ideal of civilization," but she also quickly pointed out the possibility that the home can be broken and that a woman must be prepared for such emergencies.[70]

Strong did not believe the "gentlewoman's" involvement in business matters should be considered merely so that the home "may be preserved on its financial basis." Women needed to study, she pointed out, to interest themselves in "the stirring affairs of life, by being thinkers on all subjects and questions." The goal was the "development of the individual...to bring out the highest and best in each member for ourselves" and the ultimate reward would be "the uplifting of the community, as well as the home and society."[71] Strong's approach provided a smooth transition from domestic to public life, yet her urgency for change was clear.

For Ellis Shipp, Esther Lovejoy, Georgia O'Keeffe, Abby Williams Hill, Polly Pry, B.M. Bower, Bachelor Bess Corey, Elinore Pruitt, and other western women, ability and need took precedence over traditional gender divisions of labor. The new settlements of the West needed missionaries, teachers, doctors, architects, and a wide variety of other professionals. With such a high demand and limited supply, the West could not afford to be biased against women. Thus, independent women who wanted careers found a ready market in the West. Financial need was often the initial or underlying motivation, especially for teachers and homesteaders. However, women also wanted the independence and prestige as well as the economic rewards of their work and land or business investments.

The economic need of the region was an obvious factor in the advancement of women's occupational choices, yet the psychological correlation in creating new patterns of relationships was also important. There were fewer social taboos to remind women what they could or should not do, and they could experiment with new lifestyles and career options. With fewer cultural restraints, men's attitudes also changed. They often viewed their wives and daughters more as equals. They could teach young women skills and academic subjects previously reserved for males. Men could allow their daughters to idealize them and share their public life. The result was not an end to domesticity and motherhood, but it did introduce new alternatives for women's lives.

The modifications of western culture helped facilitate both the interest and success of women who chose professional careers and non-domestic occupations. During their education and job search, assertive western daughters often had to compete with men, but encouragement from family members gave them the confidence to attain their goals. Unlike eastern society, communities in the West needed educated and experienced professionals and were willing to overlook a woman's gender as long as she proved her ability. For these reasons, western women advanced in a variety of occupations more smoothly and more rapidly than did eastern women.

Chapter Five

Equality and Suffrage
For Women in the West

Wyoming as a State with a suffrage law brought theory into practice. Law on books solidly replaced the hazy, emotional, and intellectual arguments about what women's suffrage might be.

~Elizabeth Cady Stanton

When Dr. Agnes Matilde Wergeland, the first Norwegian woman to earn a doctorate, became a U.S. citizen in 1909, she was also among the first women to establish her right to vote.[1] It was no accident that she was one of the few women in the world with the legal right to elect her new government. Wergeland, an ardent advocate of universal suffrage, chose to live in Wyoming where women had been voting since 1869.

Born in Kristiania, Norway in 1857, Agnes Matilde Wergeland was the youngest of six children. Like her cousins, Henry Wergeland and Camilla Collett who were both famed Norwegian writers, Matilde also showed early signs of this talent. Unfortunately, her father proved improvident and failed to support the family. When Wergeland was four, her mother went to work as a matron at Gaustad Asylum and tried to manage the family's needs. She provided for Matilde's basic education but was limited in resources. Matilde had to wait to continue her higher education until her older brother completed his education at the University of Munich.

After more education in Norway, including piano under the direction of the famous Edvard Grieg, Wergeland could find no jobs open to her. Friends managed to send her to Munich where she studied under the famous historian, Dr. Konrad Maurer. She returned to Norway but again found no position. After benefactors provided funds so she could complete her doctorate degree in Zurich and still no opening was available to her in Norway, she decided to accept a scholarship at Bryn Mawr in Pennsylvania in 1890.

Unfortunately, her job search in the United States was similar to her experience in her home country. Bryn Mawr desired her as a student but provided little opportunity for her as an instructor. The majority of the faculty were men even though Bryn Mawr was a university for women. After an unsuccessful attempt to get a job at the University of Chicago, she joined the faculty of the University of Wyoming. There she was respected as an intelligent, thinking person and enjoyed equal rights. Her salary was equivalent to what men were receiving for the same position, and she was soon promoted to full professorship.

Matilde Wergeland loved her adopted home. The cool climate and the snowy Rocky Mountains reminded her of her home in Norway, yet this new home offered her something her native country would not. Her lifetime hope was that Norway would someday encourage, rather than discourage the talents of her citizens and end the cycle that "one could only get ahead by depriving others."[2] After Dr. Wergeland's death in 1914, friends and admirers set up scholarship funds at both the University of Wyoming and the University of Kristiania, Norway for women who were interested in interrelations between Norway and the United States.

Wergeland was an excellent early role model for early twentieth-century women. She struggled throughout much of her early life to develop her talents and convince the world that women were capable, intelligent individuals. Although most of the world at that time was generally not tolerant of non-domestic women, Wergeland eventually found a place that was. In sparsely populated Wyoming, she found what the rest of the U.S. and her native country had denied her: simple but equal respect for her abilities and desires.

Wergeland's experience is not unique. Many nineteenth- and early twentieth-century women discovered that the West was more willing to accept women's equality than was the tradition-bound culture of the eastern seaboard.

Female missionaries, teachers, and doctors in the nineteenth century represented the beginnings of social power and economic independence for women and led to early stages of their development of political power in the West. New state constitutions and laws were adopted to fit the unique needs and unusual social conditions of the western environment. These new laws and the acceptance of unusual legal practices in western states and territories helped to expand the status of women and make their participation in legal and political activities socially acceptable.

Dorothy Gray, who has applied Frederick Jackson Turner's thesis to women of the West,[3] contends that while the East was "growing more repressive for women and more constrictive of their being" (as a result of Victorianism), the West not only offered new opportunities but required the strongest, most independent and competent women and men to take advantage of the promising potentials of the region. While the development of the West has often been seen as an exercise in physical survival, it can also be credited for allowing for social growth that was inhibited in eastern society. Western women, she points out, were scarce, valuable, and valued. Because they were expected to pull their own weight, women became independent and achieved full rights when they reached for them. Gray concludes that because eastern culture has permeated American thought, mere *images* of the western woman have unfortunately prevailed over the real history of western women.[4]

T.A Larson has suggested that women's rights were advanced more quickly in the West because legislators in the new states and territories were frequently willing to adopt new laws and legal codes. The female suffrage movement itself would have failed if western territories and states had not been willing to experiment with the principal of female equality.[5]

Beverly Beeton, who has researched the political aspects of woman's suffrage in the Rocky Mountain states and territories, contends that these states adopted woman's suffrage "as a matter of expediency, not ideology." In Utah and Idaho, the political debate over the suffrage issue centered on the Mormon practice of polygamy. Those who opposed the religious sanction of multiple wives believed that if these women received the vote, they would end the practice. Conversely, Mormons were so confident in how their women stood on this issue, they wanted women to vote in order to prove to the world that their wives were not mistreated.[6]

Early accounts of Wyoming Territory indicate that because the region needed a larger population in order to become a state, legislators thought that votes for women might attract more women into the state, thereby stabilizing the population. After the law was passed, a rumor was spread claiming that the Democratic legislature had attempted to embarrass the Republican governor by forcing him to veto the bill. Obviously, he did not comply. Although woman's suffrage was a logical human rights argument in 1869, it was still theory when the Wyoming legislators decided to accept the risk of experimenting with it as territorial law. Nevertheless, both political parties were afraid to take full responsibility for promoting such a controversial issue.[7]

Sidney Howell Fleming, a specialist on Wyoming suffrage, contends that one of the motives for the passage of woman's suffrage in Wyoming following the Civil War was a strategy of reform rather than one of justice. Fleming suggests that it was "a way of going on, burying in peace what war had not decided."[8] A few southerners tried to escape the carpetbaggers of the South under

Reconstruction by fleeing to the West where free land was available.[9] They met up with former abolitionists from the northern region, and they faced a Republican governor. Compromises became necessary to sooth over old war wounds and unite a heterogeneous group whose goal was to establish a new state.

In 1869, Colonel William Bright introduced the woman's suffrage bill because he believed his intelligent wife was more qualified to vote than the freed slaves of the southern state from which he had recently migrated. His wife Julia later reported in an interview that "Mr. Bright and I, and Mrs. Morris, had talked this over many times—the right to vote." Colonel Bright finally came up with an argument that he thought would be convincing to other men: "if by a Civil War we can liberate millions of black men who can go to the polls and vote, why is not my mother, my wife and sister equally able to exercise the right of government."[10]

Although Bright's prejudice can be construed as negative reasoning today, Bright had genuine respect for his wife and his neighbor, Esther Hobart Morris. To honor them publicly with their request for suffrage, however, would put his business and career at risk. Therefore, he decided to propose an argument that other men would have difficulty rejecting. Indeed, during the legislative debate, Representative Waller admitted that he did not favor women's vote, but he did believe women were more worthy of the ballot than another race. Besides, he was afraid to suggest to his wife that he thought her less qualified than an uneducated, former slave.[11]

Bright, a southern Democrat, did not stand alone on this issue. One of his strongest supporters was a Republican and former abolitionist from Connecticut. Appointed Secretary of State for the Territory, General Edward M. Lee encouraged Bright to step down from his role as chair of the council in order to introduce the bill. A few years before, Lee's proposed amendment to the Connecticut constitution in 1867 to provide for woman's suffrage failed. Lee, therefore, may have given Bright some ideas on wording and strategy. Later, Lee's sister tried to convince the public that Lee had been the inspiration behind Bright; however, it appears he was but one of several supporters.[12]

Historical arguments which focus on racial prejudice fail to account for the modifications in social patterns and the changing roles of women in the West. Those men who ventured west were a different breed of men. They learned to respect the services women provided rather than taking them for granted. Perhaps, too, because many of them came from rural or working backgrounds, they were used to observing their mothers working at a variety of tasks. Rural areas and the working class adhered less to the Cult of True Womanhood which was more practical and possible in urban culture and the upper middle classes of the northeast and the aristocratic tradition of the southeast.

Most pioneers could tolerate some level of equality because the hard life of the West forced many women to take on many new responsibilities. This became more obvious to them once the Fifteenth Amendment was proposed to grant elective franchise to former slaves. Women could then be viewed not just as social equals but as citizens and political equals. In addition, westerners had a special respect for women who excelled in the new environment (as examples in the previous chapters have shown). Thus, Wyoming men, prompted by a variety of motives including the respect they held for the work shared by western women, made official decisions to increase the public rights of women.

Kansas allowed limited voting rights for women even earlier than Wyoming. In 1859 the state adopted property and guardianship rights for women equal to those for men and granted woman suffrage in school district elections. Then in 1887, women's municipal suffrage was added, and the first woman mayor in the United States, Susanna Madora Kinsey Salter, was elected. One year later, more Kansas women became involved in city government when Syracuse elected a woman town councilor and Oskaloosa elected an entire council of women which included the mayor and four councilwomen. Women's campaign for full suffrage, however, did not succeed in the state until 1912.[13]

Innovative laws in other western states and territories helped extend equality rights for women in the region. Legal action was taken to promote equality issues much earlier than eastern states were willing or able to modify existing inequities in established laws and constitutions. Thus, by 1915 when the woman's suffrage rights movement began to lobby successfully at the federal level, all western states, except Texas, had already granted some form of female franchise. Few states in the eastern half of the U.S. had done so and none had yet granted full suffrage rights.[14]

Equality Through New Laws

In addition to suffrage rights, western legislators considered other measures of equality, including equal pay for equal work. This was an issue that made much more sense in the West than in the East. Since women in eastern states rarely competed directly with men for professional work, the demands of woman's rights leaders for such legislation seemed inconsequential. Women in the working class, on the other hand, did compete with men for factory work, but equal pay in such a situation would actually have been a disadvantage for women; they would have lost their jobs to men. In most jobs (including school teaching), women were hired to work simply because they were willing to work for less pay.

If equal pay legislation had come into effect, men would have been rehired in the industries where women had replaced them for lower wages.[15]

In contrast, the balance of power was different in the West. Because the newer regions desperately needed qualified workers, gender division of labor was not forcefully practiced. Women and men commonly worked at the same types of jobs, but the traditional response was to pay women less. In 1869, Wyoming decided to deal with the inequities of gender-determined salaries. One of the first laws passed by the territorial government supported equal pay for equal work. Section nine of the original school act declared that "in the employment of teachers no discrimination shall be made in the question of pay on account of sex when the persons are equally qualified."[16]

Evidence shows that the movement toward economic equality made an impact on women who lived and worked in the West. One such example was Agnes Wright Spring who grew up on Wyoming and Colorado ranches. She graduated from the University of Wyoming and was attending graduate school at Columbia University when the United States entered World War I. Classes were dismissed because many of the students enlisted. One of her friends, a soldier dressed in his new uniform, mentioned to Wright that she ought to apply for his journalism job. He reported that the position paid $25 a week, and he was not going to keep it since he was going off to war. Wright applied for the job and received an offer for only $15 a week. When she questioned the editor about the discrepancy, he reminded her that she was just a girl. At first she was taken aback, but then gave him a firm response: "Then I'm going back to Wyoming where women get equal pay for equal work."[17]

Other states also addressed the issue of equal pay for equal work. California passed a law in 1870 equalizing teaching salaries for men and women. Superintendents of Public Education in the state believed in the professionalism of teaching for men and women and translated this conviction into providing for life diplomas and equalization of salaries. "It is but simple justice," Superintendent Fitzgerald announced in 1870, "that for the same work in quality and quantity a woman should receive the same pay as a man." California legislation equalized salaries that same year. For Fitzgerald this was neither a political issue about women's rights nor about "the intellectual inferiority of the one sex to the other." He stressed that it was "only a question of simple justice."[18]

In spite of intents, disparity existed between the overall ratio in male and female salaries. The discriminating factor was based not specifically on gender identity, but rather on ability. It was believed at the time that teachers of secondary and higher education should receive higher salaries because job qualifications for teachers of older students required more education and experience. Since more men taught the upper levels while women dominated the teaching of younger children, the average male salary was legally higher than the average female salary.

Fitzgerald promoted equal pay for equal work in principle but believed it took more knowledge and skill to teach older students. Most women taught for only a few years before marrying, so they usually did not pursue the profession as a life-long career. Consequently, they did not receive the extra education and experience required for upper division classes. The spirit of equal pay for equal work, according to Fitzgerald, was to reward abilities of talented women who dedicated their lives to education. Fitzgerald reflected the dominant western thinking when he remarked, "when God has given a woman the ability to do the highest work and in equal measure, she ought to be as free as man to do it and to be well paid for it."[19] Although this system was blind to the special skills and career dedication of elementary school teachers, a legal precedence for equal pay had been set.

In most states the inequity of salaries continued even though by 1880 a trend toward female dominance in the teaching profession, particularly at the grammar school level, was clearly evident in both the East and the West.[20] For example, in California the number of new certificates granted to teachers in 1873 included 973 women and 428 men. In 1879 women again exceeded men 744 to 251.[21] The pay for women, however, was not quite so advantageous. Salaries reflected the higher regard for upper level educators who were usually men. Average salaries for women were $460 compared to $554 for men.[22] Indeed, California women averaged only about eighty percent of the male salary. This, however, was closer pay equity than in the East where, on the average, women received only a third to half of men's teaching salaries.[23]

New Property and Divorce Laws

Another area of early law reform concerning women was divorce and property laws. Under the old common law practice of *femme couverture* imported from England, women had no legal right to own property, not even their own wages, nor did they have the freedom or protection to sue for divorce to end a bad marriage. In most cases, men assumed legal custody of children. Men could divorce their wives and leave them without any financial means of support, but women had no reciprocal rights. Early woman's rights leaders abhorred the inequities of the law and argued for new property and divorce laws. In the East, the proposed changes were controversial and made only slow progress, but in the West, states began to implement new laws protecting women's status under the law.

Esther Morris, an western immigrant, experienced both circumstances. In Illinois, she became frustrated with the lack of women's rights. On the other hand, her life in Wyoming was the model of empowerment for women.

During her early life, Esther Hobart Morris suffered from loss of male support and unjust property laws, yet she managed to maintain "a confident bearing, ready wit and great human sympathy."[24] Born in Spencer, New York in 1814, she was the eighth of eleven children. Orphaned at age eleven, her older siblings helped raise her, and she developed a rewarding talent in hat-making. Her love of the beautiful and original, together with her skill, brought success to her millinery shop. She acquired a small fortune before her marriage to Artemus Slack at age 28.

She was an unusual woman who could assert herself in the face of injustice. As a teenager, she had been an "early and earnest worker" against slavery. During an abolitionist meeting at the Baptist church in her hometown, the pro-slavery members of the community became so incensed that they threatened to tear down the building "if the ladies would [only] leave the church." Young Esther bravely stood up in the pew and announced: "This church belongs to the Baptist people and no one has a right to destroy it. If it is proposed to burn it down, I will stay here and see who does it."[25]

Her marriage to Slack, a railroader, in 1841 was brief. He died leaving property to Esther and their son. When Esther went to Illinois to settle her husband's estate, she was distressed to discover that women had no right over their husband's property nor even their own children. She vowed to devote her life to women's rights.

She exercised one of her first acts of civil protest in the years following her marriage to John Morris in 1845. On election day, Esther voted alongside her husband. Even though she knew her vote did not count, "she would do her duty, and it was not her fault if it was not counted."[26]

In 1845, John, Esther, and their three sons moved to the gold mining town of South Pass City in Wyoming Territory. John opened a saloon. Esther provided medical help to a community where "law and order and medical help were three stagecoach days away."[27] Her flower gardens were noted for the cheerful color they brought to the dusty mining town. Most importantly, Esther asserted her political concerns. She helped convince her neighbor, Colonel William H. Bright, to introduce a bill in the first territorial legislature to grant woman's suffrage. In 1870 her reputation for justice led to her appointment as the world's first woman justice of the peace.

Morris could be assertive when she saw injustice, but she was also witty and humble. When finally allowed to vote where her ballot actually counted, Morris took along her physician "to see if it [voting] would make her sick. Her physician stood by, and pronounced her in good health."[28] Later, in a letter addressed to Isabella Beecher Hooker that was to be read before the Woman Suffrage Convention in Washington, D.C., she acknowledged the significance of her acceptance to her appointment as the first woman justice of the peace: "Circumstances have transpired to make my position as justice of the peace a test of woman's ability to hold public office." She also pointed out that it had not been an easy job because of her lack of experience: "I feel that my work has been satisfactory, although I have often regretted I was not better qualified to fill the position. Like all pioneers, I have labored more in faith and hope."[29]

Esther Hobart Morris (1814–1902)
Wyoming suffragist and Sweetwater County Justice of the Peace
American Heritage Center Collections University of Wyoming

Without the label of radical, Esther Hobart Morris managed to help advance political equality for women. She is remembered as the "Mother of Equal Rights," and a nine foot bronze statue of her represents Wyoming, the "Equality State," in Statuary Hall in the Capitol Building in Washington, D.C. Morris's success did not derive from a socially prominent life. She overcame great emotional and personal loss and was able to develop skills, confidence, and independence in spite of being orphaned and widowed.

Morris' campaign for suffrage rights was not the only advancement in women's rights that Wyoming Territorial legislators enacted in 1869. When Republican Governor John A. Campbell convened that first territorial legislature, he proposed that widows be given guardianship of their minor children, the right to acquire and possess property, and equal pay for equal work. The Democrat-dominated house supported these measures.

Perhaps Governor Campbell's interest in women's legal rights came from the experience of a young woman in Washington, D. C. Isabella Crane Wunderly, who suffered a difficult childhood, became Mrs. John A. Campbell in 1872. Her father died when she was four. Her mother could not support the family, so they moved in with an aunt and uncle. Isabella performed domestic chores for her aunt and studied her lessons with the uncle. Those years of the girl's life were marked by "narrowness, repression, hard work, interrupted education, little pleasure or love."[30]

Later, Isabella went to live with another aunt and uncle in Washington, D. C. after the death of their only daughter. This uncle, Joseph Carey, was Chief Justice of the Court of Claims in 1862. Fifteen-year-old Isabella was awed by the capitol city and the wartime pageantry. She watched the soldiers parade through the city. Although she spent most of her time serving as nurse and companion to her ailing aunt, she was also able to attend social functions where she met John Campbell, a general in the army. They married several years later after he accepted the appointment from President Grant to the governorship of the newly formed territory of Wyoming.

Isabella Campbell's impoverished, fatherless childhood was not atypical. Concern for widows and the defenseless position of married women in regard to property was a highly debated issue of the mid-nineteenth century. One of the earliest objectives of woman's rights activists was the passage of women's property rights. Until late in the century, women could not legally participate in their husbands' purchases, nor could they prevent men from spending the wife's earnings in whatever manner they chose. Likewise, women were forced to suffer the consequence of their husband's poor investment decisions and had no legal protection from creditors after the husband's death.

Fortunately, most western states made provisions for this problem in their constitutions or early legislation. For example, Oregon passed a special "Married Woman's Sole Trader's Bill" in 1872 to protect woman's personal earnings. The law "enabled women needing its provisions to register themselves as 'sole traders' in the office of the county clerk, thus protecting their personal earnings, outside of the mutual living expenses of the family, from dissipation by the husband's creditors."[31] California, Texas, and Nevada had clearly established property rights for married women by the 1880s that were more in line with Spanish customs than English common law as practiced in eastern states.[32]

Mari J. Matsuda points out that western states were quick to adopt married women's property acts. Texas in 1845, California in 1849, Oregon in 1857, and Kansas in 1859 wrote these rights directly into their state constitutions. Matsuda also observes that such "provisions preceded major eastern legislation such as the New York Married Women's Property Act of 1860."[33] Married women's property and guardianship rights had become so common in the West by 1869 that Wyoming's first territorial legislators unanimously included these rights.

The earliest state to enact married women's property rights was Mississippi in 1839. Other states soon followed, though the East and Southeast tended to focus more on equity rights while the West adopted equality rights. Equity rights provided for a woman to maintain ownership of family property in her own name after marriage even though control of the property might go to her husband or a family trustee. Equality rights adopted by western states were more similar to the Hispanic tradition practiced in the Southwest which gave a married woman right to equal ownership with her husband and rights to separate control of her own property.[34]

While most western states revised common law by codifying the law to provide for married women's property rights, several states including California, Texas, New Mexico, Arizona, Nevada, Washington, and Idaho incorporated a civil law system of community property. This provided more protection for the property rights of married women by designating her an equal partner in all property acquired by either wife or husband during the marriage.[35]

Divorce was another area where western states adopted more liberal laws. Glenda Riley describes western states as "havens for those seeking divorce." She points out that first the prairie states led the way and then the plains states and territories provided easier divorce laws and regularly granted divorces. More women than men sought divorce in the western region and were more likely to receive custody of their children than women in the older eastern states. Illinois and Iowa had earned the reputation as divorce centers during mid-century, but this label was extended to North Dakota and Oklahoma by the 1890s because of their shorter residency requirements. Western laws expanded the grounds for divorce to include desertion, impotency, cruelty, drunkenness, criminal or "infamous" behavior, and imposition of personal indignities.[36]

In her study of Montana women, Paula Petrik contends that "although impetus for reforming marriage and divorce law was an eastern phenomenon, Montana and other western territories set the pace in marital dissolution from the late nineteenth century into the twentieth century."[37] Examples from her study show that western women had more freedom and economic independence than did eastern women because of earlier and better divorce and property rights laws.

Robert Griswold came to a similar conclusion. His work on divorce in California contradicts the oppressive viewpoint that women were helpless victims of Victorian domestic principles. In California, marriage and divorce patterns indicate that women had options. With help from friends and relatives, women could and did take the initiative to take action independent of their husbands.[38]

Divorce and property rights were the results of western women's modifications of woman's proper sphere. Frontier daughters, in particular, did not see themselves in terms of conventional nineteenth-century definitions of womanhood; they had become much more independent. They found alternatives to marriage as a means of economic security, and they began to seek their political right to vote in order to maintain and expand their newfound social and economic rights. Petrik contends that the vote was an emblem of western women's new definition of their gender: "Women of all ages came to believe that the vote validated their civic aspirations and underpinned their personal autonomy."[39]

One of these women was May Arkwright, an illegitimate child born in the coal mining community of Washingtonville, Ohio in 1860. As an adult, she struck out on her own and became a millionaire from a silver mine investment in Idaho. Even with all her wealth, she was never accepted by the higher social circles. She identified with working men and women and refused to confine herself to the restrictions of a cultured societal norm for women. She worked for suffrage in both Idaho, which passed in 1896, and in Washington, which passed in 1910. Unlike eastern suffragists, she did not fit the mold of an educated and refined woman. Another difference was that she believed in the "goodness and fairness" that she commonly found in western men.[40]

May Arkwright was raised by her father and grandfather. Her mother had disappeared soon after her birth.[41] She learned many of her domestic skills from growing up with her father who encouraged her to learn to cook. Her cooking skills were a source of pride to her and provided her with funds to invest in a silver mine that eventually paid off. Blueberry pies were her specialty in her boardinghouse restaurant in Idaho. Her pride in her baking skills is evident in a novel she wrote in 1900 where her experience is reflected in two of the female characters: "The first young ladies to arrive at the new mining camp…made more money baking and selling elderberry pies (the only fruit in the country), for which they received one dollar each, than most men made washing gold."[42]

May's father was not her most significant mentor. Beginning at age nine, May's life was shaped by her grandfather. Her father pulled her out of school so that she could care for her blind grandfather.[43] The nurturing and love between the two, however, was mutual. Her grandfather's special interest was in keeping up with all the economic and political theories of the time. Because she was his faithful escort to all soapbox lectures and the debates among her grandfather's friends, May's informal education was full of all the "isms" that her grandfather patiently explained to her after each lecture.[44]

The highlight of this political education was the young girl's introduction to William McKinley. While she was only ten years old, May and her grandfather attended a speech by the candidate during the early years of his career. Following the speech, May's grandfather invited McKinley to spend the night with them. May served him homemade doughnuts and cider. He praised her cooking but paid her an even more important compliment. He stated that woman was the "intellectual equal of man and should be his political equal."[45] This was the first she had heard about woman's suffrage. She had listened quietly to them discussing war and reconstruction, but this new issue on women's rights made her aware for the first time that she could not expect the same economic and political rights as men.

The event made an important impact on her life. As an adult, May Arkwright Hutton not only cultivated the political activism her grandfather had instilled in her as a young girl, but she became an energetic campaigner for woman's suffrage and woman's political equality. Her grandfather stimulated a confidence in her that allowed her to develop a strong, independent, and vigorous life. Several times she gave credit to her grandfather for the inspiration of her energies. His personal philosophy for her was to "[h]itch you wagon to a star, girlie. You may never reach the eminence to which you aspire, but place no limit on your aspirations."[46] In a letter to her brother in 1908, she mentioned that grandfather would have been proud of her activities in the woman's suffrage campaign.[47]

Aside from her close relationship with her grandfather, Arkwright's youth was full of hardships. She worked in a boardinghouse where she met underpaid and overworked coal miners of her community. She was married at least once before departing for Idaho in 1883, but her husband took their money and deserted her shortly after their wedding.[48]

She was not a woman to give up. After reading in the papers and broadsides of the wealth of the silver mines in Idaho, she convinced forty of the local miners to migrate with her to get rich in the West. They left by railroad which had recently been completed into the Idaho Panhandle, and concluded the last leg of their journey into Coeur D'Alene by steamboat.

After arriving at her destination, Arkwright knew she was no coal miner, but realized she could earn money cooking for the miners. She worked for Jim Wardner's boardinghouse restaurant until she had enough saved away to run her own boardinghouse. Arkwright had good business sense and carefully collected her $6.50 a week board from each miner every Saturday evening meal right after they got paid. One of her boarders was Levy "Al" Hutton, a railroad engineer. As an orphan, Al had been unwanted and poor. This was a background with which May could identify, and they found a mutual need and companionship with each other. They married in 1887 and settled in a house in Wallace, a new community in the area.

May Hutton's life as a married woman was not the model of Victorian gentility. First of all, she was a huge woman, 225 pounds, used to working around miners. She was not afraid of using strong, unfeminine language, and her gaudy dress and lack of education did not fit the social model of the more elite of the town. She was not included in the social register, but she was not much concerned. She preferred an active life, and she was soon involved in supporting miners who wished to unionize. She continued to be an avid reader and even tried writing. The result was a poorly written novel that jumbles together the labor problems of the Idaho mining war of 1899, the heroic leadership of an Indian woman, and a romantic love story of a captured white girl who grows up with the Indians but returns to eastern society.[49]

The novel became a best seller in the northwest, but Awkright Hutton ended up buying back most of the copies later so that she would not be sued by the big mining corporations whose activities she condemned in the book. Unable to make her fortune in a writing career, the Hutton couple continued to invest in a small mining venture with sixteen other working-class people. The mine finally began to pay off in 1901, and the Hutton's became millionaires.

Even with this newfound wealth, Hutton still did not fit into high-class social circles, but she entertained plenty of important political figures. She and her husband moved into a larger house in Wallace, hired a girl to help with the house, but Awkright Hutton continued to cook for her guests including Teddy Roosevelt, Clarence Darrow, William Jennings Bryan, William Borah, and Carrie Chapman Catt. These political friendships she was able to establish would provide her clout during her woman's suffrage activities and political aspirations.

In 1904, Hutton ran for Idaho state legislature on the Democratic ticket. Women of her state already had the vote, but she wanted to prove they had political equality. She did some heavy personal canvassing and succeeded in winning the nomination much to everyone's surprise. Her hard campaign against her Republican opponent did not win her a seat on the legislature, but she made a good showing. She was only eighty votes short of victory and blamed her defeat on the mine owners who contributed $20,000 to make sure she and her labor sympathies would not have a voice in Idaho. She believed, however, she had won the vote of the women.[50]

The Huttons followed the trend of the wealthy and moved to nearby Spokane, Washington in 1906. The move to Washington put her back on the suffrage trail. By taking this new residency, she lost her privilege to vote. In 1905, she had joined the National American Woman Suffrage Association and attended the national convention in Portland. Since Washington had not yet enfranchised women, Hutton was soon actively involved in the campaign. At first Hutton worked as a subordinate to Emma Smith DeVoe of Illinois who had come to Washington specifically to organize the suffrage campaign. Gradually, however, Hutton became disenchanted with DeVoe's campaign methods and decided to organize her own campaign in eastern Washington. In 1909, Hutton increased her drive for suffrage membership in the Spokane area in order to send enough delegates to the Washington Equal Suffrage convention and unseat DeVoe. DeVoe, who feared losing her presidency, refused to seat the delegates from the eastern part of the state under the guise that their names had been released only two days prior to the convention. Hutton's supporters rented a hall and met across the street while the original convention reelected DeVoe. However, at the national convention, the disunity resulted in both sides being allowed to attend, but none of the Washington delegates were allowed to vote.

The separation dividing the western faction led by DeVoe and Cora Smith Eaton and the eastern faction led by May Arkwright Hutton was based on personality conflicts between the leaders. Patricia Voeller Horner contends that the "social differences" between Hutton and DeVoe "may have contributed to their counterproductive power struggle."[51] Hutton did not have the social graces, education, or refinement of the typical eastern suffragist. In contrast, DeVoe was educated, a professional organizer, and carried herself as a "lady." DeVoe was described by her contemporaries as "sweet, womanly, and tactful," while Hutton was accused of using "profane and insulting" language and of associating with prostitutes. Her past history of running a boardinghouse was considered bad enough, but rumor was spread that she ran a "bad house, kept for immoral purposes."[52]

For her part, Hutton did not attempt to emulate society ladies. She "felt a class division between herself and most upper-class women because they had not had to work the way she had."[53] Hutton was accused of giving little money to political causes though she was exceptionally active in personal participation. However, both May and Al Hutton were renowned for their generosity to orphanages and poor families.[54]

Following the passage of woman's suffrage in Washington state, Hutton turned her political interest fully toward the Democratic Party. In 1912, she pushed her state political party to elect the first woman to the National Democratic Convention to be held in Baltimore.[55] She, of course, was to be that delegate. In spite of her preference for William Jennings Bryan over her state's choice for Champ Clark, they elected her to attend the national convention. Hutton faithfully cast her vote for Clark as her state's choice but ended up switching to Woodrow Wilson when Clark failed to make a showing and Bryan directed his supporters to unite behind Wilson.

Hutton's next aspirations were for a seat in the Senate. Unfortunately, she had been suffering from diabetes for some time and in 1914 became seriously ill from Bright's disease. She lost nearly one hundred pounds and had no energy left for political campaigns. She died in October of 1915 from heart failure at the age of fifty-five.

Five years after her death, Al Hutton completed the Hutton Settlement. It was a dream that he and May had shared. He, as an orphan, and she, as essentially motherless, had a special compassion for orphans and unwed mothers. It was a part of what had drawn them together. Childless, they hoped they could make life better for children. After their move to Spokane, May Hutton quickly found her way onto the board of directors at the Florence Crittendon Home for unwed mothers. She contributed generously to the children's home, baked turkeys in her own kitchen for needy families, and invested in a shoe store and gave away new shoes to the poor. Their dream residence for unwanted children was to be a home, not an institution. They planned to build a series of little cottages with a real home environment, pets, and responsibilities.

May Arkwright Hutton was a large, ambitious, and independent, but very loving and caring woman. She fit into male company comfortably on an equal basis and was not afraid of their strong language, but she also held a tender spot for women, children, and working-class laborers. She believed women to be men's intellectual equals and fought for the right to be their economic and political equals as well. With a focus on justice and the right kind of persuasion, she knew that western men would vote for woman's suffrage.

Some of her contemporaries accused her of being unfeminine with masculine mannerisms, but she was respected by the working class and needy. She had earned her way in life and refused to be bullied by "proper society." Unfortunately, civilization and high society were already catching up with her home in urbanized Spokane and there were few women to follow her model. However, she had helped bring more political equality for women through her work in woman's suffrage and as a leader in political party participation and running for office.

Woman's suffrage was the single most unifying objective during the woman's rights movement of the nineteenth century, but leaders also sought other reforms, such as married women's property rights, more liberal divorce laws, and dress and health reforms. However, only the suffrage movement attracted women from all spectrums, from the conservative Women's Christian Temperance Union to the most militant feminists. Political scientist Robert J. Dinkin has observed that "women in the initial suffrage states often showed a political sophistication beyond that of their nonvoting sisters. They were much more likely to join partisan clubs and discuss important issues. As a group, they probably exhibited a stronger preference for political and social reform than women elsewhere." The fact that women were able to vote in the West was a motivation for women of the East to become more involved. Dinkin suggests that the "accomplishments" of western women "may have influenced reform-minded women in some of the eastern and midwestern states to get involved in the partisan realm even if lacking the vote. Clearly, the actions of these politicized women in the early suffrage states provided models for others of the sex to follow in the years to come."[56]

In the East, voting rights for women was a goal they finally achieved in 1920. In the Rocky Mountain region, however, woman's suffrage became a reality much sooner. It began as an experiment in the Wyoming Territory in 1869, expanded to other mountain states in the 1890s, and succeeded along the Pacific coast in the 1910s. It served as a symbol of the personal autonomy western women had achieved and did not end with mere voting rights. Western women began to participate in public office as well.

Chapter Six

Western Women In Public Office

There can be no corruption now in government without the consent of women.

~Nellie Tayloe Ross

Wyoming, the first state to permanently grant full suffrage to women, was also the first territory to appoint and elect women into public office. Before becoming the first female justice of the peace in the United States in 1870, Esther Hobart Morris had taken an active role in convincing Councilman Bright to introduce the woman's suffrage bill in the first Wyoming Territorial Legislature. She was the type of woman who men looked to when they recognized the female right to legal equality. Morris was a large woman, close to six feet tall, but more importantly, she was unafraid to speak out against injustice. She was particularly concerned with the legal inequities that denied women the right to control their own property. Morris believed in justice and is known for her motto: "Justice first, then after that the law."[1]

The first woman to be *elected* to the office of justice of the peace was Mary A. Garrett, a citizen of Wyoming. Prior to her election in 1902, Garrett served as postmaster at Rock Creek beginning in 1888. Her neighbors respected her and believed her to be qualified for the position. As a rancher, she had acquired skills valued in the West: becoming "a marvelous 'shot' and a fearless and intrepid rider." Most importantly, her neighbors believed she could "hold her own in any situation."[2]

The first woman to be elected to a state office and the first woman to be appointed to an office requiring the confirmation of the U.S. Senate was Estelle Reel Meyer. She was born in Pittsfield, Illinois in 1862 and attended schools in

Pittsfield, Chicago, St. Louis, and Boston. After living in cities in both the East and Midwest, she chose to move west where her brother owned a stage and freight business in Cheyenne, Wyoming. He was mayor of the capital city; and Estelle taught school there for six years.[3]

In 1888 she was elected County Superintendent of Schools in Laramie County which included the Cheyenne school system. She excelled in this administrative position and decided to run for State Superintendent of Public Instruction in 1894. She was elected by the largest vote recorded for a candidate in the state at that time. In conjunction with this position, she also served as Registrar of the Land Board which helped bring in revenues for the school systems. Later, she headed the state's penal and reform institutions. As Secretary of Charities and Reform, she recommended that inmates be provided with reading material and be encouraged to continue their education. She also worked for better treatment of inmates in insane asylums. Her term in office was so successful that she was considered for the gubernatorial race, but she declined the nomination.[4]

In 1898 President William McKinley appointed Reel to the position of National Superintendent of Indian Schools, and the Senate unanimously confirmed her appointment. It was the first time the Senate confirmed a woman appointee. Her appointment was reaffirmed by Presidents Theodore Roosevelt and William Howard Taft. She served as Superintendent for twelve years until her marriage to Cort Meyer in 1910.

An early advocate of "practical" education, Reel stressed self-support and industrial training for Native American children. She particularly noted that the education of Indian girls had been sadly neglected. After observing the degraded culture of Native Americans, she believed that the closest path toward self-respect that she could help provide was self-support. She could not tolerate the idea that Indians should remain helpless victims and defenseless wards of the state. She hoped her educational programs would provide Native Americans a chance to regain some measure of their self-respect and self-reliance.[5]

The experiences of Morris, Garrett, and Reel as leaders in women's involvement in political office were repeated by others. Wyoming women were the first to serve on juries, first to hold public office, and first to vote on all local, state, and federal issues from 1870 on. Although office-holding women did not attain numbers equal to men, women in the state did not believe there was any discrimination or misconduct on the part of men. Mary Bellamy, Wyoming's first woman legislator elected in 1910 (and the second in the nation—Colorado having elected the first), pointed out that "there is no sex antagonism here and consequently no opposition to women's holding office." She also mentioned that even at that early date, it was "suggested that a woman run for the governorship, and there was no opposition to the idea."[6]

Bellamy spoke for many western women when she answered a reporter's query as to why more women had not been elected to office in the state. She replied that most women do not want the responsibility of public office: "There are few unmarried women, and the married ones are too busy at home." She did not believe, however, that women were selfish in this regard: "many of them are willing to be office-holders if they think they can help the state." She cited the example of Jean Brooks who served as a major on her father's staff as commander of the state militia and as deputy governor during her father's term as governor. Bellamy remarked that she believed "that almost any office the women might want they could get."[7]

Wyoming men were not a problem in the women's movement toward political participation. Bellamy reported that, "…men are usually willing to elect those [women] that run. You see in Wyoming, when it comes to politics, the men don't think of women as women but as citizens." Women of the state believed men accepted them as political equals: "They are willing to accord us equal rights with themselves, to consider what we want, and if it seems desirable, to grant it." Bellamy believed that it was for this reason, Wyoming women never felt compelled toward militancy: "it has never been necessary for women to become office-holders. Between the men and the women of this state there is a sympathetic understanding and the best kind of cooperation…working together for the good of Wyoming."[8]

Mary (Godat) Bellamy was one of the younger generation of pioneers to Wyoming. She was born in Missouri in 1861, but her family moved to Galena, Illinois while she was young. After her father died, she and her mother moved west in 1873. Bellamy attended college at the University of Wyoming. She was one of the founding members of the Cheyenne Women's Club in 1894 and encouraged the club to affiliate with the General Federation of Women's Clubs in 1896.

After Bellamy and her husband moved to Laramie in 1898, Bellamy organized another women's club and became Superintendent of Albany County Schools. In 1910, she was elected to the state legislature from the same county. Her most important concerns were for the rights of women and children. She helped pass a reform measure to incarcerate women prisoners separately from men in Wyoming, and she helped set up provisions for a separate institute for boys at the Wyoming Boys Institute. Another change she introduced to the state legislature was more liberal provisions in probate law for married women who served as administrators and executors.[9] Bellamy recalled the unfair laws used against her mother when she had attempted to settle their property in Illinois after her husband (Mary's father) died. They had been forced to move west for new beginnings, and as a legislator, she wanted to make sure Wyoming women did not suffer the same abuse of law.

Already a privileged voter, Bellamy worked for national woman's suffrage. She served as President of the Wyoming State Society of Women Voters and helped with the Oregon campaign for state suffrage. In 1915 she served as Wyoming's delegate to the National Council of Women Voters Convention in San Francisco and was instrumental in inviting the council to Wyoming for their 1916 convention.

Bellamy recognized the antagonism that went with suffrage movements in England and the eastern United States. She and other western women were anxiously aware that their political equality was not available to their eastern contemporaries. One professional woman remarked that she had been offered the position of dean of women at two large eastern universities but had turned down both jobs. She said she "prefer[red] a state with less pay, fewer immediate attractions and suffrage, than national recognition, more compensation and a step backward in the evolution of political rights."[10]

Wyoming citizens were careful to avoid any connection to radicalism; they wanted the world to view their experiment with woman suffrage as a natural human right that worked calmly and smoothly. They wanted no one to accuse them of turning the world upside down; however, they were not afraid to advance the political power of women when it was practical and useful.

The example of early Wyoming women officeholders was repeated in other western states. By 1900, Kansas claimed fifteen women mayors and "dozens" more were "chosen to serve on town councils," according to Robert J. Dinkin. He also notes that forty percent of the vote in Idaho in 1898 was by women who made up only 40% of the population. The state elected three women to the legislature, four county treasurers, fifteen county superintendents of public instruction and the state superintendent of schools.[11]

Another political scientist Kristi Anderson points out that in 1920 the governor of New Mexico "appointed both Hispanic and Anglo women to every state board, a woman became assistant secretary of state, and women moved into control of the public welfare board." The positions of secretary of state and superintendent of public instruction tended to become "'traditional' women's offices." Several states, which Anderson points out were mostly in the West, had repeatedly elected women to this highest position in public education. Anderson's statistics also point out that by the 1930s, "New England and western states led in the number of women elected to legislative and other [state] offices" while "southern states lagged far behind in the extent to which women ran for and won legislative office."[12]

The Victorian ideal of femininity which required women to be domestic, submissive, and dependent was unworkable in the West, particularly for women who had learned to work side by side with fathers, brothers, and husbands. The West challenged them with rugged terrains, harsher and drier climates, and new gender relationships. The more exceptional women, such as Esther Morris, Mary Garrett, Mary Bellamy, and Estelle Reed Meyer, adapted to the new environment and excelled at vital public roles. What made them advance more quickly than other women was their willingness to offer their services to their community, state, or country. Each of these women found their self-identity to be more suitable to the public sphere where they could be independent and self-reliant.

Women who held public office in the West, like those who worked in professional fields, developed their confidence from the encouragement of male role models, especially fathers and brothers. They recognized their abilities and talents to succeed in areas that had been traditionally reserved for men. They also realized that they could not rely on standard laws and eastern customs to protect their rights as humans. Their environmental and social conditions taught them they could work with men to achieve equality.

Congresswoman

Western women did not believe themselves to be limited to local and state offices. By the early twentieth century after most western states had granted full woman's suffrage, women began to direct their efforts toward national office. One of the most important political offices was opened to women by Jeannette Rankin of Montana, the first woman elected to the United States House of Representatives. She was the daughter of Montana pioneers, highly motivated and encouraged by her father during her youth, and elected to office with the help of her brother as campaign manager.

A young Jeannette Rankin (born in 1880) became involved in the suffrage movement late in the campaign but had a very strong impact on the passage of laws at both the state and national levels. The suffrage movement was the perfect arena for her concern about the corrupt government she had observed in both her home state of Montana and the slum areas of eastern cities she visited. The political experience she gained by working for woman's suffrage gave her the training and the motivation to run for Congress in 1916. Rankin correctly believed she could push the Nineteenth Amendment through the House of Representatives. She could not have achieved national status, however, without the help and support of her family and community.

John Rankin took a special interest in Jeannette, his eldest child, and encouraged his daughter to accompany him around the ranch, sawmill, and logging camps. He was always ready to listen to her and build her confidence with compliments. Rankin once remarked, "He was very proud of me—always flattered me."[13] As she grew older, she proved worthy of his esteem; she was bright, energetic, and always tried to make herself useful. One day while Rankin was out watching her father and his hired hands put hay into the barn with new machinery, one of the mechanisms jammed. Since her father could not leave the wild team to investigate, Rankin walked around to the side of the machine, quickly recognized how to solve the problem, and reported back to her father. He immediately instructed his men to do as she said. When the task was completed, he teased his men: "You haven't the sense enough to do it yourself; you have to let a little girl tell you what to do."[14] Rankin later recalled this moment with pride.

Rankin's father continued to be her role model through her adolescent years. She recalled that she and her father discussed everything. One topic that her father often brought up with the family was the military. His perspective had a lasting impact on Rankin's political views. She recognized that the army was quite prominent in Montana, but her father had little respect for the service. Mr. Rankin often pointed out the murderous behavior of the U.S. Army toward the Indians. Rankin was particularly saddened by the deaths of the Nez Perce tribe who left Idaho and fled through Montana where they were stopped by the army on their way to seek refuge in Canada. When Rankin was still a child, she saw five Indians hanged in her town. At the time, she had been conscious that it was wrong, even outrageous.[15] These childhood observations and the influence of her father had much to do with her later pacifism and commitment to world peace.

Rankin did not especially enjoy school and believed she learned more by working on the ranch. Nevertheless, she graduated from high school and decided to attend the University of Montana. She had difficulty trying to decide what field to study but finally narrowed her choices to either teaching or nursing. She had been quite successful in doctoring the animals around the ranch, but her father convinced her that she was too independent minded for nursing. He urged her to complete her bachelor's degree in education. Soon after she graduated in 1902, her father died.[16]

Rankin decided she wanted to do something more significant with her life than to teach school as her mother had. After reading about Jane Addams and her work in the Chicago slums, Rankin decided to investigate the field of social work. She worked for four months in a settlement house in San Francisco and then decided to go back to school to learn how she could do more. In 1908 she enrolled in the New York School of Philanthropy (the forerunner of Columbia University's School of Social Work). While working among the impoverished of the city, she concluded that the only solution to the poverty problem was government regulation. However, she was not sure government would provide the necessary solutions because the existing system was so corrupt.

Around this same time, Rankin became acquainted with the woman's suffrage movement in New York. If women became involved in legislative decisions, she quickly concluded, then much of the corruption and poverty could be cleared away. Back in high school, she and her brother Wellington had often discussed the problems with government and noted the exploitive nature of the big coal companies that controlled her state. During her work in the city, she began to realize that corruption existed on all levels of government. Once she accepted the premise that the root of the evil was male immorality, she became committed to the suffrage campaign and believed that women's vote would help alleviate the problems of the country.

When Rankin moved to Seattle in 1910 to work in another settlement house, she became involved in the state's successful campaign to become the fifth state in the nation to enfranchise women. At first, she worked alone canvassing for woman's suffrage during her spare time until she learned that a suffrage organization was already in operation. Suffragists had been acting covertly in an attempt to avoid opposition from the liquor interests. Rankin joined the campaign and learned how to canvass the "anti's." The strategy worked; the state broke the fourteen year lapse since the first four Rocky Mountain states had passed full suffrage rights for women. (Utah and Idaho had become the third and fourth states to grant full suffrage in 1896.)

From 1911 to 1914, Rankin was among the strongest promoters of woman suffrage when she returned to Montana. She believed in working at the grass roots level which was the strategy she had learned from working on campaigns in New York and Washington. She organized support in each precinct and toured the state lecturing from trains and on street corners. Because Rankin was an eloquent speaker, she found herself in great demand.

After her success and high visibility in the state from the suffrage campaign, Rankin decided to seek the Republican nomination for Congress. Her brother Wellington, who was by now a well-established attorney and successful rancher, supported her whole heartedly and volunteered to serve as her campaign manager. Despite the fact that she was a woman, she had an advantage over the seven men who ran against her. At the time, the two representatives from the state were still being elected at large; districting had not yet been determined. Because of her many speaking engagements during the suffrage campaign, she was better known across the state than any of her opponents. Rankin received three times as many votes as the next highest candidate even though the election was, overall, a landslide for the Democratic Party.

Jeannette Rankin (1880–1973)
Congresswoman, Montana

Rankin is chiefly remembered in the history books for her first vote in the House. On her first day in office in 1917, President Wilson asked Congress for a declaration of war. Rankin was clearly and vocally an advocate of peace, but her pacifism had not yet been tried. She received heavy pressure from suffragists not to make a bad impression. Her vote of no, they believed, would seriously damage the national woman's suffrage movement. The worst blow to Rankin came from her own brother. Wellington believed the Axis Powers had to be stopped, and he was thinking of enlisting. Despite all the opposition, the Congresswoman held firm to her convictions and cast her unpopular "no" vote with the declaration that "I want to stand by my country but I cannot vote for war. I vote no."[17]

In spite of the infamy of her vote, Rankin was able to achieve important advancements for woman's suffrage. In January 1918, Congresswoman Rankin placed the suffrage bill on the agenda. She then provided herself as a good model. She later pointed out, "I operated as a Congressman. I was polite and sensitive, and I didn't do the wrong thing, and all the men had to do was to watch men. I didn't have to say anything."[18]

Rankin did, indeed, plan her strategy carefully. What she considered her greatest success was in silencing her strongest opponent, Joe Walsh of Massachusetts. Since he was "violently opposed" to woman's suffrage, she usually tried to avoid him. One day, however, she was asked to speak in his district. When she addressed his constituents, she told them of all the good things he had done in Congress. She then pointed out that he had only one fault: he opposed woman's suffrage. She reminded them, however, that they, as his electors, were to blame because they had not converted him.[19]

Shortly before the bill came to a vote, Congresswoman Rankin went to Walsh's office to ask a favor. She said, "I don't want you to do anything against your conscience. If you are against woman's suffrage, I'm not going to ask you to vote for it. But I *am* going to ask you *not* to make a speech against it." She knew Walsh's speeches were dangerous and could convert any borderline voters. When Walsh asked her what he should say if asked, she told him to simply leave the room with no reply. He admitted he had some difficulty voting against woman suffrage but did not specify, and out of respect, she did not inquire.[20]

When the votes came in, the ayes won by only one vote. Walsh surprised everyone by extending his favor to Rankin one step further. When anyone who had voted yes approached him hoping that he would convince them to change their vote, Walsh replied, "If you change your vote, I'll change mine."[21] Thus, Rankin had managed to sway the influence of her strongest opponent.

Rankin's successful impact on the House vote was due to her ability to work with men and effectively use their political strategies. She was a prudent leader, and in her words, she was "a good Congressman." She firmly insisted that she had not done "any female things" to get her way. She refused to flirt with men and conscientiously played the game by their rules.[22]

Rankin had mastered the techniques of politics, but she also realized that not all women were ready to participate in political activities. After all, government administration was a male domain where women had been forbidden for centuries. Rankin realized that because of this prohibition there were discrepancies between women's unused abilities and their current level of practiced behavior. She believed women needed the vote to end government corruption, but she also realized that most women were not prepared for that responsibility. When women were confronted with public issues, Rankin pointed out, they generally "won't *think* about it." Instead they think, "what it'll do to my husband's job; what'll it do to my dress. Will I have to wear the same dress two or three times?" Because of their submissive training, women "won't give, and they won't think." Rankin believed women capable, but they had not yet been trained or motivated to think politically.[23] Most women, especially those in the East, had not had the advantage of learning to communicate in the male-dominated public world. western women had an advantage because they had more opportunities to work with men and participate in public activities where both genders were involved.

Rankin noticed a distinction in women's political abilities between the women of the West and those in her temporary home in the South. According to Rankin, women who had been voting for decades and had participated in the suffrage campaign "were so much more advanced in their thinking than the states that had never had a state convention." In contrast, she observed that women in the South Carolina League of Women Voters "were always doing things the wrong way…because they didn't know anything about political procedures." She believed that state by state campaigns for suffrage had ultimately been the better strategy because they prepared women for the technical aspects of public decision-making.[24]

Jeannette Rankin was a strong role model for twentieth-century women. She promoted suffrage rights at both the state and national levels and proved that women were politically capable. Her early successes can be attributed not only to her intelligence and diligence, but also her environment. Her mother had been a model of women's intellect and as a teacher had indicated that women had economic alternatives to marriage and domesticity. Her father served as a strong role model and devoted himself to developing his daughter's abilities and confidence. He taught her to be independent and placed education above domestic concerns. Her state supported her campaign for woman's suffrage and shortly after put her into one of the nation's highest offices. It did not matter that she was a woman. She merely had to prove herself a concerned and capable citizen who had mastered the strategies of politics and was willing to serve in a public office.

Western Women Governors

In 1924 women's political history made another advance. Two women, both from western states, were elected to the governorship. The most obvious qualification for both women was that they followed their husbands into office. One of them, however, was to prove that her political abilities went beyond her marriage contract.

"Ma" Ferguson of Texas ran in the gubernatorial race because her husband had completed all his eligible terms but was not ready to give up control of the office. Ma Ferguson took over the official position as Governor of Texas, but her status was merely symbolic. Her husband continued to make the decisions and control the administration.

The situation was different, however, for Nellie Tayloe Ross of Wyoming. Her husband died while in office. She had shared his work, his interests, his plans, and his responsibilities from the day they were married. She had always been behind him and provided him with constructive criticism as he struggled through the preparation of legal briefs, speeches, and campaign strategies.

Governor Ross, a Democrat, faced strong Republican opposition during the 1922 gubernatorial race. His victory had been hard-won. Therefore, when he died suddenly, the Democrats were afraid of losing control. They believed Nellie Ross could best carry on the work and programs her husband had started. They asked her to run for office. Realizing the stupendous weight of this request, not only because of responsibilities of such a high office but also because she was the first woman to do so, Ross at first refused. She saw herself as a humble mother and wife, recently widowed and in mourning.

The Democratic Party took advantage of her dedication to her husband and convinced her that she must complete her husband's work. The Chairman of the State Democratic Committee, who had been a close friend of her husband's, coaxed her into accepting the nomination. He asked her to consider her husband's "unfinished work" in the gubernatorial office "as a child he has left to be nourished, and you are the one who must assume the task."[25] Her natural abilities, however, took her far beyond her marital obligation. She later became active in the Democratic Party at the national level and was the first woman to be appointed Director of the Mint.

Nellie Tayloe, born in 1886 in St. Joseph, Missouri, married William Bradford Ross, an attorney from Tennessee, in 1902 and moved west as a teenage bride. She fulfilled her role as wife and mother for twenty years before her political career began. That role included studying politics, history, and law to help her husband through the early years of his career. "So eager was my interest in my husband's advancement," Ross later wrote, "that when he wanted to test the effect of his theories of the law by discussion with me, he could depend on finding a ready listener and one not unwilling to expose any fallacies I thought I could detect."[26]

Nellie Tayloe Ross (1876–1977), Wyoming Governor, 1924–1926
Nellie Tayloe Ross Papers, America Heritage Center, University of Wyoming

Ross's involvement and educational interest in her husband's work was a natural continuation of her childhood. Her father, James Tayloe, was a merchant by profession, gentleman farmer by avocation, and definite proponent of education. He believed in education for all his children including his only surviving daughter Nellie. She was the sixth child born into the family. (Several babies born before her had died in infancy). After Tayloe moved his family to Kansas during the early years of Nellie's schooling, public education became a difficult venture for the fragile little girl. To make sure she learned her basics, Mr. Tayloe hired a private tutor. Nellie was a motivated student and earned excellent marks. Although she never attended college, she may have received some additional education, or at least an interest in law and history, from her three brothers, particularly Samuel who became a judge.[27]

Ross cited two other sources for her informal education that prepared her for office. During the early years of marriage, she and her husband took turns reading classical literature to each other. This, she believed, not only gave her extensive knowledge but helped develop her speaking voice. Another source of educational and political advancement for her was her membership in the prestigious Cheyenne Woman's Club. This small group limited its membership to twenty-five in order to concentrate all activities on the group's education.[28]

The greatest credit for her education, Ross gives to her husband: "I had long realized that the strong, good man at my side was the vital influence in the molding of my character and thought." While he lived, she believed her "individuality was almost submerged in his." However, after she found herself on her own after his death, she recognized that instead of submergence, her close association with her husband had helped her to develop "a more clearly defined and independent individuality with real self-reliance based upon convictions and experience."[29]

It is unclear at what point Ross completed her husband's "unfinished work" and when she began to work from her own agenda. She later remarked that she was not so much surprised by the idea of taking over for her husband as she was by how much knowledge she had absorbed. When "confidential disclosures" crossed her desk to which she was "already thoroughly familiar," she felt a surge of confidence. Thus, when "difficult new questions arose," she was comfortable about confronting them. She also said that "the thought often occurred to me that probably none of those other governors, looking down at me from the walls above, knew at first any more about such matters than I did." Her solution, she believed, was similar to what her predecessors had followed: "investigate and learn."[30]

Although no act of her administration made front page news, at least one activity made national news. In 1926 she managed to delay the building of a proposed dam on the Colorado until all states that had an interest in the "distribution of the impounded water" had a chance to participate in an agreement.[31] Her "ability as leader in the state" was reflected in several bills which the legislature passed. These included new coal mine regulations, a new banking code, an enlarged farm-loan fund, and a child-labor law barring employment of children under sixteen in hazardous occupations.[32]

Ross, the thirteenth governor of the state, had a successful two-year term, but she was not reelected. Her administration went smoothly and without incident. One source reported that she attended "strictly—and quietly to business." She instigated no drastic measures; she granted no pardons, "set or upset" no precedents, defied no lawless order, and vindicated no family honor to arouse public resentment toward a woman in office.[33]

When it came time for re-election, Ross chose not to campaign. She wanted her success in office to speak for itself; she did not want to be caught up in the political debates. Perhaps one of the issues that most hurt her chance for re-election was her failure to respond to accusations made against her by women activists in the state. Theresa A. Jenkins, an active Republican who had been nationally active during the suffrage movement, accused Ross of having done nothing for the state or for women. First, Jenkins pointed out that the woman governor never took part in the suffrage campaign, was never a delegate to "a Woman's Suffrage Convention, to a Woman's Christian Temperance meeting...or to a meeting of any kind, in any place, or at any time, to do anything for the advancement of the women and children of the state."[34] At this point in her life, Ross was not an activist. She was not trying to turn the world upside down; she simply fulfilled a role in which she believed she was needed.

The second contention against her was an unjust accusation. Jenkins feared that with the water rights of the state in jeopardy, Ross was not the best person to have in office. Ross, however, had already proved she could detain the dam project until all states involved could participate. Ross's mistake was her failure to take advantage of an active campaign in which she could respond to these accusations and emphasize her political strengths and successes.

Jenkins doubted Ross's commitment and service to women, but it was not an issue that remained in question for long. After completion of her two-year term, Nellie Tayloe Ross became a popular nation-wide speaker. The people of the country wanted to know about this woman who held such a high office. Ross did not disappoint them. During a summer tour with the eastern Chautauqua Association, the former woman governor won the respect of those she addressed. The *Madison Sentinel* of South Dakota reported her to be "without question the finest woman speaker ever to appear on the Chautauqua program." She was an excellent speaker with a clear, confident voice and "quiet dignity."[35] The *Kinsley Graphic* of Kansas also gave her a glowing report: "She speaks clearly, logically, and closed a wonderful talk [entitled "Women in Politics"] with an appeal for women to use their political power for the world peace, the greatest human need today." The reporter described her as "delightful to meet, a woman of culture, refinement and great personal power."[36]

With such national recognition, the Democratic Party selected her to serve as vice-chairman of the National Democratic Committee. In this capacity, she was acknowledged for her outstanding abilities by President Franklin Roosevelt who appointed her in 1933 to become the first woman Director of the Mint. She held this position competently for twenty years and was reappointed by Democratic and Republican Presidents alike until her retirement in 1953.

Nellie Tayloe Ross was a bright woman who learned ably and quickly. Brought up in a conventional home, she learned to love her place as a wife and mother. In one of her speeches she proclaimed that home, wifehood, and motherhood "fulfills her highest destiny." Yet she was a realist and acknowledged that not all women would have the same experience, nor should they. She pointed out that "there is so much work to be done in the world outside [the home] not only useful but absolutely essential to the happiness and well being of civ[ilization]." Because of this, every woman in the U.S. had finally achieved "freedom of choice that enables her to find that avenue of service to which she is most inclined and for which she is best fitted."[37]

The Ross children were all boys, but had she had a daughter, Ross would surely have encouraged her to be educated, to be prepared for whatever service best suited her. In a speech, Ross pointed out that "through education...woman is learning her potentialities, and through it her latent genius is finding release." She also pointed out that she would indeed recommend politics as a pursuit for women. Above all else women needed to concern themselves with world peace. Politics gave them a new voice of power: "Time was when women could only weep over the tragedy of war but now they share with men responsibility for the solution of that problem."[38] One of Ross's favorite sayings was that "there can be no corruption now in government without the consent of women."[39]

Enfranchisement and political office for women meant that they could finally participate directly and actively in government. Likewise, laws of western states and territories which guaranteed equal pay for teachers were a significant beginning. It marked a new recognition of women's economic rights and intellectual abilities. It did not protect women who wished to compete in all former male occupations, but it opened the door to new possibilities. Even more importantly, women's votes began to count, beginning with Wyoming's woman's suffrage law in 1869. It was a slow process, but the door was opened. Having just one state willing to experiment with a twenty-one-year-old idea (the 1848 Seneca Falls Convention officially recognized the movement for woman's suffrage), was the beginning of a legal and firm commitment. It took another 21 years before additional states began to add the voting rights of women, and 51 years to make it a Constitutional amendment; but once the experiment survived the test in one state, it provided a successful model for others.[40]

Women did not achieve these early stages of equality by themselves. Supportive fathers and strong male role models helped put the idea in young women's minds, and once there, brothers and husbands either directly or inadvertently helped nurture women's evolution toward equality. Courageous male leaders took the risk of proposing equality rights, and they counted on rational female models to prove themselves worthy of their trust. Many women like Esther Hobart Morris, Estelle Reel Meyer, Jeannette Rankin, and Nellie Tayloe Ross rose to the occasion with admirable grace and dignity, alleviating many of the fears that women's equality would mean a radical uprooting of centuries-old traditions.

Chapter Seven

Conclusion
Equality for Women in the Facilitating Environment of the American West

Historically, the West has not been just a region of exploration and conquest; it has been a symbol of hope, of vision, of new beginnings. People from eastern states, from Europe, even from Asia migrated to the West not for the many hardships that they were to endure but for hope of opportunities that it represented. Many of them failed and others destroyed the land and cultures as they made their fortune, but the "West of the Imagination" has remained an important American tradition.[1]

In early histories, the image of hope, adventure, and new beginnings represented by the West was applied predominantly to men; however recent work has added a female dimension.[2] Many women migrated west by choice with their own hopes and dreams and found new beginnings and opportunity. In this study, I have provided a variety of examples of these women. I have also shown ways in which the environment and social conditions of the West helped promote new opportunities for women and thus advanced early laws and practices toward equality. In this manner, women continued to elevate their gender from its long tradition of inferior economic and submissive political status.

Women's inferior status came about as civilization supposedly became more advanced. To what degree cultural progress was actually a positive value was challenged by Henry Nash Smith in *Virgin Land*. He criticized contemporary writers who believed in "the theory of social stages which places the West below the East." Smith remarked that this theory was dependent on the notion that "civilization" steadily increases "as one moves from primitive simplicity and coarseness toward the complexity and polish of urban life."[3] Urban polish which included theater, ballet, and other high culture depended upon leisure time and wealth of a select class. What the theory ignored were the slums, poverty, class stratification, and human degradation that was the negative and more intense result of nineteenth-century urbanization and industrialization.

The deteriorating status of women was a part of the "civilizing" influence of cities and industry. The growth of wealth and refinement, according to Julia Spruill, was the factor most detrimental to women's "initiative, energy, and independence." Spruill contends that self-reliant colonial women found precedence for their participation in business and public life from pre-seventeenth-century English women. "English women of the aristocracy" before the seventeenth century commonly took an interest "in national affairs," and English women of the lower classes were usually "engaged in what today we call gainful occupations." Following the Restoration, however, seventeenth-century English women became more interested in "wealth and the vogue for frivolous entertainments." The result was "a rapid deterioration in the physique, the morale, and the general efficiency of upper-class women." Colonial women at first could not afford this luxury; but as wealth and urbanization began to take over colonial life, American women began to emulate the ornamental lifestyle of English women. Nevertheless, there were still pockets of self-reliant colonial women, and their expanded role was a result of their environment. "Because of the rural character of their lives and the general influence of the frontier," Spruill asserts, "[eighteenth-century] American ladies were less idle and artificial than those in England" although they were not as "daring and independent" as their mothers "of the preceding century."[4]

Following the Revolution, the new ideology of republicanism included a new role for women that gave them more prestige. Education for girls was given new consideration. According to Mary Beth Norton, there were three arguments that helped shape the new role of women. First, it was determined that instead of "unsexing" women, education would make them "better wives, mothers, and mistresses of households." Second, a feminine-focused education could help cultivate "proper behavior." Third, the requirements for a virtuous republican citizenship depended on the involvement of women who were considered more virtuous by nature. Educated mothers were needed to train their sons to become good citizens of the republic.[5]

Although the republican motherhood ideology recognized the domestic status of women to be valuable and made women less subordinate to men, this definition of womanhood eventually became more restrictive. Norton concludes that "woman's domestic and maternal role came to be seen as so important that it was believed women sacrificed their femininity if they attempted to be more (or other) than wives and mothers." The result was that Victorian womanhood gradually replaced republican womanhood.[6]

As settlers began to migrate westward, they took their social standards with them, including the ideals of Victorian womanhood. However, when they succeeded, Victorian ideals and traditions became a deterrent to equality rights for women. Westerners discovered that the frontier environment required that new laws and customs be created. It was the relaxation of Victorian standards that allowed opportunities for the advancement of equality rights for women to occur. This happened more quickly in the West than in the East because the West was less culturally "civilized."

The lives of assertive western daughters, in particular, reveal that there was a period in the settlement of the West when women made significant advances toward equality and independence. As this book has shown, their success was based on the distinct influence of a new environment where daughters adapted more readily than did their emigrant mothers. The first generation had a tendency to identify with the traditional standards of their Victorian upbringing and maintain emotional and psychological ties with the family and friends "back home." Daughters, on the other hand, were more apt to accept the frontier environment as the norm and look to non-traditional women and male role models. Daughters were freer to experiment with both "male" and "female" work, privileges, and responsibilities.

In terms of work, women who emigrated west on their own initiative in order to advance their careers or own their own land found the western environment more permissive. The West also took the lead in offering co-education and gave better salaries and positions to female teachers. In terms of legal and political rights for women, the West clearly took the lead. Suffrage was granted to western women much more readily in western states and territories than in eastern states.

In order for equality to occur, a society will go through three stages of change. The first stage is a rejection of the old models of relationships. That necessitates the second stage where the subordinate group finds alternative models with which to identify. If positive new models are adopted, then the society will move to the third stage which is a blending of the roles of the formerly subordinate group with the dominant group on a more equal basis.

These stages have been applied in this study to the development of the U.S. West. Differences between generations existed in terms of behaviors and attitudes which affected the change in the public lives of women. The lives of the assertive western daughters were substantially different from their emigrant mothers. They were the first generation to fully adapt to the conditions of a new region. They shared similar hopes, disappointments, and a common disillusionment with the domestic ideology of their mothers' generation. Because their mothers did not experience the unique conditions of the western environment in their own youths, they were unable to provide the model by which their daughters could learn to adapt. The non-traditional women were forced to develop new styles based on their own experiences and to discover new role models suitable to their unique situation.

From these new models they learned autonomy, confidence, skills, and goals that went beyond domesticity. The primary issue was that the daughters did not wish to be limited to the single option of domestic wife and mother that their own mothers represented. The rejection of mothers as role models led to the assertive daughters looking to women in non-traditional careers or male mentors whom they could idealize and imitate. From them, they learned autonomy, confidence, skills, and goals that went beyond domesticity. Young girls in the West spent more time in the outdoors than had their Victorian mothers. In work and in play, they participated in activities with fathers, brothers, and other males. Many were interested in the natural environment and indigenous cultures.

Although gender divisions of labor and social conventions were more relaxed in the West, the young women who grew up there were still subject to some restrictions. However, most were able to overcome those obstacles placed upon them by outmoded expectations of family and communities. In general, assertive western women found that Victorian culture, represented by their mothers and grandmothers, restricted their endeavor-oriented nature while the frontier environment allowed them more career options and political freedoms.

Once social obstacles were overcome, assertive western women could move into the third stage which allowed them to blend into the public sphere with men. They found an unprecedented opportunity for independence, self-realization, and professional advancement. The professional trend for women in the West began with the emigration of women as missionaries, teachers, and writers. Although these occupations existed in the East, there were more positions available and a greater depth of opportunity and more abundant demand in the West. First generation migrants also found their domestic labors more valued in the West where they could earn good incomes from cooking meals or doing laundry for bachelors. Their economic pursuits tended to be more domestic-oriented, however, while their daughters tended to pursue careers in non-traditional fields. Assertive women became professors, doctors, architects, artists, journalists, homesteaders, and business owners. Financial need was often the motivation, especially for teachers and homesteaders, but the assertive generation also wanted the independence and prestige in addition to the economic rewards of their work and investments. Because there was a high demand and limited supply, western-ers could not afford to discriminate against women.

Economic need, however, was not the only factor. A new psychology of inter-personal relationships was also necessary. Fewer social taboos meant western women could experiment with new lifestyles and career options. Men's attitudes also changed as they began to view their wives and daughters more as partners and equals. Father figures could allow daughters to idealize and imitate them, and they could teach young girls skills and subjects formerly taught only to boys. As a result, western women found career alternatives that went beyond domesticity.

The beginnings of social power and economic independence for women led to early steps toward political power in the West. New state constitutions and laws were adopted to fit the unique needs and unusual social conditions of the western environment. These new laws and the acceptance of unusual legal practices in western states and territories helped to expand the status of women and make their participation in legal and political activities socially acceptable. Enfranchisement and political office for women meant that they could finally participate directly and actively in government. Likewise, laws of western states and territories which guaranteed equal pay for teachers supported a significant beginning. It marked a new recognition of women's economic rights and intellec-tual abilities. It did not protect women who wished to compete in every former male occupation, but it opened the door to new possibilities.

Later twentieth-century career-oriented women continued to try to overcome social prejudices that defined them as intellectually and politically inferior, and confined them to a separate, domestic sphere. Westerners had developed prece-dence for female independence and equal opportunity. It was an attitude that became legendary even though it was later diluted and less expansive once west-ern states and cities were established and leisure time and luxuries became avail-able.

One classic study has revealed that during the war years of the 1940s, western women were more independent and open to change. They were more likely to approve equal standards for women and men than were women in the other regions of the country. D'Ann Campbell concludes from a 1943 survey of women that "just as western women led crusaders for the rights to vote and for coeducation, in 1942 they were pioneers in the new morality."[7]

Even as late as the 1960s, the trend continued. Jo Ann Robinson, one of the female leaders of the Montgomery bus boycott of 1955, chose to move to the West where she believed she would find more freedom than she had in the South. According to Virginia Scharff, who describes Robinson's activities and mobility in *Twenty Thousand Roads: Women, Movement, and the West,* the ideas and myths of regions continue to impact people's attitudes and choices: "In American history, the concept of the West has always been hitched to the possibility of mobility, of transformation, of progress." This "state of mind (or myth, perhaps)" stands in sharp contrast to the "regional identity of the South" which Robinson left behind. In the South of the 1950s, "people know their places, and places can be fixed in time and space" especially when considering the perspective of "white supremacy" where "their claims to be able to fix place *and* race on the notion that social and political boundaries are real, obvious, formidable, and permanent." Scharff points out that "the South long maintained its regional distinctiveness not by moving, but by standing firm against motion and change and fluidity"[8] which stands in sharp contrast to the evolutionary mobility of the West.

The West of the 1960s represented more mobility and freedom for some women of the Northeast as well. Maggie Fahin, born in Connecticut, believed the West provided her more individual freedom and professional equality. At age 40, she became an ordained minister, served a rural congregation in Wyoming, and founded an ecumenical ranch in the Wind River Mountains. Fahin once remarked, "Nowhere else in this world am I so totally alive. Nowhere else do heaven and earth seem so close to being one." Wilderness was an important part of her ecumenical ranch program, and she recorded that "wilderness is a creative step forward because it has its own patterns and…tends to breed a kind of humility." In contrast, the city "is tamped with mankind's own imagination and living patterns." Fahin saw the wilderness as a place of renewal.[9]

The second of two daughters, Fahin was her mother's favorite. She was quiet and never caused her mother any problems. Because she was Nathalie's "golden girl," her every want and need were automatically met by her adoring mother. This over- protectiveness on the part of her mother was later considered a disadvantage to her development. A biographer contends that "Maggie was given no early need to communicate or interact with others in a normal way, a gap in her learning process that would profoundly frustrate her self-expression throughout life."[10]

Her mother clung to her in a manner that Fahin would later describe as unhealthy: "As a young child I could do no wrong. What a strange and terrible bondage." As an adult, she recognized her underdeveloped self: "I protected my inner world from invasion." She withdrew from the external world where she was often misunderstood and hurt. To protect her inner self, she cautiously guarded her thoughts and feelings.[11]

Living in an environment that allowed her few opportunities for self expression, Fahin remained quiet and withdrawn. Two events in her youth, however, helped strengthen her self-awareness. On the first occasion, she discovered a new form of communication. A friendly hired hand lifted her onto the back of a gentle, shaggy pony. She quickly developed an emotional affinity with the soft, warm animal and felt the rhythm of its strides. Her biographer points out, "She'd known immediately here was someone with whom she could interact. With the pony, the simplest of gestures and words brought response."[12]

The second occasion of her self development was at age fourteen when she and her mother and sister took a vacation at a Wyoming dude ranch. She was deeply inspired by the rugged blue mountains, and they became a lifelong source of strength. Equally important, Fahin learned to interact with people. For the first time in her life, she made friends with people who understood her and shared her love for horses. She idealized Lew, the wrangler, and Einar Anderson, the big Swede from a neighboring ranch. They responded to her enthusiasm and her love of their country. Because she shared their special understanding of horses, they invited her to tag along with them. Anderson became her idealized role model and remained a close friend during her later Wyoming ranch years.

At age 14, she quickly noted the freedom and total lack of formality and reserve in Wyoming ranchers. When she stated this observation to her sister Katie, "Everyone seems so free—so friendly," Katie responded, "Of course. They've learned the social shackles we're used to are folderol."[13]

Fahin's reflections in her journal pinpoint the differences between the East and West and the impact these two regions had on her life. She recalls that at age twelve she was alone when she sustained an injury. At that moment, she realized that controlling her emotions was the New Englanders way of showing maturity. In contrast she points out that "the reason I felt so freed in Wyoming" was because "people were simply themselves."[14] With sadness, Fahin left the dude ranch and the mountains and returned home to a more civilized society.

Approaching her fortieth year, Fahin began to rebel. With the children nearly grown and her husband away much of the time, she saw little purpose in her life and began looking for things to do. She volunteered to work with disadvantaged youth. She also decided to go back to school to renew her interest in theology.

Eventually, she purchased Ring Lake Ranch which was to become an ecumenical retreat. Fahin had many problems with the weather, the construction, thefts, rats, and free-loaders who took advantage of her generous nature. Fortunately, Einar Anderson, the big Swede who had befriended her when she was fourteen, lived nearby and helped her find ways to overcome her difficulties. Both of her children were also supportive and helped her establish her dream. The retreat became world-renowned.

Maggie Baker Fahin died February 7, 1984 near her beloved mountains. As a twentieth-century woman, she had the unique opportunity to experience what many pioneer women of the previous century had learned. Life was rugged in the unsettled West, but it challenged them to ignore refined social customs and explore their individual abilities and interests. The rustic environment took away social restrictions and reflected the possibilities of a more wholesome life.

Thus, Fahin was able to capture a little of the facilitating environment that women of the late eighteenth and nineteenth centuries experienced. As civilization caught up in the West, women lost much of what they had gained. The components that created the environment were lost; harsh conditions and lack of cultural refinements, a relaxation of gender boundaries, the inspiration from male mentors, and the greater demand than supply of professionals either disappeared or became considerably less influential. Fortunately, not all of the gains in equality were lost or forgotten. Suffrage and equal pay were important first steps towards equality for women. Therefore, the facilitating environment of the frontier experience set into motion an important social change for women that continued into the late twentieth century.

For many women and minority groups around the world, equality remains an elusive dream. U.S. citizens abhor the subjugation of women in certain countries while the U.N. attempts to defend human rights. Equal Rights for all humans is still a major issue. While positive alternative models (stage two of this theory) are readily available, most cultural groups are unable to reject the old models (stage one) and are afraid to allow the blending of old, segregating roles (stage three). The problem is we expect revolutionary change through wars, protests, and demands. For the process to be successful, however, evolutionary steps must be taken to change the attitude of backward cultures to accept the value of Human Equality.

Appendix A

Dates of States Granting Full Suffrage

	DATE	STATE
1	1890	Wyoming
2	1893	Colorado
3	1896	Utah
4	1896	Idaho
5	1910	Washington
6	1911	California
7	1912	Oregon
8	1912	Arizona
9	1912	Kansas
10	1914	Nevada
11	1914	Montana
12	1917	New York
13	1918	Michigan
14	1919	Oklahoma
15	1919	South Dakota

19th Amendment to the U.S. Constitution: Ratified August 18, 1920

Appendix B

Selected List of Western Women

NAME	LIFE SPAN	WESTERN STATES	OCCUPATION
Archer, Kate Rennie	1863–1960	California	Teacher, Poet
Atkins, Mary	1819–?	California	Educator
Atherton, Gertrude	1857–1948	California	Novelist
Austin, Mary Hunter	1868–1934	California	Author, Naturalist
Beecher, Catharine	1800–1878	Ohio, Wisconsin	Teacher, School Founder
Bellamy, Mary (Godat)	1861–1966	Wyoming	First Woman Elected to a State Legislature
Beard, Frances B. (Birkhead)	1850?–?	Iowa, Wyoming	Teacher, Principal, Superintendent
Bower, Bertha (Muzzy)	1871–1940	Montana, California	Author of Western Fiction
Bowman, Sarah A.	1812–1866	Missouri, Texas, Arizona	Hotelkeeper, Army Laundress, Cook, Restaurant Operator
Bull, Martha (James)	?–1944	Wyoming	Store Manager, Postmistress
Campbell, Leonel Ross "Polly Pry"	1857–1938	Colorado	Journalist, Political Activist
Carr, Emily	1871–1945	British Columbia, California	Artist
Carr, Jean	Served 1875–1880	California	Deputy Sup't of Public Education
Cather, Willa Sibert	1873–1947	Nebraska	Author
Cashman, Nellie	1850?–1925	Arizona, Alaska	Mine Investor, Business Owner, Promoter of Community Activities

NAME	LIFE SPAN	WESTERN STATES	OCCUPATION
Cooper, Sarah B.	1835–1896	California	Helped establish Free Kindergarten in San Francisco
Culbertson, Mary	Not available	Wyoming	Woman Homesteader
Cunningham, Imogen	1883–1976	Oregon, California	Photographer, Artist
Dean, Dr. Maria M.	1883 Began homeopathic practice	Montana	Medical Doctor Local Politics
Duniway, Abigail Scott	1834–1915	Oregon	Publisher, Suffragist
Eastman, Elaine Goodale		[See Goodale, Elaine]	
Fahin, Margaret "Maggie" (McFarlan)	1922–1984	Wyoming	Minister, Owner of Ranch, Owner Ecumenical Retreat
Farnham, Eliza W.	1815–1863	Illinois, California	Writer, Reformer
Folz, Clara Shortridge	1849–1934	California	Attorney, Suffragist
Fix, Georgia (Arbuckle)	1852–1918	Nebraska	Medical Doctor
Garrett, Mary A. (Banner)	1863–1925	Wyoming	Postmaster, Justice of the Peace
Goodale, Elaine	1863–1953	South Dakota	Teacher, Supervisor
Gray, Mary Augusta (Dix)	1810–1881	Oregon	Missionary
Haskell, Ella L. (Knowles)	1860?–?	Montana	1st Woman Lawyer of the State
Hearst, Phoebe (Apperson)	1842–1919	Missouri, California	Philanthropist
Hebard, Alice Marven	1859–1928	Iowa, Wyoming	Teacher
Hebard, Dr. Grace Raymond	1861–1936	Iowa, Wyoming	Engineer, Professor, Historian
Hill, Abby Williams	1861–1943	Iowa, Washington	Commissioned Artist
Howell, Helen	Not available	Wyoming	Woman Homesteader
Hunt, Helen (Fisk)		[See Jackson, Helen Hunt]	

NAME	LIFE SPAN	WESTERN STATES	OCCUPATION
Hutton, May (Arkwright)	1860–1915	Idaho, Washington	Cook, Mine Owner, Politics
Jackson, Helen Hunt	1830–1885	California, Colorado	Author, Commissioner of Indian Affairs
Jenkins, Theresa A.	1853–1936	Wyoming	Suffragist, Delegate to Republican Nat'l Convention
Johnson, Elizabeth Ellen "Lizzie"	1840–1924	Texas	Ranchwoman, Writer, Financier
Jones, Barbara, "Ma'am"	Not available	Arizona, New Mexico	"Medicine Woman," Teacher, Trading Post Operator
Lockey, Mary	1874–1939	Montana, California	Educator, School Founder
Lovejoy, Esther (Clayson) [a.k.a. Esther Pohl]	1869–1967	Oregon	Medical Doctor, International Health
Maxwell, Martha (Dartt)	1831–1881	Wisconsin, Colorado	Naturalist, Taxidermist
Meyer, Estelle Reel		[See Reel, Estelle]	
Morgan, Julia	1872–1957	California	Architect
Morris, Esther Hobart (McQuigg)	1814–1902	Wyoming	1st Woman Justice of the Peace
Moses, Phoebe Ann [a.k.a. Annie Oakley]	1860–1926	Ohio	Sharpshooter, Entertainer with Wild West Show
Newcomb, Frances Johnson	1887–1970	Wisconsin, New Mexico	Teacher, Recorder of Navajo Stories and Art
Newman, Sarah Jane "Sally Scull"	1817?–1866?	Texas	Rancher, Horse Trader
Oakley, Annie		[See Moses, Phoebe Ann]	
O'Keeffe, Georgia	1887–1986	Wisconsin, New Mexico	Artist
Pariseau, Esther	1823–1902	Washington	Mother Superior, Architect
Parkhurst, Emily (Swett)	1850?–?	California	Teacher, Writer, Organizer of Women's Writing Assoc.
Pry, Polly		[See Campbell, Leonel Ross]	
Rankin, Jeannette	1880–1973	Montana	Politics, Congressman

NAME	LIFE SPAN	WESTERN STATES	OCCUPATION
Reel, Estelle	1862–1959	Wyoming, Washington	Teacher, Sup't of Schools, Nat'l Sup't of Indian Schools
Richards, Clarice E.	1875–1945	Colorado	Rancher, Post-Mistress, Author
Ross, Nellie Tayloe	1886–1977	Wyoming	Governor, Director of the Mint
Sabin, Florence	1871–1953	Colorado	Medical Researcher
Scudder, Laura	1881–1959	Washington, California	Nurse, Lawyer, Businesswoman
Shipp, Ellis (Reynolds), M.D.	1847–1939	Utah	Medical Doctor, Instructor
Scull, Sally		[See Newman, Sarah Jane]	
Shelley, Kate	1866–1912	Iowa	Child Farmer, Train Operator
Snyder, Grace (McCance)	1882–19??	Nebraska	Homesteader
Spring, Agnes (Wright)	1894–1988	Colorado, Wyoming	Historian, Author
Stewart, Elinore (Pruitt)	1876–1933	Oklahoma, Colorado, Wyoming	Woman Homesteader
Strong, Harriet Williams (Russell)	1844–1926	California	Rancher, Businesswoman, Inventor
Truax, Nettie	Not available	Wyoming	Educator, Sup't of County Schools, State Legislator
Wergeland, Dr. Agnes Matilde	1857–1914	Wyoming	Writer, University Professor
Wheeler, Mary C.	Not available	Montana	Teacher, Artist, Suffragist
Whitman, Narcissa (Prentiss)	1808–1847	Oregon	Missionary
Wiggins, Kate Douglass	1856–1923	California	Educator
Wissler, Susan	Mayor 1911	Wyoming	Town Mayor
Wood, Sara Bard (Field)	1882–1974	California	Poet, Suffragist

Notes

Preface

1. John Mack Faragher, *Women and Men on the Overland Trail* (New York: Yale University Press, 1979); Lillian Schlissel, *Women's Diaries of the Westward Journey* (New York: Schocken Books, 1982); Julie Roy Jeffrey, Frontier Women: *The Trans-Mississippi West 1840–1880* (New York: Hill and Wang, 1979).

2. Teresa Jordan, *Cowgirls: Women of the American West, An Oral History* (Garden City, NY: Doubleday & Company, Inc., 1984).

3. Lillian Schlissel, *Women's Diaries of the Westward Journey* (New York: Schocken Books, 1982) and "Women's Diaries on the Western Frontier." *American Studies* 18 (Spring 1977): 87–100.

4. Nancy Chodorow, *The Reproduction of Mothering: Psychoanalysis and the Sociology of Gender* (Berkeley: University of California Press, 1978).

5. Welter described the belief in these four attributes as the "cult of true womanhood"; Barbara Welter, "The Cult of True Womanhood: 1820–1860," *American Quarterly*, 18 (Summer, 1966):151–74.

6. Carol Fairbanks and Sara Brooks Sundberg, *Farm Women on the Prairie Frontier: A Sourcebook for Canada and the United States* (Metuchen, NJ: Scarecrow Press, 1983). Fairbanks and Sundberg have asserted that the westering experience and settlement were very similar in Canada and the United States.

7. Patricia Nelson Limerick, *The Legacy of Conquest: The Unbroken Past of the American West* (W.W. Norton & Co.: New York, 1987). Frederick Jackson Turner, "The Significance of History," presented at the Chicago meeting of the American Historical Association, 1891 reprinted in *Frontier and Section: Selected Essays of Frederick Jackson Turner*, ed. Ray Allen Billington (Englewood Cliffs, NJ: Prentice Hall, Inc., 1961).

8. Walter Webb, *The Great Plains: A Study in Institutions and Environment* (Boston: Ginn, 1931; Lincoln: University of Nebraska Press, Bison Book Printing, 1981), 505.

9. Lois W. Banner, *Elizabeth Cady Stanton: A Radical for Women's Rights* (Boston: Little, Brown and Company, 1980); Kathryn Kish Sklar, *Catharine Beecher: A Study in American Domesticity* (New York: W.W. Norton & Company, 1976); and Jean Strouse, *Alice James: A Biography* (Boston: Houghton Mifflin Co., 1980).

Chapter One

1. Harriott Stanton Blatch, Address to the National Woman's Congressional Committee, recorded by Dr. Grace Raymond Hebard in "Fifty Years Ago," Cathedral Hall, Laramie, Wyoming, Nov. 11, 1919, 17, 20 in Woman's Suffrage Collection, Folder #1, American Heritage Center (AHC), University of Wyoming, Laramie, Wyoming. Emphasis added.

2. Ibid.

3. Dr. Grace Hebard, "Where Are We 47 Years Later," address to the National Congressional Committee, recorded in "Fifty Years Ago," 5.

4. For more detail, see Sidney Howell Fleming, "Solving the Jigsaw Puzzle: One Suffrage Story at a Time." *Annals of Wyoming* 62 (Spring 1990): 22–72.

5. Edith M. Phelps, ed., *Selected Articles on Woman Suffrage, Debaters' Handbook Series*, 3rd ed., (White Plains, N.Y.: The H. W. Wilson Company, 1916), 47.

6. Note: The geographic location of the study has not been limited to a specific place or time. The *West* and *western frontier* of this study represent an environment rather than a specific locale. During the nineteenth century, the American West referred to different locations at different times, beginning in the Midwest during the early part of the century, expanding to the Mississippi River and quickly beyond to Texas, Oregon, and California during mid century, returning to the plains states of Kansas and Nebraska, and finally filling in the Rocky Mountain Region with Colorado, Wyoming, Montana, Utah, and Idaho by the end of the century. The *West* or w*estern frontier* is used in this study, therefore, to refer to various, newly settled territories that did not yet have the population base and organization in which Victorian divisions of gender, class, culture, and ethnicity could dominate behavioral pattern.

7. Barbara Miller Solomon, *In the Company of Educated Women: A History of Women and Higher Education in America* (New Haven: Yale University Press, 1985), 53.

8. Sandra L. Myres, *Westering Women and the Frontier Experience 1800–1915* (Albuquerque: University of New Mexico Press, 1982), 258.

9. T.A. Larson, "Women's Role in the American West," *Montana, the Magazine of Western History* 24 (Summer 1974).

10. Frederick Jackson Turner, "The Significance of the Frontier in American History," presented at the Chicago meeting of the American Historical Association, 1893, reprinted in Billington, *Frontier and Section*.

11. Ibid., 37–38.

12. Ibid., 42–43.

13. Ibid. Emphasis added.

14. Kathryn Kish Sklar, *Catharine Beecher: A Study in American Domesticity* (New York: W.W. Norton & Company, 1976),

15. Anne Seagraves. *Daughters of the West*. (Hayden, Idaho: Wesanne Publications, 1996) 42.

16. Ibid., 19–20.

17. *St. Louis Post*, 1895, quoted in Ibid., 21.

18. Judy Alter, "Pioneer Doctor," *The Women Who Made the West*, ed. by the Western Writers of America, (Garden City, N.Y.: Doubleday & Company, Inc., 1980), 130–140.

19. Orrin A. Engen, *Writer of the Plains, A Biography of B.M. Bower,* (Culver City, Calif.: The Pontine Press, 1973).

20. Winifred Black Bonfils, T*he Life and Personality of Phoebe Apperson Hearst* (San Francisco: Printed for William Randolph Hearst by John Henry Nash, 1928), 5.

21. Mr. and Mrs. Fremont Older, *George Hearst: California Pioneer* (Los Angeles: Westernlore, 1966), 114–115.

22. Ibid., 115, 117.

23. Barbara Welter, "The Cult of True Womanhood: 1820–1860," *American Quarterly* 18 (Summer 1966):151–74.

24. Edward Clarke, *Sex in Education; or, A Fair Chance for the Girls,* (Boston: J.R. Osgood & Co., 1873). See also a discussion of the effect of Clarke's theories in Carroll Smith-Rosenberg, "The New Woman as Androgyne: Social Disorder and Gender Crisis, 1870–1936," *Disorderly Conduct: Visions of Gender in Victorian America*, (N.Y.: Oxford University Press, 1985), 245–296.

25. Smith-Rosenberg, 264.

26. Catharine Beecher, *Suggestions Respecting Improvements in Education, Presented to the Trustees of the Hartford Female Seminary* (Hartford: Packard & Butler, 1829); Beecher, *The True Remedy for the Wrongs of Woman; with a History of an Enterprise having that for its Object* (Boston: Phillips, Sampson & Co., 1851). For a review of the writings of Beecher's contemporaries see Barbara Welter, *Dimity Convictions: The American Woman in the Nineteenth Century* (Athens: Ohio University Press, 1976).

27. Sklar, 88 [emphasis added].

28. Ibid., 31.

29. Ibid., 8, 63.

30. Ibid., 28.

31. Ibid., 53.

32. Most of the woman's rights issues were considered "radical" at the time of introduction, including higher education for females, property rights for married women, and equal suffrage. The term, *feminism*, was not widely applied until very late in the twentieth century suffrage campaign. The label was not introduced into the U.S. until the early 1900s, so none of the women in the following descriptions would have considered themselves *Feminists*. Likewise, the terms *Domestic Feminists* and *Separatist Feminists* have been only recently coined and were not used by nineteenth century women. For a history of "The Birth of Feminism" and the introduction of the term *feminism*, see Nancy Cott, *The Grounding of Modern Feminism*, (New Haven: Yale University Press, 1987), especially 11–50.

33. Cott, *The Grounding of Modern Feminism*, 4, 16.

34. Ibid., 16.

35. Karen Blair, *The Clubwoman as Feminist: True Womanhood Redefined, 1868–1914*, (N.Y.: Holmes & Meier Publishers, Inc., 1980), 4.

36. Harriet Beecher Stowe, *Uncle Tom's Cabin*, (Boston: John P. Jewett & Co., 1851). The two sisters coauthored three books between 1869 and 1873 to promote domestic science. The first was *The American Woman's Home, or Principles of Domestic Science* (1869). The second was a revision to be used as a textbook: *Principles of Domestic Science; As Applied to the Duties and Pleasures of the Home. A Text Book for the Use of Young Ladies in Schools, Seminaries, and Colleges* (1870). The second revision was published in 1973, *The New Housekeeper's Manual: Embracing a New Revised Edition of the American Woman's Home; or, Principles of Domestic Science. Being a Guide to Economical, Healthful, Beautiful, and Christian Homes*. All three were published in New York by J. B. Ford & Co.

37. Catharine E. Beecher and Harriet Beecher Stowe, "The Christian Family," *The American Woman's Home*, as quoted in Barbara M. Cross, ed., *The Educated Woman in America: Selected Writings*, (N.Y.: Teachers College Press, 1965), 83.

38. Ibid., 84.

39. Catharine Beecher, *The True Remedy for the Wrongs of Woman; with a History of an Enterprise having that for its Object*, (Boston: Phillips, Sampson & Co., 1851), 233.

40. Beecher, *Suggestions Respecting Improvements in Education, presented to the Trustees of the Hartford Female Seminary*, (Hartford: Packard & Butler, 1829), 16.

41. Mrs. Dorcas James Spencer, *A History of the WCTU of North and Central California*, (Oakland: West Coast Printing Co., 1911).

42. Ibid., 38.

43. Sarah M. Severance, *An Extra Session of California Legislature*, Political Science Study Series, Vol. II, No. 2, National American Woman Suffrage Association, New York, September 1896.

44. *17th Annual Report of the Woman's Christian Temperance Union of California*, 1896.

45. Sarah J. Severance to Caroline (Seymour) Severance, San Jose, CA, December 28, 1911, Caroline Severance Collection, Huntington Library, San Marino, CA.

46. Ella Gile Ruddy, Ed., *The Mother of Clubs: Caroline M. Seymour Severance; an Estimate and an Appreciation*, (Los Angeles: Baumgardt Publishing Co., 1906), 32.

47. Alice Marian Chapman, *Madame Severance: The Founder of Woman's Clubs*, (Thesis for M.A., University of Southern California, 1930), 9.

48. Statement by Severance to John Riis, quoted in Chapman, 35 and Ruddy, 18.

49. A list of members is recorded in Chapman, 35.

50. "Constitution and By Laws of the L.A. Woman's Club," Caroline Severance Collection, Huntington Library.

51. Caroline Severance notes, Severance Collection, Huntington Library.

52. *Seventh Annual Report of the WCTU of Southern California*, 1889, 80–83.

53. Chapman, 42.

54. From her notebook of quotes, Caroline Severance Collection, Huntington Library.

55. Caroline Severance, an address to the New England Woman's Club, 1881, Ruddy, 33.

56. Letters, Box 23, Severance Collection, Huntington Library.

57. S.M. Severance to Caroline Severance, San Jose, California, July 30, 1911, Caroline Severance Collection, Huntington Library.

58. Susan Look Avery to Caroline Severance, Louisville, Kentucky, March 9, 1905, Severance Collection, Huntington Library.

59. Catharine Beecher, *The Evils Suffered By American Women and American Children: The Causes and the Remedy*, (N.Y.: Harper & Bros., 1846) 6.

60. Ibid., 12.

61. Mary Maples Dunn, "Saints and Sisters: Congregational and Quaker Women in the Early Colonial Period," *Women in American Religion*, Janet Wilson James, Ed. (Philadelphia:, 1980), 45.

62. Barbara Leslie Epstein, *The Politics of Domesticity: Women, Evangelism, and Temperance in Nineteenth Century America* (Middletown, Conn: Wesleyan University Press, 1981).

63. Estelle B. Freedman, *Their Sister's Keepers: Women's Prison Reform in America, 1830–1930* (Ann Arbor: The University of Michigan Press, 1981).

64. Estelle B. Freedman, "Separatism as Strategy: Female Institution Building and American Feminism, 1870–1930," *Feminist Studies* 5 (Fall 1979): 512–29.

65. Carroll Smith-Rosenberg, "The New Woman as Androgyne," *Disorderly Conduct*, 256.

66. Ibid.

67. Ibid., 257.

68. New York *Herald*, 12 September 1852, reprinted in Stanton, Anthony, and Gage, *History of Woman Suffrage*, Vol. 1, 854.

69. Smith-Rosenberg, 286.

70. Ibid., 288.

71. Ibid., 281.

72. Civilization is generally associated with the advancement of humanity. However, the civilization of nineteenth century western civilization was male-dominated and male privileged. As this study point outs, the advancement of civilization was actually detrimental to women while the less civilized settlements of the West were beneficial to women's status. For discussions on the male-orientation of Western civilization, see Karen Horney, M.D. *Feminine Psychology*, (W.W. Norton and Company, 1967; and Simone deBeauvoir, *The Second Sex*, trans. by H.M. Pashley, (N.Y.: Alfred A. Knopf, 1953, c. 1949).

73. Lois W. Banner, *Elizabeth Cady Stanton: A Radical for Woman's Rights*, (Boston: Little, Brown and Company, 1980).

74. Nancy F. Cott, *The Grounding of Modern Feminism*, (New Haven: Yale University Press, 1987), 25–26.

75. Cott, 26.

76. "Alice Paul's Triumphs for Equality," *Alice Paul Institute*, 2004 <http://www.alicepaul.org/docs/triumphs.htm> (accessed 5 March, 2004).

77. Kristi Anderson, *After Suffrage: Women in Partisan and Electoral Politics before the New Deal* (Chicago and London: The University of Chicago,1996), 170, 12, 149.

78. See Sarah M. Evans, *Born for Liberty: A History of Women in America* (New York: The Free Press, 1989), especially "Feminizing Public Spaces," 70–93. Evans cites Catharine Beecher as the leader of this strategy: "Beecher's insistence on women's moral superiority and on women's moral mission in a democratic society extended women's sphere beyond the private home and thrust it into the public sphere." The result of Beecher's "close identification" between moral issues and womanhood "made any setting a domestic one and any action womanly if its end was the virtue of society." (71) See also Barbara J. Harris, *Beyond Her Sphere: Women and the Professions in American History* (Westport, Ct.: Greenwood Press, 1978); Glenda Riley, *Inventing the American Woman: A Perspective on Women's History, 1607–1877* (Arlington Heights, Illinois: Harland Davidson, Inc., 1986); and Ryan, *Cradle of the Middle Class.*

79. Catharine E. Beecher, *The Evils Suffered by American Women and American Children: The Causes and the Remedy* (New York: Harper & Bros., 1946); and *The True Remedy for the Wrongs of Woman; with a History of an Enterprise having that for its Object* (Boston: Phillips, Sampson & Co., 1851). See also, Kathryn Kish Sklar, *Catharine Beecher: A Study in American Domesticity.*

80. A twentieth century parallel was "Rosie, the Riveter" propaganda used during World War II to encourage women to work in the defense industry. Welding and riveting were considered masculine skills; however, with a shortage of male factory workers during the war, housewives had to be convinced that they were qualified. Therefore, posters and advertising compared riveting to sewing. Riveting a bolt in an airplane was comparable to sewing a button on a shirt. The intent of this campaign was to put women in the work force. Domestic qualifications were used as a strategy to make women's work in the defense industry—previously seen only as a male domain—appear socially acceptable.

81. For a discussion of separatism in eastern women's rights campaigns, see Freedman, "Separatism as Strategy"; and Carroll Smith-Rosenberg, "The New Woman as Androgyne: Social Disorder and Gender Crisis, 1870–1936," *Disorderly Conduct: Visions of Gender in Victorian America* (New York: Oxford University Press, 1985).

82. Among the first to acknowledge the diversity of experience for westering women was Glenda Riley. Her book on *Frontierswomen* in 1981 challenges male stereotypes and myths about passive women of the West and stresses the diversity of women's experiences. She claims that the images of "saints in sunbonnets," "Madonna of the prairie," and "pioneer in petticoats" have "done more to cloud than to illuminate women's true involvement in the western experience." Her analysis of settlers' diaries and letters has shown that in challenging the trail, women also challenged the nineteenth century myths about the "weaker" sex. Many women emerged as "valuable partners in the frontier experience." Frontierswomen learned to adapt and to improvise. When confronted with frontier conditions, reality differed from ideals. Riley contends that "although they may have paid lip service to the nineteenth-century ideal of a 'proper lady,' most Iowa frontierswomen were too deeply immersed in a system of economic partnership with men to really believe in it or practice it." (Glenda Riley, *Frontierswomen: The Iowa Experience.*)

Another historian who has researched the diversity of women's experience is Sandra L. Myres. Myres contends that there was no typical overland experience: "Individual women experienced different conditions and reacted in varying ways to the Westward journey." According to Myres, life after the trail produced a diversity of experience for women. Some of the more assertive activities on the part of women included direct participation in money-raising and decision-making at both the family and community levels. Hard work and self-reliance paid off in the respect women earned for both their domestic skills and their expanded roles in the public domain. Although western women's view of themselves did not radically change, Myres contends that their public roles, self-reliance, and economic opportunities were greatly expanded.

The adaptive behavior of pioneer women in Riley's study and the assertive behavior of women in Myres's study could be considered possible catalysts for early success of woman's suffrage in the West. More specifically, frontier women's extensive participation in the business world helped promote the reputation of hardy, independent women of the West. These historians demonstrate that the experience for women of the West had more than one dimension. (Sandra L. Myres, *Westering Women*, 98, 102).

83. Harriette Andreadis, "True Womanhood Revisited: Women's Private Writing in Nineteenth Century Texas," *Journal of the Southwest* 31 (Summer 1989): 179–204, especially 203. Questions were adapted from her list on page 179.

84. Emily Jones Shelton, "Lizzie E. Johnson: A Cattle Queen of Texas," *Southwestern Historical Quarterly* (January 1947): 349–366.

85. Elizabeth Jameson, ""Women as Workers, Women as Civilizers: True Womanhood in the American West," in Armitage and Jameson, *The Women's West*, 145–164.

86. Ibid., 159.

87. Ibid.

88. Ibid., 159, 160.

89. Katherine Harris, "Homesteading in Northeastern Colorado, 1873–1920," 165–178, especially 167, 169, 173–74.

90. Dr. Grace Raymond Hebard, manuscript notes for an address to The National Woman's Congressional Committee presented in Cheyenne, Wyoming, 1916[?], Woman's Suffrage Folder #1, University of Wyoming (AHC).

91. "Woman Suffrage in Wyoming," Woman Suffrage Leaflet, Vol. II, no. 19, published by the American Woman Suffrage Association, Boston, Mass., May 1, 1889, Woman Suffrage Folder, (AHC), Laramie, WY. [Italics from the original.]

92. Ex-Chief Justice Fisher, of Cheyenne, Wyoming, in letter to *Daily New Era*, Lancaster, Pa., Dec. 11, 1883, quoted in *Woman Suffrage Leaflet*.

93. Mrs. L. W. Smith, quoted in *Woman Suffrage Leaflet*.

94. Hon. John W. Kingman, quoted in Ibid.

95. Jameson, 160.

96. Ibid., 161. (Emphasis added.)

97. Ibid.

98. Marie Jahoda, "Notes on Work," in *Psychoanalysis—A General Psychology: Essays in Honor of Heinz Hartmann*, eds. Rudolph M. Loewenstein, Lottie M. Newman, Max Schur, and Albert J. Solnit (New York: International Universities Press, Inc., 1966); and Anthony Storr, *Solitude: A Return to the Self* (New York: Ballantine Books, 1988).

99. Mary Maverick, diary entry, February 14, 1856 (entry excluded from published diary) quoted in Andreadis, "True Womanhood," 193.

100. Ruth B. Moynihan, Susan Armitage, and Christiane Fischer Dichamp, *So Much Work to Be Done: Women Settlers on the Mining and Ranching Frontier* (Lincoln: University of Nebraska Press,1990), xvi-xxviii.

101. This definition and use of the generational category is taken from Lewis S. Feuer, *The Conflict of Generations: The Character and Significance of Student Movements* (New York: Basic Books, Inc., Publishers, 1969), 25; and Mead, *Culture and Commitment*, 43.

Chapter Two

1. This is a description from some of her closest acquaintances. Quoted in Antionette May, *Helen Hunt Jackson: A Lonely Voice of Conscience* (San Francisco: Chronicle Books, 1987), 3.

2. Helen Hunt Jackson, *A Century of Dishonor: A Sketch of the United States Government's Dealings with Some of the Indian Tribes* (New York: Harper & Brothers, 1881).

3. Helen Hunt Jackson, *Ramona* (Boston: Roberts Brothers, 1884).

4. Biographical details taken from May, *Helen Hunt Jackson*.

5. Ibid., 4.

6. Ibid.

7. Ibid., 22–33.

8. Carole Smith-Rosenburg, "The Hysterical Woman: Sex Roles and Role Conflict in Nineteenth-Century America," *Disorderly Conduct: Visions of Gender in Victorian America,* (N.Y.: Oxford University Press, 1985).

9. Kate Chopin, *The Awakening*, (G.P. Putnam's Sons, 1964), first published in 1899; Charlotte Perkins Gilman, *The Yellow Wallpaper*, (Old Westbury, NY: The Feminist Press, 1973), originally published Boston: Small, Maynard, 1899.

10. Letter from Alice James to William James, quoted in Strouse, Alice James, ix.

11. Some examples of Henry James's books are *What Maisie Knew, The American,* and *The Ambassadors.*

12. Quoted in Jean Strouse, *Alice James: A Biography* (Boston: Houghton Mifflin Co., 1980), xiii.

13. Quoted from a Dr. Coombs in Catharine E. Beecher, *The True Remedy for the Wrongs of Woman*, (Boston: Phillips, Sampson & Co., 1851), pp. 40–41. [Beecher's italics.]

14. Elliott West,*Growing Up With the Country: Childhood on the Far Western Frontier* (Albuquerque: University of New Mexico Press, 1989), 257.

15. Adrietta Applegate Hixon, *On to Oregon! A True Story of a Young Girl's Journey Into the West* (Wesler, Idaho: Signal-American Printers, 1947), 17.

16. Elinor Richey, *Eminent Women of the West* (Berkeley: Howell-North Books, 1975), 18–21.

17. Ibid., 29.

18. Lucille McDonald, "Mother Joseph," *The Women Who Made the West*, The Western Writers of America Series (Garden City, N.Y.: Doubleday & Company, Inc., 1980), 120–129.

19. "The Doctor Was an 'Adventuress,'" *Today's Health*, August 1970 in Olive Burt Collection, Box 14, (AHC), Laramie, Wyoming.

20. Agnes Wright Spring, "Stage Stop on the Little Laramie," *Persimmon Hill* 4, 2 (1974): 4–17; "A True Woman of the West," *Colorado Heritage News* (March 1987); Olga Curtis, "The Beloved Historian," *Empire Magazine*, 21 October 1979, 46–47, 49; Agnes Wright Spring Collection, American Heritage Center (hereafter cited as AHC), Laramie, Wyoming.

21. Mary Proctor Mothershead, "History of W. T. Proctor," *Homestead Fever: History of Denton, Danvers, Coffee Creek,* compiled by Denton Heritage Committee, (Great Falls, Mont.: Blue Print and Letter Company, 1977), 288.

22. Roberta Cheney, "From Rags to Riches," *The Women Who Made the West*, 220–239; and Patricia Voeller Horner, "May Arkwright Hutton: Suffragist and Politician," *Women in Pacific Northwest History, An Anthology*, Karen J. Blair, ed. (Seattle: University of Washington Press, 1988), 25–42.

23. Ibid.

24. Elyce Wakerman, *Father Loss: Daughters Discuss the Man That Got Away* (New York: Henry Holt and Company, 1984).

25. Benjamin, *Father and Daughter*, 14. See also Wakerman, *Father Loss: Daughters Discuss the Man That Got Away* (New York: Henry Holt and Company, 1984); and Cath, Gurwitt, and Gunsberg, *Fathers and Their Families*.

26. Annie Fern Swartwout, *Missie: The Life and Times of Annie Oakley* (Blanchester, Ohio: Brown Publishing Co., 1947).

27. Benjamin, *Father and Daughter*.

28. Swartwout, *Missie*.

29. Ibid.

30. Ibid., 16.

31. No records have been found to indicate why Annie chose "Oakley" for her stage name. Shirl Kasper, *Annie Oakley* (Norman: University of Oklahoma Press, 1992), 23; and Glenda Riley, *The Life and Legacy of Annie Oakley*, The Oklahoma Western Biographies, (Norman: University of Oklahoma Press, 1994), 20.

32. Wakerman, *Father Loss*, 131–32.

33. Wakerman, *Father Loss*, 130–131.

34. Lyle Bruere and Ruth Van Ackeren, "Heroine of Honey Creek," in *The Women Who Made Who Made the West*, 62.

35. Ibid., 66.

36. Ibid.

37. Ibid., 67.

38. Sigmund Freud, "Some Psychical Consequences of the Anatomical Distinction Between the Sexes," (1925). Reprinted in Jean Strouse, Ed., *Women and Analysis: Dialogues on Psychoanalytic View of Femininity* (N.Y.: Dell Publishing Co., Inc.), 1974.

In terms of the Oedipus Complex, the boy figuratively desires to "kill" his father out of jealousy toward the man who competes with him for mother's attention. If the father is out of the way, the boy can then "marry" his mother. That is, he can receive more of her admiring attention. In more literal terms, the boy learns that he is expected to model himself after his father. He becomes overwhelmed by the loneliness and isolation of his inevitable self-reliance and longs to return to the safe, nurturing attention of his mother.

In contrast, girls discover they have no penis and despise their mothers "who sent [them] into the world so insufficiently equipped." (Freud, 33) A girl then turns to her father for his penis, which is his symbol of autonomy. Since she can never have a penis of her own (i.e., to be independent), the young female child desires to "marry" her father who can give her a "penis-baby." In other words, she longs to be "daddy's girl" so that she can enjoy, at least for a while, the *symbolical* autonomy and strength she experiences with the special attention of her male parent.

During the Oedipal conflict for girls, the female never reaches castration anxiety like boys. According to classical theory, the boy's fear for his organ prompts him to leave his mother and idealize his father. In contrast, the girl is already "castrated"; therefore, she never really leaves the stage of father love. She becomes like her mother in order to learn how to attract father and other men. Most of her energies thereafter are expended in this desire for masculine attention.

The feminine cycle of the Oedipal Complex suggests that a girl lives to attract men. This attraction is where she gets her pleasure and finds purpose for her life. Furthermore, after she "gets her man," then she can "possess a penis" by living through and for her son. In an unfortunate sense, she becomes a *selfless* creature who lives *selfishly* to attract the attention of others. The result is a weak self-identity. [Interpretation of Elyce Wakerman, *Father Loss: Daughters Discuss the Man That Go Away* (N.Y.: Henry Holt and Company, 1987)].

39. Biographical material was taken from Barbara Welter, "The Mystical Feminist," *Dimity Convictions: The American Woman in the Nineteenth Century*, (Athens: Ohio University Press, 1976); Barbara M. Cross, ed., *The Educated Woman in America: Selected Writings*, (N.Y.: Teachers College Press, 1965); and Margaret Fuller, *Woman in the Nineteenth Century*, Arthur B. Fuller, editor, (Boston: J.P. Jewett & Co., 1845).

40. Margaret Fuller as quoted in Barbara Welter, "Mystical Feminist," 158.

41. Fuller, *Woman in the Nineteenth Century*.

42. Julia Cherry Spruill, *Women's Life and Work in the Southern Colonies* (University of North Carolina Press, 1938; reprint, New York: W. W. Norton & Company, Inc., 1972), 308–311.

43. This pattern is evident in women's literature following the Civil War such as *Mrs. Burton Harrison, The Carlyles: A Story of the Fall of the Confederacy* (1905); Mary Johnson, *The Long Roll* (1911); and Virginia Boyle, *Brokenbourne* (1897).

44. Robert Riegel, *American Feminists* (Lawrence: University of Kansas Press, 1963) briefly noted that there was a tendency in woman's rights leaders of the nineteenth century to have been influenced during their childhood by their fathers. A negative, incestuous relationship is documented in Linda Gordon, *Heroes of Their Own Lives: The Politics and History of Family Violence, Boston 1880–1960* (New York: Viking Penguin Press, 1988).

45. John Demos, "The Changing Faces of Fatherhood," in *Past, Present, and Personal: The Family and the Life Course in American History* (New York: Oxford University Press, 1986), 42.

46. Nancy F. Cott, *Bonds of Womanhood: 'Woman's Sphere' in New England, 1780–1835* (New Haven: Yale University Press, 1977).

47. Ruth H. Bloch, "Untangling the Roots of Modern Sex Roles: A Survey of Four Centuries of Change," *Signs* 4 (Winter 1978); Carl Degler, *At Odds: Women and Family in America From the Revolution to the Present* (New York: Oxford University Press, 1980), 73.

48. Degler, *At Odds*.

49. Philippe Aries, *Centuries of Childhood: A Social History of the Family*, trans. Robert Baldick (1960; reprint, New York: Vintage Books, 1962); and John Demos, *A Little Commonwealth: Family Life in Plymouth Colony* (New York: Oxford University Press, 1970).

50. See Degler, *At Odds*, 66–67, 71.

51. Ibid., 73–74.

52. Mary Ryan, *Cradle of the Middle Class: The Family in Oneida County New York 1790–1865* (New York: Cambridge University Press, 1981), 232.

53. Ibid., 235–37.

54. Demos, "The Changing Faces of Fatherhood," 51–54.

55. Degler, *At Odds*, 74, 77.

56. Degler, *At Odds,* 73; and Demos, "The Changing Faces of Fatherhood," 42.

57. Nancy Chodorow, *The Reproduction of Mothering: Psycho-analysis and the Sociology of Gender* (Berkeley: University of California Press, 1978). Chodorow concludes that "the separation of domestic and public spheres…has been sharpened through the course of industrial capitalist development, producing a family form reduced to its fundamentals." These fundamentals, according to Chodorow, are gender divided with "women's mothering and maternal qualities and heterosexual marriage" on the one hand and "male dominance" on the other. (Chodorow, 10).

Chodorow uses the Oedipus Complex for a classic description of the role fathers play in their daughters' early lives. In the Oedipal theory, it is believed that the role of the father is a heterosexual one. He teaches his son to separate his identity from his mother and behave more like a man. Conversely, the father encourages his daughter to imitate her mother to obtain his (and her future husband's) love.

58. Ibid., 219.

59. For an account of first generation western women's adherence to domesticity, see Jeffrey, *Frontier Women*; Glenda Riley, *The Female Frontier*; and Robert L. Griswold, "Anglo Women and Domestic Ideology in the American West in the Nineteenth and Early Twentieth Centuries," in Schlissel, Ruiz, and Monk,*Western Women: Their Land, Their Lives*, 15–33.

60. Heinz Kohut, M.D., *The Analysis of the Self: A Systematic Approach to the Psychoanalytic Treatment of Narcissistic Personality Disorders*, The Psychoanalytic Study of the Child Monograph No. 4 (Madison, CT: International Universities Press, Inc., 1971).

61. Ernest S. Wolf, M.D., *Treating the Self: Elements of Clinical Self Psychology*, (N.Y.: The Guilford Press, 1986), 183–4.

62. Lora Heims Tessman, "Fathers and Daughters: Early Tones, Later Echoes," *Fathers and Their Families*, eds. Stanley H. Cath, Alan Gurwitt, and Linda Gunsberg, (Hillsdale, NJ: The Analytic Press, 1989), 197–223.

63. See, for example, the lives of Catharine Beecher, Alice James, and Margaret Fuller in Kathryn Kish Sklar, *Catharine Beecher: A Study in American Domesticity* (New York: W.W. Norton & Company, 1976); Jean Strouse, *Alice James: A Biography* (Boston: Houghton Mifflin Co., 1980); and Barbara Welter, *Dimity Convictions: The American Woman in the Nineteenth Century* (Athens: Ohio University Press, 1976).

64. Lora Heims Tessman, "Fathers and Daughters: Early Tones, Later Echoes," 197–223.

65. Jessica Benjamin, *Father and Daughter: Identification with Difference—A Contribution to Gender Heterodoxy* (Paper delivered at the Los Angeles Psychoanalytic Society and Institute, Los Angeles, California, February 21, 1991), 10.

66. Ibid. [Her emphasis.]

67. Ibid., 12.

68. Ibid.

69. For example, see West, *Growing up with the Country*; and Paula Petrik, *No Step Backward*.

70. Margaret Mead, *Culture and Commitment: The New Relationships Between the Generations of the 1970s* (The Natural History Press/Doubleday & Co., Inc., 1970; reprint, N.Y.: Columbia University Press, 1978). See especially Chapter Two.

71. Ibid.

72. See, for example, the lives of Catharine Beecher, Alice James, and Margaret Fuller in Kathryn Kish Sklar, *Catharine Beecher: A Study in American Domesticity* (New York: W.W. Norton & Company, 1976),; Strouse, *Alice James: A Biography* (Boston: Houghton Mifflin Co., 1980), 88; and Barbara Welter, *Dimity Convictions: The American Woman in the Nineteenth Century* (Athens: Ohio University Press, 1976).

73. Ibid., 43.

74. Oral history of Betty Davis in Teresa Jordan, *Cowgirls: Women of the American West, An Oral History*, (Garden City, N.Y.: Doubleday & Company, Inc., 1984), 66.

75. Oral history of Carole Horn in Jordan, *Cowgirls*, 50.

76. Oral history of Marie Bell in Jordan, *Cowgirls*, 24.

77. Oral history of Elsie Lloyd and Amy Chubb in Jordan, *Cowgirls*, 9.

78. Biographical details taken from Elinor Richey, *Eminent Women of the West* (Berkeley, Ca: Howell-North Books, 1975).

79. Ibid.

80. John Swett, "First Biennial Report, Superintendent of Public Instruction, 1863–65," *Appendix to Journal of Legislation*, Vol. II, Doc. 1, 43–45.

81. John Swett, "Higher Professional Training," *Pacific School and Home Journal*, No. 8, San Francisco, August 1879, 255.

82. Tribute to the memory of Emily Tracy (Swett) Parkhurst, *California Illustrated Magazine,* 1892 as recorded in John Swett, *Public Education in California: Its Origin and Development, with Personal Reminiscences of Half a Century*, (N.Y.: American Book Company, 1911), 17.

Chapter Three

1. Judy Skalla, "Beloved Healer," *The Women Who Made the West*, The Western Writers of America Series, (Garden City, N.Y.: Doubleday & Company, Inc. 1980), 155.

2. Ellis Reynolds Shipp, M.D., *Life Lines, Poems.* Salt Lake: Skelton Publishing Company, 1910). See especially "Memories of Childhood," 19–20; "My Mother," 160; and "Anna," 235.

3. Quoted in Ibid., 153.

4. Ibid., 155.

5. Ibid., 159.

6. Ibid., 160–61.

7. Ibid., 159, 161.

8. Quoted in Ibid., 154.

9. See Glenda Riley, *The Female Frontier: A Comparative View of Women on the Prairie and the Plains* (Lawrence, KS: University Press of Kansas, 1988), especially Chapter 9; and the Introduction to Ruth B. Moynihan, Susan Armitage, and Chistiane Fischer Dichamp, eds., *So Much Work to Be Done: Women Settlers on the Mining and Ranching Frontier* (Lincoln: University of Nebraska Press, 1990). This topic will be discussed more fully in the next chapter.

10. Carroll Smith-Rosenberg, "The Female World of Love and Ritual: Relations Between Women in Nineteenth Century America." *SIGNS* 1 (Autumn 1975), 1–19.

11. Lucille McDonald, "Mother Joseph," *The Women Who Made the West*, The Western Writers of America Series (Garden City, N.Y.: Doubleday & Company, Inc., 1980), 122.

12. Mrs. Catherine Sager Pringle, "Narcissa Prentiss Whitman," in *Souvenir of Western Women,* ed. Mary Osborn Douthit (Portland, Oregon: Presses of Anderson & Duniway Company, 1905), 17.

13. Rosalind A. Keep, *Fourscore and Ten Years: A History of Mills College* (Mills College, California, 1945).

14. "She Left School Fifty Years Ago, But Dr. Grace Raymond Hebard Has Been at School Mostly Since," *The Press Union*, Iowa City, June 4, 1932; Paul Frison, "Dr. Hebard, Wyoming's Foremost Historian is True Daughter of Her Pioneer Parents," *The Wyoming News*, undated; "Historical Study of Alice Marven Hebard," compiled by the American Association of University Women, 1960–61; and "Funeral for Dr. Hebard, Famed Wyoming Historian, to be Today," *Wyoming Eagle*, October 13, 1936; all in Grace R. Hebard File, Historical Research and Publications (hereafter cited as HPR), Division of Parks and Cultural Resources, Dept. of Commerce, Cheyenne, Wyoming.

15. Elinor Richey, "Jeannette Rankin: Woman of Commitment," in *Eminent Women of the West*, 180–207; and Malca Chall and Hannah Josephson, *Jeannette Rankin: Activist for World Peace, Women's Rights, and Democratic Government*, Suffragists Oral History Project (Berkeley: Regents of the University of California, 1974).

16. Richey, *Eminent Women*, 19–20.

17. "The Doctor Was an 'Adventuress,'" *Today's Health*, August 1970, in Olive Burt Collection, Box 14, (AHC), Laramie Wyoming.

18. Sara Holmes Boutelle, *Julia Morgan, Architect* (N.Y.: Abbeville Press Publishers, 1988), 21; and Elinor Richey, "Julia Morgan: Architect with Empathy," *Eminent Women of the West*, 237–263.

19. Judy Alter, "Pioneer Doctor," *The Women Who Made the West*, 130–140.

20. T. A. Larson, "Women's Role in the American West," *Montana, the Magazine of Western History* 24 (Summer 1974), 6.

21. Alice Kessler-Harris, *Out to Work: A History of Wage-Earning Women in the United States* (New York: Oxford University Press, 1982), 126.

22. Barbara Mayer Wertheimer, *We Were There: The Story of Working Women in America*, (New York: Pantheon Books, 1977), 256–257.

23. Ruth B. Moynihan, Susan Armitage, and Christiane Fischer Dichamp, *So Much Work to Be Done: Women Settlers on the Mining and Ranching Frontier* (Lincoln: University of Nebraska Press, 1990).

24. Mary Austin, *Earth Horizon* (New York: The Literary Guild, 1932), 115. [Her emphasis.]

25. Alice Kessler-Harris, *Out to Work*, Chapters 2–3.

26. Ibid., Chapter 5.

27. Ibid., Chapters 4–5. See also, Barbara J. Harris, *Beyond Her Sphere: Women and the Professions in American History*, Contributions to Women's Studies, No. 4 (Westport, Connecticut: Greenwood Press, 1978).

28. Barbara J. Harris, *Beyond Her Sphere*, 121.

29. Carroll Smith-Rosenberg, "The New Woman as Androgyne: Social Disorder and Gender Crisis 1870–1936," *Disorderly Conduct: Visions of Gender in Victorian America* (New York: Oxford University Press, 1985), 245–296. See especially 256–257: "Loving and living with other women, within the separatist environment of women's colleges, settlement houses, and reform organizations…the New Women amassed greater political power and visibility than any other group of women in American experience…Sadly, their struggle for autonomy often led to estrangement from their own mother and female kin, who remained within the old female world and who feared the attraction the new world held for their daughters…M.Carey Thomas's mother hesitated long before permitting Thomas to be one of the first women to attend Cornell University. Jane Addam's stepmother insisted that Addams fulfill all duties genteel society expected of a young bourgeois girl…[and] bitterly resented Addam's refusal to marry."

30. Elizabeth Jameson, "Women as Workers, Women as Civilizers: True Womanhood in the American West," in *The Women's West*, ed. Susan Armitage and Elizabeth Jameson (Norman: University of Oklahoma Press, 1987), 150–51, 159–60.

31. Katherine Harris, "Homesteading in Northeastern Colorado, 1873–1920: Sex Roles and Women's Experience," in *The Women's West*, 167, 169, 171.

32. Anne M. Butler, *Daughters of Joy, Sisters of Mercy: Prostitutes in the American West, 1865–1890* (Urbana: University of Illinois Press, 1985).

33. Sandra Myers, *Westering Women and the Frontier Experience 1800–1915* (Albuquerque: University of New Mexico Press, 1982), 241.

34. "Mary Murdock Compton," oral narrative to Henria Packer Compton, in Christiane Fischer, ed., *Let Them Speak for Themselves: Women in the American West, 1849–1900* (Hamden, Ct.: Archon Books, 1977).

35. "Luzena Stanley Wilson, `49er. Memories recalled years later for her daughter Correnah Wilson Wright," in Fischer, *Let Them Speak for Themselves.*

36. Diary of Cora Babcock, South Dakota Historical Society, Pierre, SD, as cited in Myres, *Westering Women*, 242.

37. *Report of the Secretary of the Helena Board of Trade for the Year 1878* (Helena: Fisk Brothers, 1879), 27; Appendix 2, Table 10 as quoted in Paula Petrik, *No Step Backward: Women and Family on the Rocky Mountain Mining Frontier, Helena Montana 1865–1900* (Helena: Montana Historical Society Press, 1987), 25.

38. Wertheimer, *We Were There*, 209.

39. Kathryn Kish Sklar, *Catharine Beecher: A Study in American Domesticity*, (N.Y.: W.W. Norton & Company) 1976, 94.

40. Quoted in Pamela Herr, "Reformer," *Women Who Made the West*, The Western Writers of America, (Garden City, N.Y.: Doubleday & Company, Inc., 1980), 206.

41. Ibid., 207.

42. Ibid.

43. Julie Roy Jeffrey, "Narcissa Whitman: The Significance of a Missionary's Life," *Montana, the Magazine of Western History* 41 (Spring 1991), 4.

44. Ruth Moynihan, *Rebel for Rights: Abigail Scott Duniway* (New Haven: Yale University Press, 1983).

45. Kessler-Harris, *Out to Work*.

46. Polly Welts Kaufman, *Women Teachers on the Frontier* (New Haven: Yale University Press, 1984).

47. Mary Ryan, *Cradle of the Middle Class: The Family in Oneida County New York 1790–1865* (New York: Cambridge University Press, 1981); and Nancy F. Cott, *Bonds of Womanhood: 'Woman's Sphere' in New England, 1780–1835* (New Haven, 1977).

48. Mrs. Catherine Sager Pringle, "Narcissa Prentiss Whitman," *Souvenir of Western Women*, ed. Mary Osborn Douthit (Portland, Oregon: Presses of Anderson & Duniway Company, 1905), 17–20.

49. Ibid.

50. Lucille McDonald, "Mother Joseph," in Western Writer of America, *The Women Who Made the West* (Garden City, New York: Doubleday & Co., Inc., 1980), 122–23.

51. Kaufman, *Women Teachers on the Frontier*.

52. Sara M. Evans, *Born for Liberty: A History of Women in America* (New York: The Free Press, 1989), 148f.

53. Sarah Deutsch, *No Separate Refuse: Culture, Class, and Gender on an Anglo-Hispanic Frontier in the American Southwest, 1880–1940* (New York: Oxford University Press, 1987), 63–64.

54. McDonald, "Mother Joseph," 128.

55. Nancy F. Cott, "Young Women in the Second Great Awakening in New England," *Feminist Studies* 3 (1975): 15–29. See also Kaufman, *Women Teachers on the Frontier*.

56. Sklar, *Catharine Beecher: A Study in American Domesticity*; Barbara Miller Solomon, *In the Company of Educated Women: A History of Women and Higher Education in America* (New Have: Yale University Press, 1985); Helen Lefkowitz Horowitz, *Alma Mater: Design and Experience in the Women's Colleges from Their Nineteenth-Century Beginnings to the 1930s* (Boston: Beacon Press, 1984); and Ann Douglas, *The Feminization of American Culture* (New York: Alfred A. Knopf, 1977).

57. Catharine E. Beecher and Harriet Beecher Stowe, *The American Woman's Home; or, Principles of Domestic Science Being a Guide to the Formation and Maintenance of Economical, Healthful, Beautiful, and Christian Homes* (New York: J.B. Ford & Company, 1869).

58. Barbara Welter, *Dimity Convictions: The American Woman in the Nineteenth Century* (Athens: Ohio University Press, 1976), Chapter 9.

59. Sklar, *Catharine Beecher: A Study in American Domesticity*.

60. Kaufman, *Women Teachers on the Frontier*.

61. Ibid., xvii.

62. Horowitz, *Alma Mater: Design and Experience in the Women's Colleges*.

63. Solomon, *In the Company of Educated Women*, 21.

64. Fred John Sales, "A History of the Superintendency of Public Instruction in the State of California, 1850–1932," (Ph.D. dissertation, University of Southern California, 1935),16–19. For a summary of Froebel's methods, see Samuel Chester Parker, *The History of Modern Elementary Education* (Totowa, N.J.: Littlefield, Adams & Co., 1970), 431–486.

65. Rosalind A. Keep, *Fourscore and Ten Years: A History of Mills College* (Mills College, California, 1945).

66. William Ferrier, *Ninety Years of Education in California, 1846–1936* (Berkeley: Sather Gate Book Shop, 1937), 252–53; and Keep, *Fourscore and Ten Years*, 86, 94–104. For a review of other women as college presidents, see Solomon, *In the Company of Educated Women*, 47–49; and Horowitz, *Alma Mater*. Ada L. Howard, a Mount Holyoke graduate, served as nominal president at Wellesley College under the direction of its founder, Fowle Durant. The most well-known female college president was M. Carey Thomas. She was offered the position at Bryn Mawr in 1894 after a very close vote. This was four years after Mrs. Mills accepted the presidency in California.

67. Carroll Smith-Rosenberg, "Androgyny" in *Disorderly Conduct*, 259. See also Ferrier, *Ninety Years of Education in California*, 252–53. Commendations for Mills College physical exercise program is recorded in Keep's *Fourscore Years* and the private publication of *Mills College for Young Women*, (San Francisco, 1903).

68. State Superintendent Ezra S. Carr, "Report to the Governor, October 1, 1879," *Appendix to the Journals of the Senate and Assembly of the 23rd Session of the Legislature of the State of California*, Vol. II. (Sacramento: State Office, 1879), 23.

69. Ibid., 23.

70. Two-thirds of Mills alumnae married within ten years of graduation. See *Mills College Statement*, 1937.

71. William Bartlett, "The Founder and Builder," Address given at Founders Day, Mills College, May 11, 1894, (San Francisco, private publication, 1894), 6–7.

72. Harriet Williams (Russell) Strong, Strong Collection, Huntington Library, San Marino, California.

73. This summary of California education is discussed in Sales, "A History of the Superintendency of Public Instruction in the State of California, 1850–1932." In 1873 the University was moved to its permanent location at Berkeley.

74. Miller, *In the Company of Educated Women*, 52–55; Mabel Newcomer, *A Century of Higher Education for Women* (New York: Harper & Row, 1959), 29–30.

75. Ezra Carr to UC Regents, 10 November 1870, Carr Manuscript Collection, Huntington Library, San Marino, CA.

76. Ibid.

77. "Report of UC Regents to Governor, August 1, 1879," *Appendix to the Journals of the Senate and Assembly of the 23rd Session of the Legislature of the State of California*, Vol. II, State Office, Sacramento, 1879, 16, 53, 59, 70–71.

78. Sales, "A History of the Superintendency of Public Instruction in the State of California, 1850–1932," 37; and Roy Cloud, *Education in California: Leaders, Organizations, and Accomplishment of the First Hundred Years* (Stanford: Stanford University Press, 1952), 21–22.

79. John Swett, *Public Education in California: Its Origin and Development, with Personal Reminiscences of Half a Century* (New York: American Book Company, 1911), 17.

80. Carr, "Report to the Governor."

81. Andrew J. Moulder, *Commentaries on the School Law with the Elements of School Architecture; Laws Relating to the School Lands, Forms an Instruction* (Sacramento: John O'Meara, State Printer, 1858), 37–38.

82. John Swett, *First Biennial Report, Superintendent of Public Instruction, 1863–65; Appendix to the Journal of Legislation*, Vol. II, Doc. 1, 43–45.

83. Carr, "Report to Governor."

84. John Swett, "Higher Professional Training." *Pacific School and Home Journal* 8 (August 1879), 255.

85. *Bulletin, Mills College*, 13.

86. "San Francisco," *Pacific School and Home Journal*, August 1887, 275; and Roy Cloud, *Education in California*, 50.

87. Alice Marian Chapman, "Madame Severance: The Founder of Woman's Clubs" (Thesis for M.A., University of Southern California, 1930), 42; and Ferrier, *Ninety Years of Education in California*, 168–175.

88. Cloud, *Education in California*, 57, 58, 60.

89. Jeanne C. Carr, "The Industrial Education of Women," *Appendix to the Journals*, 239–40.

90. Ibid., 243.

91. Frank C. Jordon, Sec. of State, *California Blue Book, Legislative Manual or State Roster* (Sacramento Printing, 1924), 450.

92. Sales, "A History of the Superintendency of Public Instruction in the State of California, 1850–1932," 219.

93. See, for example, Agnes Smedley, *Daughter of Earth* (Old Westbury, New York: Feminist Press, 1973), and Elizabeth Corey, *Bachelor Bess: The Homesteading Letters of Elizabeth Corey, 1909–1919*, ed. Philip L. Gerber (Iowa City: University of Iowa Press).

94. "Tribute to the memory of Emily Tracy (Swett) Parkhurst," *California Illustrated Magazine*, 1892 as recorded in John Swett, *Public Education in California: Its Origin and Development, with Personal Reminiscences of Half a Century* (New York: American Book Company, 1911), 17.

95. Sigvald Stoylen, "Dr. Matilde Wergeland," *Sons of Norway Magazine* in Wergeland Collection, AHC, Laramie, Wyoming.

96. Hebard Collection, American Historical Center (AHC), Laramie, Wyoming.

Chapter Four

1. Virginia Scharff, *Twenty Thousand Roads: Women, Movement, and the West* (Berkeley: Univeristy of California Press, 2003), 95.

2. Reported by May Preston Slosson, "In Memoriam, Grace Raymond Hebard," published by the Faculty of the University of Wyoming, June 1937, Grace Raymond Hebard file #2 (HRP, Cheyenne).

3. The territories of Wyoming and Utah both granted women the vote in 1869. Utah women actually voted first in a local election in the spring of 1870 while Wyoming women did not vote until a general election in September. However, Wyoming has been given credit as the first to grant woman suffrage because of the higher status of the election and because Wyoming never withdrew woman's voting rights. Utah retracted women's right to vote soon after it was initiated and did not reissue that privilege until 1896.

4. Scharff, *Twenty Thousand Roads*, 96.

5. Boutelle, *Julia Morgan, Architect,* 21; and Richey, "Julia Morgan: Architect with Empathy,"*Eminent Women of the West* (Berkeley: Howell-North Books, 1975), 237–263.

6. Richey, "Jeannette Rankin" Woman of Commitment," *Eminent Women of the West,* 180–207; and Malca Chall and Hannah Josephson, *Jeannette Rankin: Activist for World Peace, Women's Rights, and Democratic Government.*

7. Elliott West,*Growing Up With the Country: Childhood on the Far Western Frontier* (Albuquerque: University of New Mexico Press, 1989), 257.

8. Ibid., 21.

9. "The Doctor Was an 'Adventuress,'" *Today's Health,* August 1970, in Olive Burt Collection, Box 14, (AHC), Laramie Wyoming.

10. Letter to her sister Mary, September 2, 1876, quoted in Maxine Benson, *Maxine Maxwell: Rocky Mountain Naturalist,* Women in the West Series (Lincoln: University of Nebraska Press, 1986). Biographical details have been taken from Benson's work.

11. Laurie Lisle, *Portrait of an Artist: A Biography of Georgia O'Keeffe* (Seaview Books, 1981; reprint N.Y.: Washington Square Press, 1987), 17.

12. Letter from O'Keeffe to Mitchell Kennerly, January 20, 1929, quoted in Lisle, *Portrait of an Artist,* 26.

13. Lisle, *Portrait of an Artist,* 15, 17, 26.

14. Elinore Pruitt Stewart, *Letters of a Woman Homesteader,* (The Atlantic Monthly Company, 1912, 1914; Boston: Houghton Mifflin Company, 1988), 15–17.

15. Mrs. Alfred H. (Cora M.) Beach, ed. and comp., "Mrs. Mary A. Garrett, First Woman to Be Elected Justice of the Peace in the World," in *Women of Wyoming* (Casper, Wyoming: S.E. Boyer & Company, 1927), 425.

16. Erik Erikson, "Womanhood and the Inner Space," *Identity, Youth and Crisis* (N.Y.: Norton, 1968).

17. Kay Graber, ed., *Sister to the Sioux: The Memoirs of Elaine Goodale Eastman* (Lincoln: University of Nebraska Press, Bison Books, 1978).

18. Eliza W. Farnham, *Life in Prairie Land* (N.Y.: Harper and Brothers, 1846; reprint Nieuwkoop, Netherlands: B De Graaf, 1972) as quoted in Pamela Herr, "Reformer," in *Women Who Made the West,* 210.

19. Clarice E. Richards, *A Tenderfoot Bride: Tales from an Old Ranch,* (N.Y.: F. H. Revell Co., 1920; reprint Lincoln: Univeristy of Nebraska Press, Bison Book, 1988), 87.

20. Ibid., 128–29, 226.

21. Anita Pollitzer, "That's Georgia," *Saturday Review,* November 4, 1950, quoted in Lisle, *Portrait of an Artist,* 63.

22. Lisle, *Portrait of an Artist,* 62–63.

23. Stewart, *Letters of a Woman Homesteader.*

24. Gretel Ehrlich, "Foreward," in Stewart, *Letters of a Woman Homesteader,* xiii-xxi.

25. Stewart, *Letters of a Woman Homesteader,* 215.

26. Joseph R. Blackstock, *Report on Laura Scudder* (Monterey Park, Calif.: Historical Society, 1974).

27. Laura Scudder, "High Sierras," quoted in Blackstock, *Report on Laura Scudder,* 14.

28. Alice Kessler-Harris, *Out to Work: A History of Wage-Earning Women in the United States* (New York: Oxford University Press, 1982), 58.

29. Margaret Fuller, *Woman in the Nineteenth Century,* Authur B. Fuller, editor, (Boston: J.P. Jewett & Co., 1845).

30. Harriet Beecher Stowe, *Uncle Tom's Cabin; or, Life Among the Lowly* (Boston: John P. Jewett & Company, 1852; reprint New York: Harper & Row, Publishers, 1965).

31. Harris-Kessler, *Out to Work.*

32. Dorothy Nafus Morrison, *Ladies Were Not Expected: Abigail Scott Duniway and Women's Rights* (N.Y.: Artheneum, 1977. Reprint. Western Imprints, The Press of the Oregon Historical Society, 1985); Ruth Moynihan, *Rebel for Rights: Abigail Scott Duniway* (New Haven: Yale University Press, 1983).

33. Helen Hunt Jackson, *A Century of Dishonor* (New York: Harper and Brothers, 1881); and *Ramona* (Boston: Roberts Brothers, 1884). For details on her life, see Antionette May, *Helen Hunt Jackson: A Lonely Voice of Conscience* (San Francisco: Chronicle Books, 1987).

34. Mary Lou Pence, "Polly Pry," *The Women Who Made the West,* ed. by the Western Writers of America, (Garden City, N.Y.: Doubleday & Company, Inc., 1980), 104–119.

35. Ibid.

36. Ibid.

37. Vera L. Norwood, "Heroines of Nature: Four Women Respond to the American Landscape," *Environmental Review* 8 (Spring 1984): 34–56.

38. Mary Austin, *Woman of Genius* (Garden City, N.Y.: Doubleday, Page & Co., 1912).

39. Orrin A. Engen, *Writer of the Plains, A Biography of B.M. Bower* (Culver City, Calif.: The Pontine Press, 1973).

40. Ibid., 3.

41. Ibid., 2.

42. Ibid., 4.

43. B.M. Bower, *Jean of the Lazy A* (Toronto: McClelland, Goodchild, & Stewart, 1915).

44. See, for example, Martha Maxwell. Her childhood interest in wildlife and her companionship with farm animals developed into a career as a wildlife specialist and taxidermist. Maxine Benson, *Martha Maxwell: Rocky Mountain Naturalist* (Lincoln: University of Nebraska Press, 1986).

45. Anthony Storr, *Solitude: A Return to the Self* (New York: Ballantine Books, 1988), xiii.

46. Ibid., xiv.

47. Judy Scalla, "Beloved Healer," *The Women Who Made the West*, 152–163.

48. Morgan and Flora North, interviewed by Suzanne B. Riess, *The Julia Morgan Architectural History Project* (Berkeley: The Bancroft Library Regional Oral History Office), Vol. II, 161, 170.

49. Sara Holmes Boutelle, *Julia Morgan, Architect* (New York: Abbeville Press Publishers, 1988), 45.

50. Morgan North to Reiss, *The Julia Morgan Architectural History Project*, 199.

51. Boutelle, *Julia Morgan, Architect*, 8–9, 83–86.

52. Ronald Fields, *Abby Williams Hill and the Lure of the West* (Washington State Historical Society, 1989).

53. Emily Carr, *Growing Pains: The Autobiography of Emily Carr* (Toronto: Oxford University Press, 1945).

54. Doris Bry and Nicholas Callaway, eds.*Georgia O'Keeffe: In the West* (N.Y.: Alfed Knopf, 1989); Laurie Lisle, *Portrait of an Artist* (Seaview Books, 1980; revised edition, New York: Washington Square Books, Pocket Books, 1986), 62–64, 100–101.

55. Riley, *The Female Frontier*, especially chapters five and six; Sheryll Patterson-Black, "From Pack Trains to Publishing: Women's Work in the Frontier West," in *Western Women in History and Literature*, ed. Sheryll Patterson-Black and Gene Patterson-Black (Crawford, Nebraska: Cottonwood Press, 1978); Myres, *Westering Women*, especially chapter nine.

56. Barbara J. Harris, *Beyond Her Sphere: Women and the Professions in American History*, Contributions to Women's Studies, No. 4, (Westport, Connecticut: Greenwood Press, 1978), 88–90.

57. Judy Skalla, "Beloved Healer," *The Women Who Made the West*.

58. "Dr. Esther Lovejoy State Pioneer," *Oregon Journal*, February 14, 1968, in Olive Burt Collection, Box #14, AHC, Laramie, Wyoming.

59. Elinore Pruitt Stewart, *Letters of a Woman Homesteader* (The Atlantic Monthly Company, 1913; reprint, Boston: Houghton Mifflin Company, 1988); and Elizabeth Corey, *Bachelor Bess: The Homesteading Letters of Elizabeth Corey, 1909–1919*, edited by Philip L. Gerber, (Iowa City: University of Iowa Press, 1990).

60. Glenda Riley, *The Female Frontier: A Comparative View of Women on the Prairie and the Plains* (Lawrence: University Press of Kansas, 1988), 134.

61. Ibid., 137.

62. The practice was common enough that B.M. Bower created three women characters whose cabin was built on the corner of their three adjacent claims in *The Flying U's Last Stand* (New York: Grosset & Dunlap Publishers, 1915).

63. Sandra L. Myres, *Westering Women and the Frontier Experience 1800–1915*, Histories of the American Frontier, (Albuquerque: University of New Mexico Press, 1982), 259.

64. Mary W. M. Hargreaves, "Women and the Agricultural Settlement of the Northern Plains," *Agricultural History* 50 (January 1976), 182.

65. Riley, *The Female Frontier*, 133.

66. See, especially, Teresa Jordan, *Cowgirls: Women of the American West, An Oral History* (Garden City, New York: Doubleday & Company, Inc., 1984).

67. Harriet Williams (Russell) Strong Collection, Huntington Library, San Marino, CA.

68. Harriet Williams (Russell) Strong, undated letter, no addressee, Strong COLL L11–6, HS 854 [c.1915], Harriet W.R. Strong Collection, Huntington Library, San Marino, California.

69. "East Favors Suffrage: Prominent Club Woman Tells of Splendid Organization in New York, All Classes Interested," *Los Angeles Express*, Saturday, January 14, 1911, Harriet W.R. Strong Collection, Huntington Library.

70. Mrs. H.W.R. Strong, "Thirty Years Ago," *The Clubwoman*, November 1926, extracts from an address delivered by Mrs. H.W.R. Strong at the beginning of her second year as president of the Ebell Club in 1895, Strong Collection, Huntington Library, San Marino, CA.

71. Ibid.

Chapter Five

1. Biographical details have been taken from Sigvald Stoylen, "Dr. Matilde Wergeland," *Sons of Norway Magazine* in Wergeland Collection, AHC, Laramie, Wyoming.

2. Ibid.

3. Frederick Jackson Turner, "The Significance of the Frontier in American History," presented at the Chicago meeting of the American Historical Association, 1893; and Walter Prescott Webb, *The Great Plains* (New York: Grossett & Dunlap, 1931). For examples of challenges to this thesis, see discussion in Chapters One and Two.

4. Dorothy Gray, *Women of the West* (Millbrae, California: Les Femmes, 1976).

5. T.A. Larson, "Woman Suffrage in Wyoming," *Pacific Northwest Quarterly* 56 (April 1965): 57–66.

6. Beverly Beeton, *Women Vote in the West: The Woman Suffrage Movement 1869–1895* (New York: Garland Publishing, Inc., 1986).

7. These types of reasoning are proposed in the early history of Wyoming by Grace Hebard, Suffrage Collection, American Heritage Center (AHC), University of Wyoming, Laramie. For published summaries of these accounts see Beeton, *Women Vote in the West*; and Michael A. Massie, "Reform Is Where You Find It: The Roots of Woman Suffrage in Wyoming," *Annals of Wyoming* (Spring, 1990): 2–21.

8. Sidney Howell Fleming, "Solving the Jigsaw Puzzle: One Suffrage Story at a Time," *Annals of Wyoming* (Spring 1990): 27.

9. Dr. Lewis E. Theiss, "Wyoming Led Off," *Christian Science Monitor*, July 8, 1958, in Woman Suffrage File #2, AHC.

10. From an interview with Mrs. Bright by Dr. Grace Raymond Hebard, quoted in Hebard's address to The National Woman's Congressional Committee [1916], in Woman's Suffrage File #1, AHC.

11. Elizabeth Cady Stanton, Susan B. Anthony, and Matilda Joslyn Gage, eds., *History of Woman Suffrage 1876–1885*, vol. 3 (New York: Arno & The New York Times, 1969), 674.

12. Mary Lee Stark, "One of the First Wyoming Women Voters Tells How Franchise Was Granted. Many Wrong Statements Are Corrected in Article." No author or publisher, in Esther Hobart Morris Collection, File #2, AHC.

13. Dennis A. Jones, "Immigrant Women in Kansas in the Early Days," *Kansas Quarterly* 18 (Summer 1986), 15.

14. Edith M. Phelps, ed., *Selected Articles on Woman Suffrage, Debaters' Handbook Series*, 3rd ed., (White Plains, N.Y.: The H. W. Wilson Company, 1916), 47.

15. Alice Kessler-Harris, *Out to Work: A History of Wage-Earning Women in the United States* (New York: Oxford University Press, 1982).

16. *Council Journal of the Legislative Assembly of the Territory of Wyoming, First Session, 1869* (Cheyenne: Tribune Office, 1870), 20.

17. Agnes Wright Spring, "But You're a Girl," *The Arrow of Pi Beta Phi* (Spring, 175), 42–44, in Agnes Wright Spring bio-file #2, AHC, Laramie, Wyoming; and "A True Woman of the West," *Colorado Heritage News* (March 1987), published by the Colorado Historical Society, in Agnes Wright Spring writings file, AHC.

18. Rev. O. P. Fitzgerald, "Equalization of Salaries—Simple Justice," *The California Teacher*, November 1870, 131–32.

19. Ibid.

20. Polly Welts Kaufman, *Women Teachers on the Frontier* (New Haven: Yale University Press, 1984), xxi-xxii.

21. State Superintendent Ezra S. Carr, "Report to Governor, October 1, 1879," *Appendix to the Journals of the Senate and Assembly of the 23rd Session of the Legislature of the State of California*, vol. II (Sacramento: State Office, 1879), supplementary pages.

22. Ibid., 19.

23. Nancy Hoffman, *Woman's 'True' Profession: Voices from the History of Teaching* (Old Westbury, N.Y.: The Feminist Press, 1981), 10.

24. Mae Urbanek, "Justice of the Peace," *The Women Who Made the West*, ed. by the Western Writers of America, (Garden City, N.Y.: Doubleday & Company, Inc., 1980), 202.

25. Chicago *Tribune*, June 17, 1894, quoted in "Esther Hobart Morris and Suffrage," prepared by the Staff in the Archives and Western History Dept. of the Library, University of Wyoming, Esther Hobart Morris Collection, folder #2, (AHC), 3–4.

26. San Francisco *Chronicle*, February 16, 1872, in Esther Hobart Morris Collection, File #2, (AHC).

27. Urbanek, "Justice of the Peace," *The Women Who Made the West*, 202.

28. San Francisco *Chronicle*.

29. Letter to Mrs. Hooker from Mrs. Esther Hobart Morris, J.P., undated, South Pass City, Wyoming Territory, in Suffrage Folder #2, (AHC).

30. Mrs. Alred H. Beach, Ed., "Mrs. John Campbell," *Women of Wyoming*, (Casper, WY: S.E. Boyer & Company, 1927), 53–59.

31. Abigail Scott Duniway, "A Few Recollections of a Busy Life," *Souvenir of Western Women,* ed. by Mary Osborn Douthit (Portland, OR: Presses of Anderson & Duniway Company, 1905), 11.

32. See Horace G. Platt, *The Law as to the Property Rights of Married Women; As Contained in the Statutes and Decisions of California, Texas, and Nevada,* (San Francisco, Sumner Whitney & Co., 1885).

33. Mari J. Matsuda, "The West and the Legal Status of Women: Explanations of Frontier Feminism," *Journal of the West* 24 (January 1985), 50.

34. Matsuda, "The West and the Legal Status of Women," 50; Norma Basch, "Equity Vs. Equality: Emerging Concepts of Women's Political Status in the Age of Jackson," *Journal of the Early Republic* 3 (Fall 1983): 297–318; and Sarah Deutsch, *No Separate Refuge: Culture, Class, and Gender on an Anglo-Hispanic Frontier in the American Southwest, 1880–1940* (New York: Oxford University Press, 1987), 45.

35. Matsuda, "The West and the Legal Status of Women," 50.

36. Glenda Riley, *The Female Frontier: A Comparative View of Women on the Prairie and the Plains* (Lawrence: University of Kansas Press, 1988), 21–22, 81.

37. Paula Petrik, *No Step Backward: Women and Family on the Rocky Mountain Mining Frontier, Helena, Montana 1865–1900* (Helena: Montana Historical Society, 1987), 98.

38. Robert L. Griswold, "Apart But Not Adrift: Wives, Divorce, and Independence in California, 1850–1890," *Pacific Historical Review* (1980): 265–283.

39. Petrik, *No Step Backward,* 116.

40. Patricia Voeller Horner, "May Arkwright Hutton: Suffragist and Politician," *Women in Pacific Northwest History, An Anthology,* Karen J. Blair, ed. (Seattle: University of Washington Press, 1988), 38.

41. Roberta Cheney, "From Rags to Riches," The *Women Who Made the West,* 221, 230. Cheney points out that after Hutton made her wealth, she visited her father's legitimate children, her brothers and sister, in Ohio. At that time, she located her mother and paid the funeral expenses after her death. Another source assumes that Hutton's mother died while May was still a child. In this case, however, Horner was relying on an undated newspaper clipping from one of Hutton's scrapbooks. See Horner, "May Arkwright Hutton: Suffragist and Politician," *Women in Pacific Northwest History,* 25.

42. May Arkwright Hutton, *The Coeur D'Alenes, or A Tale of the Modern Inquisition in Idaho* (Denver: The APP Engraving & Printing Co., 1900).

43. Horner, "May Arkwright Hutton: Suffragist and Politician," *Women in Pacific Northwest History,* 25.

44. The following biographical details have been taken from Horner, "May Arkwright Hutton," 25–42; Cheney, "From Rags to Riches," 220–239; and James Montgomery, *Liberated Woman: A Life of May Arkwright Hutton* (Spokane: Gingko Publishers, 1974).

45. From Hutton's personal scrapbook, quoted in Horner, "May Arkwright Hutton: Suffragist and Politician," *Women in Pacific Northwest History,* 25. See also Ida Husted Harper, ed., *The History of Woman Suffrage* (National American Woman Suffrage Association), 1922, Vol. 5, 133–134.

46. Letter of Hutton to William E. Borah [Senator from Idaho], Sept. 28, 1909, Charles Gonser private papers, quoted in Horner, 27.

47. Letter of Hutton to Lyman B. Arkwright, Nov. 16, 1908, Gonser papers, cited in Horner, 38.

48. Montgomery and Cheney mention Bert Munn as her first husband. He drowned some years after leaving her. Horner cites evidence that May Arkwright married Frank Day when she was eighteen, but there is no available information on the dissolution of this marriage. There is also a discrepancy in the date of her departure for Idaho. Cheney report it was 1878 while Horner records 1883. Because Hutton is recorded to have said that she came West at the age of 23, the 1883 date is probably correct.

49. Hutton, *The Coeur D'Arlene*.

50. Statistics quoted in Horner, 28.

51. Horner, 33.

52. Eaton to Catt, Oct. 24, 1909, and Eaton to J. H. DeVoe, June 4, 1909, DeVoe Collection, Box 2, Washington/Northwest Room, Washington State Library, Olympia, quoted in Horner, 33, 32.

53. Horner, 33. For supporting evidence, see Lucile F. Fargo, *Spokane Story* (New York: Columbia University Press, 1950), 190–192.

54. Hutton's tight purse is described by Dr. Eaton in letter to DeVoe's husband, ibid. Her generosity to orphans and the poor is frequently described in Montgomery and Cheney.

55. She would not, however, be the first woman to be elected to a national nominating convention. That honor goes to Theresa A. Jenkins of Wyoming who was elected to the Republican National Convention in Minneapolis, Minnesota in 1892. In this status, she made several speeches urging national suffrage. It should be noted that Mae Urbanek, *Women Who Made the West*, 202, evidently gave this credit to Esther Hobart Morris in error.

56. Robert J. Dinkin, *Before Equal Suffrage: Women in Partisan Politics from Colonial Times to 1920* (Westport, Conn.: Greenwood Press, 1995) 101.

Chapter Six

1. Mae Urbanek, "Justice of the Peace," in Western Writers of America, *Women Who Won the West* (Garden City, New York: Doubleday & Company, 1980), 201.

2. Mrs. Alfred H. (Cora M.) Beach, Ed., "Mrs. Mary A. Garrett, First Woman to Be Elected Justice of the Peace in the World," *Women of Wyoming* (Casper, Wyoming: S.E. Boyer & Company, 1927), 425.

3. Biographical data taken from "Mrs. Cort F. Meyer, State Superintendent of Public Instruction and National Superintendent of Indian Schools," *Women of Wyoming*, ed. Beach, 39–41; "Death Takes Mrs. Cort F. Meyer at Age Ninety-six," *The Toppenish (Washington) Review*, Thursday, Aug. 6, 1956, Mrs. Cort Meyer file, Historical Research and Publications (HPR), Division of Parks and Cultural Resources, Dept. of Commerce, Cheyenne, Wyoming; "They've Seen Yakima Grow," [Yakima, Wash.] *Herald*, May 3, 1953 in Mrs. Cort Meyer file (HRP). "First Woman School Head For State Dies," *Wyoming State Tribune*, August 13, 1959, Mrs. Cort Meyer file, HRP.

4. Ibid.

5. "They've Seen Yakima Grow," *Herald.*

6. Theiss, "Wyoming Led Off," *Christian Science Monitor*, 81 in Esther Hobart Morris Collection, American Heritage Center, University of Wyoming.

7. Ibid.

8. Ibid.

9. Beach, ed. "Mary (Godat) Bellamy, Wyoming's First Woman Legislator," *Women of Wyoming*, 44–46.

10. Quote from an unidentified woman educator, in Theiss, "Wyoming Led Off," *Christian Science Monitor*," 81.

11. Robert J. Dinkin, *Before Equal Suffrage: Women in Partisan Politics from Colonial Times to 1920* (Westport, Conn.: Greenwood Press, 1995).

12. Kristi Anderson, *After Suffrage: Women in Partisan and Electoral Politics before the New Deal* (Chicago and London: The University of Chicago,1996), 115, 116.

13. Elinor Richey, "Jeannette Rankin: Woman of Commitment," *Eminent Women of the West* (Berkeley, California: Howell-North Books, 1975), 180–207; and Malca Chall and Hannah Josephson, *Jeannette Rankin: Activist for World Peace, Women's Rights, and Democratic Government*, Suffragists Oral History Project (Berkeley: Regents of the University of California, 1974), 188.

14. Chall and Josephson, *Jeannette Rankin*, 188.

15. Ibid., 191–92.

16. Richey, *Eminent Women*, 184. Much of the following biographical details have been taken from Richey.

17. Chall and Josephson, *Jeannette Rankin*, 192–193.

18. Ibid, 17.

19. Ibid., 18.

20. Ibid., 18–19. [Their emphasis.]

21. Ibid., 19.

22. Ibid., 20.

23. Ibid., 33. [Their emphasis.]

24. Ibid., 55.

25. Nellie Tayloe Ross, "The Governor Lady, Nellie Tayloe Ross, America's First Woman Governor, Tells for the First Time the Intimate Story of her Political Career," *Good Housekeeping*, Sept. 1927, 36, Ross Bio-File #2, AHC.

26. Nellie Tayloe Ross, "The Governor Lady, Nellie Tayloe Ross Tells the Intimate Story of Her Life as Wife and Mother—and as the Chief Executive of the State of Wyoming. It Is a Record of Which all Women Should Be Proud," *Good Housekeeping*, Aug. 1927, 31, in Nellie Tayloe Ross, File #2, AHC.

27. "Biographical Profile of Nellie Tayloe Ross, Director of the Mint," Reproduced from State Department Publication, July 1948, in Nellie Tayloe Ross Collection, AHC.; and Robert McCracken, "Nellie Tayloe Ross, The United States' First Woman Governor," *Wyoming State Tribune*, April 23, 1952, in Ross Collection, Newsclip File, Box #3, AHC.

28. Nellie Tayloe Ross, "The Governor Lady, Nellie Tayloe Ross Tells the Intimate Story of Her Life as Wife and Mother—and as the Chief Executive of the State of Wyoming," *Good Housekeeping*, August 1927, 30–31, 118–124, in Nellie Tayloe Ross Biographical File #2, AHC.

29. Ross, "The Governor Lady," 36.

30. Ibid., 212.

31. "A Sure Enough Woman Governor," *The Oregonian*, Portland, January 17, 1926, Ross Collection, Newsclip File, AHC.

32. Sandra Guzzo, "Happy Birthday Nellie Tayloe Ross," *Laramie [Wyo.] Boomerang*, Nov. 28, 1976, 7, Ross Collection, Newsclip File, Box #3, AHC.

33. Miss Mayme Ober Peak [of Chevy Chase, Maryland], "Governor Nellie Ross at Home," no publisher or date, Ross Collection, Box #1, AHC.

34. Theresa A. Jenkins, "An Open Answer," a letter addressed to Mr. Thomas Seddon Taliaffero, Jr., October 7, 1926, in Jenkins File, AHC.

35. Madison, S.D. *Sentinel*, title unavailable, June 20, 1930, Ross Collection, Box #1, AHC.

36. *Kinsley [Kansas] Graphic*, title unavailable, July 17, 1930, Ross Collection, Box #1, Biographical File, AHC.

37. Nellie Tayloe Ross, manuscript, Ross Collection, Box #3, AHC.

38. Ibid.

39. "Favorite Sayings of Nellie Tayloe Ross," Ross Collection, Biographical File, Box #1, AHC.

40. Wyoming granted woman suffrage as a territory in 1869. It became a constitutional right when the state officially entered the union in 1890. Three other Rocky Mountain states also granted full woman's suffrage during that decade: Colorado in 1893 and Utah and Idaho in 1896. Washington was the fifth state to grant full suffrage but did not do so until 1910. Other western states followed soon after. The Nineteenth Amendment to the U. S. Constitution which gave full suffrage rights to women in all states was not ratified until 1920.

Chapter Seven

1. Patricia Limerick contends that the "winning" of the West was not a victory. There was too much destruction of environment and culture. Problems with Indians and women and environment that were conquered in the nineteenth century were not properly resolved. She points out that many of these problems have reemerged in the twentieth. See Limerick, *The Legacy of Conquest: The Unbroken Past of the American West* (New York: W.W. Norton & Company, 1987). "West of the Imagination" is a phase coined by William H. Goetzmann and William N. Goetzmann, *West of the Imagination* (New York: W.W. Norton & Company, 1986).

2. For examples of the male adventure image see, for example, Ray Allen Billington, *The Far Western Frontier* (New York: Harper & Row, Publishers, 1956) and with Martin Ridge, *Westward Expansion: A History of the American Frontier*, 5th Ed. (New York: MacMillan Publishing Co., Inc., 1982); Joe B. Frantz and Julian Ernest Choate, Jr. *The American Cowboy: The Myth and the Reality* (Norman: University of Oklahoma Press, 1955); William H. Goetzmann, *Exploration and Empire: The Explorer and the Scientist in the Winning of The American West* (New York: W.W. Norton & Co., Inc., 1966).

For work in the area of women's positive motivations in the West see Dee Brown, *The Gentle Tamers* (New York: Putnam, 1958); Christiane Fischer, Ed., *Let Them Speak for Themselves: Women in the American West* (Hamden, Ct.: Archon Books, 1977); Dorothy Gray, *Women of the West* (Millbrae, California: Les Femmes, 1976); Teresa Jordon *Cowgirls: Women of the American West* (Garden City, N.Y.: Doubleday & Company, Inc., 1984); Polly Welts Kaufman, *Women Teachers on the Frontier* (New Haven: Yale University Press, 1984); Sandra L. Myer *Westering Women and the Frontier Experience* (Alburquerque: Univeristy of New Mexico Press, 1982); Nell Brown Propst, *Those Strenuous Dames of the Colorado Prairie* (Boulder, Colorado: Pruitt Publishing Co., 1982); Glenda Riley, *Frontierswomen: The Iowa Experience* (Ames: Iowa State University Press, 1981); Virginia Scharff, *Twenty Thousand Roads: Women, Movement, and the West* (Berkeley: University of California Press, 2003), 141.

3. Henry Nash Smith, *Virgin Land: The American West as Symbol and Myth* (1950; reprint, Cambridge, Mass.: Harvard University Press, 1970).

4. Julia Cherry Spruill, *Women's Life and Work in the Southern Colonies* (University of North Carolina Press, 1938; reprint, New York: W. W. Norton & Company, Inc., 1972).

5. Mary Beth Norton, *Liberty's Daughters: The Revolutionary Experience of American Women, 1750–1800* (Boston: Little, Brown and Company, 1980), 265.

6. Ibid., 297, 299.

7. D'Ann Campbell, "Was the West Different? Values of Young Women in 1943," *Pacific Historical Review* 47 (August 1978), 463.

8. Virginia Scharff, *Twenty Thousand Roads: Women, Movement, and the West* (Berkeley: University of California Press, 2003), 141.

9. Quoted in Betty Starks Case, *Maggie: Set Free in the Wyoming Rockies* (Greybull, Wyoming: Wolverine Gallery, 1988), 41, 119.

10. Biographical details have been taken from Case, *Maggie: Set Free in the Wyoming Rockies*.

11. Ibid., 20.

12. Ibid., 104.

13. Ibid., 81.

14. Ibid., 74.

Bibliography

MANUSCRIPT COLLECTIONS AND DOCUMENTS

American Heritage Center, University of Wyoming, Laramie Wyoming

>Mary Bellamy Papers
>Olive Burt Papers
>Grace Raymond Hebard Papers
>Theresa Jenkins Papers
>Esther Hobart Morris Papers
>Nellie Tayloe Ross Papers
>Agnes Wright Spring Papers
>Matilde Wergeland Papers
>Woman's Suffrage Collection

Historical Research and Publications, Division of Parks and Cultural Resources, Department of Commerce, Cheyenne, Wyoming

>Grace Hebard Papers
>Esther Hobart Morris Papers
>Estelle Reel/Mrs. Cort Meyer Papers

Henry E. Huntington Library, San Marino, California

>Ezra S. Carr Collection
>Caroline Severance Collection
>Harriet Russell Strong Collection
>Rare Book Collection
>   of Mills College:
>   Barlett, William, "The Founder and Builder,"
>   Address given at Founders Day, Mills College, May 11, 1894. San Franciso, private publications, 1894.
>   *Mills College for Young Women*
>   (San Francisco, 1903)

Mills College Statement, 1937

of Journals:
The California Teacher (November 1870).
Pacific School and Home Journals
(August 1879 and August 1887).

of Government Documents:
*Appendix to the Journals of the Senate and Assembly of the 23rd
Session of the Legislature of the State of California.* Vol. 2.
Sacramento: State Office, 1879.
Jordan, Frank C., Sec. of State. *California Blue Book, Legislative
Manual or State Roster.* Sacramento Printing, 1924.
Moulder, Andrew J. *Commentaries on the School Law with the
Elements of School Architecture; Laws Relating to the
School Lands, Forms and Instruction.* Sacramento: John
O'Meara, State Printer, 1858.
Swett, John. *First Biennial Report, Superintendent of Public
Instruction, 1863–1865; Appendix to the Journal of
Legislation.* Vol 2, Doc. 1.

LETTERS, JOURNALS, AUTOBIOGRAPHIES, BIOGRA-PHIES, ORAL HISTORIES, AND HISTORICAL FICTION

Austin, Mary Hunter. *Earth Horizons.* New York: Houghton-Mifflin Co., 1932.
——. *The Land of Little Rain.* Houghton Mifflin, 1903. Reprint. New York:
Penquin Books, 1988.
——. *Woman of Genius.* Garden City, N.Y.: Doubleday, Page & Co., 1912.
Banner, Lois W. *Elizabeth Cady Stanton: A Radical for Women's Rights.* Boston:
Little, Brown and Company, 1980.
Barton, Lois, ed. *One Woman's West: Recollections of the Oregon Trail and Settling
the Northwest Country by Martha Gay Masterson 1838–1916.* 2nd ed.
Eugene, Oregon: Spencer Butte Press, 1986.
Beach, Mrs. Alfred H. (Cora M.), ed. and comp. *Women of Wyoming.* Casper,
Wyoming: S.E. Boyer & Company, 1927.
Benson, Maxine. *Martha Maxwell: Rocky Mountain Naturalist.* Women in the
West Series. Lincoln: University of Nebraska Press, 1986.
Blackstock, Joseph R. *Report on Laura Scudder.* Monterey Park, Calif.: Historical
Society, 1974.

Blair, Karen J., ed. *Women in Pacific Northwest History, An Anthology.* Seattle: University of Washington Press, 1988.

Boutelle, Sara Holmes. *Julia Morgan, Architect.* New York: Abbeville Press Publishers, 1988.

Bower, B. M. *Chip of the Flying-U.* Street & Smith, 1904. Reprint. G. W. Dillingham Campany, 1906.

—-. *The Flying U's Last Stand.* New York: Grosset & Dunlap, 1915.

—-. *Jean of the Lazy A.* Toronto: McClelland, Goodchild, & Stewart, 1915.

Bry, Doris and Nicholas Calloway. Eds. *Georgia O'Keeffe: In the West.* New York: Alfred A. Knopf, 1989.

Carr, Emily. *Growing Pains: The Autobiography of Emily Carr.* Toronto: Oxford University Press, 1945.

Case, Betty Starks. *Maggie: Set Free in the Wyoming Rockies.* Greybull, Wyo.: Wolverine Gallery, 1988.

Cather, Willa. *O Pioneers.* Boston & New York: Houghton Mifflin Co., 1913.

Chall, Malca, and Hannah Josephson. *Jeannette Rankin: Activist for World Peace, Womens' Rights, and Deomocratic Goverment.* Suffragists Oral History Project. Berkeley: Regents of the University of California, 1974.

Chapman, Alice Marian. "Madame Severance: The Founder of Woman's Clubs." Thesis for M.A. University of Southern California, 1930.

Cleveland, Agnes Morley. *No Life for a Lady.* Boston: Little, Brown and Company, 1935.

Corey, Elizabeth. *Bachlor Bess: The Homesteading Letters of Elizabeth Corey, 1909–1919.* Edited by Philip L. Gerber. Iowa City: University of Iowa Press, 1990.

Douthit, Mary Osborn, ed. *The Souvenir of Western Women.* Portland, Oregon: Anderson & Duniway Co., 1905.

Engen, Orrin A. *Writer of the Plains, A Biography of B.M. Bower.* Culver City, Calif.: The Pontine Press, 1973.

Fargo, Lucile F. *Spokane Story.* New York: Columbia University Press, 1950.

Fields, Ronald. *Abby Williams Hill and the Lure of the West.* Washington State Historical Society, 1989.

Fischer, Christiane, ed. *Let Them Speak for Themselves: Women in the American West, 1849–1900.* Hamden, Conn.: Archon Books, 1977.

Gilman, Charlotte Perkins. *The Yellow Wallpaper.* Boston: Small, Maynard, 1899. Reprint. Old Westbury, N.Y.: The Feminist Press, 1973.

Graber, Kay, ed. *Sister to the Sioux: The Memoirs of Elaine Goodale Eastman.* Lincoln: University of Nebraska Press, Bison Books, 1978.

Harper, Ida Husted, ed. *The History of Woman Suffrage.* Vol. 5. National American Woman Suffrage Association, 1922.

Hixon, Adrietta Applegate. *On to Oregon! A True Story of a Young Girl's Journey into the West*. Westler, Idaho: Signal-American Printers, 1947.

Homestead Fever: History of Denton, Danvers, Coffee Creek. Compiled by Denton [Montana] Heritage Committee. Great Falls, Mont.: Blue Print and Letter Company, 1977.

Hutton, May Arkwright, *The CoeurD'Alenes, or A Tale of the Modern Inquisition in Idaho*. Denver: The APP Engraving & Printing Co., 1900.

Jackson, Helen Hunt. *Ramona*. Boston: Roberts Brothers, 1884.

James, Edward T., ed. *Notable American Women, 1607–1950, A Biographical Dictionary*. Cambridge, Mass.: Belknap Press of Harvard University Press, 1971.

Jordan, Teresa. *Cowgirls: Women of the American West, An Oral History*. Garden City, NY: Doubleday & Company, Inc., 1984.

Kasper, Shirl. *Annie Oakley*. Norman: University of Oklahoma Press, 1992.

Lisle, Laurie. *Portrait of an Artist: A Biography of Georgia O'Keeffe*. Seaview Books, 1981. Reprint. New York: Washington Square Press, 1987.

Mark, Joan. *A Stranger in Her Native Land: Alice Fletcher and the American Indians*. Lincoln: University of Nebraska Press, 1988.

May, Antionette. *Helen Hunt Jackson: A Lonely Voice of Conscience*. San Francisco: Chronicle Books, 1987.

Montgomery, James. *Liberated Woman: A Life of May Arkwright Hutton*. Spokane: Gingko Publishers, 1974.

Morrison, Dorothy Nafus. *Ladies Were Not Expected: Abigail Scott Duniway and Women's Rights*. N.Y.: Artheneum, 1977. Reprint. Western Imprints, The Press of the Oregon Historical Society, 1985.

Moynihan, Ruth. *Rebel for Rights: Abigail Scott Duniway*. New Haven: Yale University Press, 1983.

Moynihan, Ruth, Susan Armitage, and Christiane Fischer Dichamp. *So Much Work to Be Done: Women Settlers on the Mining and Ranching Frontier*. Women in the West Series. Lincoln: University of Nebraska Press, 1990.

Richards, Clarice E. *A Tenderfoot Bride: Tales from an Old Ranch*. New York: F. H. Revell Co., 1920. Reprint. Lincoln: University of Nebraska Press, Bison Book, 1988.

Richey, Elinor. *Eminent Women of the West*. Berkeley: Howell-North Books, 1975.

Riess, Suzanne B. *The Julia Morgan Architectural History Project*. Berkeley: The Bancroft Library Regional Oral History Office, Vol. II.

Riley, Glenda. *The Life and Legacy of Annie Oakley*. The Oklahoma Western Biographies. Norman: University of Oklahoma Press, 1994.

Roach, Joyce Gibson. *The Cowgirls*. 2nd ed. University of North Texas Press, 1990.

Robertson, Janet. *The Magnificent Mountain Women: Adventures in the Colorado Rockies*. Lincoln: University of Nebraska Press, 1990.

Rolvaag, O. E. *Giants of the Earth: A Saga of the Prairie*. New York: Harper & Brothers, 1927.

Seavgraves, Anne. *Daughters of the West*. Hayden, Idaho: Wesanne Publications, 1996.

Shelton, Emily Jones. "Lizzie E. Johnson: A Cattle Queen of Texas." *Southwestern Historical Quarterly* (January 1947).

Sklar, Katherine Kish. *Catharine Beecher: A Study in American Domesticity*. New York: W.W. Norton & Company, 1976.

Smedley, Agnes. *Daughter of Earth*. Westbury: The Feminist Press, 1973.

Stewart, Elinore Pruitt. *Letters of a Woman Homesteader*. The Atlantic Monthly Company, 1913, 1914. Reprint. Boston: Houghton Mifflin Company, 1988.

Strouse, Jean. *Alice James: A Biography*. Boston: Houghton Mifflin Co., 1980.

Swartwout, Annie Fern. *Missie: The Life and Times of Annie Oakley*. Blanchester, Ohio: Brown Publishing Co., 1947.

Swett, John. *Public Education in California: Its Origin and Development, with Personal Reminiscences of Half a Century*. New York: American Book Company, 1911.

Theiss, Lewis Edwin and Mary Bartol Theiss, "Pioneer of Suffrage States, Eighth and Concluding Article in the Equal Suffrage Series," in *Pictorial Review* (October 1913), in Esther Hobart Morris Collection, American Heritage Center, University of Wyoming.

Wells, Reba. "Cora Viola Howell Slaughter: Southern Arizona Ranchwoman." *Journal of Arizona History* (Winter 89): 391.

Women Who Made the West. The Western Writers of America Series. New York: Doubleday & Company, Inc., 1980.

HISTORICAL AND OTHER SECONDARY LITERATURE

"Alice Paul's Triumphs for Equality." *Alice Paul Institute*. 2004 <http://www.alicepaul.org/docs/triumphs.htm> (accessed 5 March, 2004).

Allen, Martha Mitten. *Traveling West: 19th Century Women on the Overland Routes*. El Paso: Texas Western Press, 1987.

Anderson, Kristi. *After Suffrage: Women in Partisan and Electoral Politics before the New Deal*. Chicago: The University of Chicago, 1996.

Andreadis, Harriette. "True Womanhood Revisited: Women's Private Writing in Nineteenth Century Texas." *Journal of the Southwest* 31 (Summer 1989): 179–204.

Aries, Philippe. *Century of Childhood: A Social History of the Family*. Translated by Robert Baldick. New York: Alfred A. Knopf, 1962.

Armitage, Susan, and Elizabeth Jameson, eds. *The Women's West*. Norman: University of Oklahoma Press, 1987.

Banes, Ruth A. "Autobiography and the Western Woman." *Turn-of-the-Century Women* 1 (Summer 1984): 9–21.

Banner, Lois W. "Women's History in the United States: Recent Theory and Practice." *Trends in History* 4 (Fall 1985): 93–121.

Basch, Norma. "Equity vs. Equality." *Journal of the Early Republic* (Fall 1983): 297–318.

Beecher, Catharine E. *The Evils Suffered by American Women and American Children: The Causes and the Remedy*. New York: Harper & Brothers, 1846.

—. *Suggestions Respecting Improvements in Education*. Hartford: Packard & Butler, 1829.

—. *The True Remedy for the Wrongs of Woman; with a History of an Enterprise Having That for Its Object*. Boston: Phillips, Sampson & Co., 1851.

—. *Woman Suffrage and Woman's Profession*. Hartford: Brown & Gross, 1871.

Beecher, Catharine E., and Harriet Beecher Stowe. *The American Woman's Home; or, Principles of Domestic Science Being a Guide to the Formation and Maintenance 2* New York: J. B. Ford and Company, 1869.

Beeton, Beverly. *Women Vote in the West: The Woman Suffrage Movement 1869–1896*. New York: Garland Publishing, Inc., 1986.

Berkhofer, Robert, Jr. "Space, Time, Culture, and the New Frontier." *Agricultural History* 38 (January 1964).

Billington, Ray Allen, and Martin Ridge. *Westward Expansion: A History of the American Frontier*. 5th ed. New York: Macmillan Publishing Co., 1982.

Blair, Karen J. *The Clubwoman as Feminist: True Womanhood Redefined, 1864–1914*. New York: Homes & Meier Publishers, 1980.

Blouet, Brain W., and Frederick C. Luebke, eds. *The Great Plains: Environment and Culture*. Lincoln: University of Nebraska Press, 1979.

Boose, Lynda, and Betty Flowers, eds. *Daughters and Fathers*. Baltimore: Johns Hopkins University Press, 1989.

Brown, Dee. *The Gentle Tamers: Women of the Old Wild West*. New York: Putnam, 1958. Reprint. Lincoln: University of Nebraska Press, 1981.

Butler, Anne M. *Daughters of Joy, Sisters of Misery: Prostitutes in the American West*. Urbana: University of Illinois Press, 1985.

Campbell, D'Ann. "Was the West Different? Values of Young Women in 1943." *Pacific Historical Review* 47 (August 1978): 453–464.

Cloud, Roy. *Education in California: Leaders, Organizations, and Accomplishments of the First Hundred Years.* Stanford: Stanford University Press, 1952.

Cogan, Frances B. *All-American Girl: The Ideal of Real Womanhood in Mid-Nineteenth-Century America.* Athens: University of Georgia Press, 1989.

Cott, Nancy F. *Bonds of Womanhood: 'Woman's Sphere' in New England, 1780–1835.* New Haven: Yale University Press, 1977.

—-. *The Grounding of Modern Feminism,* New Haven: Yale University Press, 1987.

—-. "Young Women in the Second Great Awakening in New England." *Feminist Studies* 3 (1975): 15–29.

Degler, Carl N. *At Odds: Women and Family in America from the Revolution to the Present.* New York: Oxford University Press, 1980.

Deknatel, Charles Y. "Regionalism and Environment: The Search for Planning Strategy and Organization in the Great Plains." *Environmental Review* 10 (Summer 1986): 107–121.

Demos, John. *A Little Commonwealth: Family Life in Plymouth Colony.* New York: Oxford University Press, 1970.

—-. *Past, Present, and Personal: The Family and the Life Course in American History.* New York: Oxford University Press, 1986.

Deutsch, Sarah. *No Separate Refuge: Culture, Class, and Gender on an Anglo-Hispanic Frontier in the American Southwest, 1880–1940.* New York: Oxford University Press, 1987.

Dick, Everett. *The Sod-House Frontier 1854–1890.* New York: Alfred A. Knopf, 1977.

Dinkin, Robert J. *Before Equal Suffrage: Women in Partisan Politics from Colonial Times to 1920.* Contributions in Women's Studies, Number 152. Westport, Connecticut: Greenwood Press, 1995.

Douglas, Ann. *The Feminization of American Culture.* New York: Alfred A. Knopf, 1977.

Epstein, Barbara Leslie. *The Politics of Domesticity: Women, Evangelism, and Temperance in Nineteenth Century America.* Middletown, Conn.: Wesleyan University Press, 1981.

Evans, Sarah M. *Born for Liberty: A History of Women in America.* New York: The Free Press, 1989.

Fairbanks, Carol and Sara Brooks Sundberg. *Farm Women on the Prairie Frontier: A Sourcebook for Canada and the United States.* Metuchen, NJ: Scarecrow Press, 1983.

Fairbanks, Carol and Bergine Haakenson, eds. *Writings of Farm Women, 1840–1940: An Anthology.* New York: Garland Publishing, Inc., 1990.

Faragher, John Mack. "History from the Inside-Out: Writing of Women in Rural America." *American Quarterly* 33 (Winter 1981): 537–57.

—-. *Women and Men on the Overland Trail.* New York: Yale University Press, 1979.

Faragher, Johnny, and Christine Stansell. "Women and Their Families on the Overland Trail to California and Oregon, 1842–1867." *Feminist Studies* 2/3 (1975): 150–166.

Ferrier, William. *Ninety Years of Education in California, 1846–1936.* Berkeley: Sather Gate Book Shop, 1937.

Fischer, Christiane, ed. *Let Them Speak for Themselves: Women in the American West, 1849–1900.* Hamden, Conn.: Archon Books, 1977.

Fleming, Sidney Howell. "Solving the Jigsaw Puzzle: One Suffrage Story at a Time." *Annals of Wyoming* 62 (Spring 1990): 22–72

Floyd, Janet. *Writing the Pioneer Woman.* Columbia and London: University of Missouri Press, 2002.

Fowler, William. *Woman on the American Frontier.* Ann Arbor: Plutarch Books, 1971.

Freedman, Estelle. "Separatism as Strategy: Female Institution Building and American Feminism 1870–1930." *Feminist Studies* 5 (Fall 1979): 512–29.

Fuller, Margaret. *Woman in the Nineteenth Century.* Edited by Authur B. Fuller. Boston: J.P. Jewett & Co., 1845.

Gallaher, Ruth A. *Legal and Political Status of Women in Iowa, 1838–1918.* Iowa City: State Historical Society, 1918.

Gilman, Charlotte Perkins. *Women and Economics.* Boston, Small, Maynard, 1898.

Georgi-Findlay, Brigitte. *The Frontiers of Women's Writing: Women's Narratives and the Rhetoric of Westward Expansion.* Tucson: The University of Arizona Press, 1996.

Goetzmann, William H. *Exploration and Empire: The Explorer and the Sicentist in the Winning of the American West.* New York: W. W. Norton & Co., Inc., 1966.

Goetzmann, William H. and William N. Goetzmann. *West of the Imagination.* New York: W.W. Norton & Company, 1986.

Gordon, Linda. *Heroes of Their Own Lives: The Politics and History of Family Violence, Boston 1880–1960.* New York: Viking Penquin Press, 1988.

Gray, Dorothy. *Women of the West.* Millbrae, Calif.: Les Femmes, 1976.

Griswold, Robert L. "Apart But Not Adrift: Wives, Divorce, and Independence in California, 1850–1890." *Pacific Historical Review* (1980): 265–283.

—-. *Family and Divorce in California; 1850–1890: Victorian Illusions and Everyday Realities*. Albany: State University of New York Press, 1982.

Hampsten, Elizabeth. *Read This Only to Yourself: The Private Writings of Midwestern Women, 1880–1910*. Bloomington: Indiana University Press, 1982.

Hargreaves, Mary W. M. "Women and the Agricultural Settlement of the Northern Plains." *Agricultural History* 50 (January 1976).

Harris, Barbara J. *Beyond Her Sphere: Women and the Professions in American History*. Contributions to Women's Studies, No. 4. Westport, Connecticut: Greenwood Press, 1978.

Hayward, C. Robert. *Victorian West: Class and Culture in Kansas Cattle Towns*. Lawrence: University Press of Kansas, 1991.

Helvenston, Sally I. "Ornament or Instrument? Proper Roles for Women on the Kansas Frontier." *Kansas Quarterly* 18 (Summer 1986): 35–47.

Hoffman, Nancy. *Woman's `True' Profession: Voices from the History of Teaching*. Old Westbury, N.Y.: The Feminist Press, 1981.

Horowitz, Helen Lefkowitz. *Alma Mater: Design and Experience in the Women's Colleges from Their Nineteenth-Century Beginnings to the 1930s*. Boston: Beacon Press, 1984.

Hough, Emerson. *The Passing of the Frontier: A Chronicle of the Old West*. New Haven: Yale University Press, 1918.

Hudson, Berkeley. "Laura Scudder Was More Than a Name." *Los Angles Times*, April 9, 1989.

Jackson, Helen Hunt. *A Century of Dishonor*. New York: Harper and Brothers, 1881.

Jackson, Louise, and Michael Day. "The Wyoming Literary and Library Association, 1870–1878." *Journal of the West* 30 (July 1991): 14–24.

Jameson, Elizabeth. "Toward a Multicultural History of women in the Western United States." *SIGNS* 13 (Summer 1988): 762–91.

Jeffrey, Julie Roy. *Frontier Women: The Trans-Mississippi West 1840–1880*. New York: Hill & Wang, 1979.

—-. "Narcissa Whitman: The Significance of a Missionary's Life." *Montana, the Magazine of Western History* 41 (Spring 1991): 3–15.

Jensen, Joan M. *With These Hands: Women Working on the Land*. Old Westbury: The Feminist Press, 1981.

Jensen, Joan M., and Gloria Ricci Lothrop. *California Women: A History*. Golden State Series. San Francisco: Boyd & Fraser Publishing Co., 1987.

Jensen, Joan M., and Darlis A. Miller. "*The Gentle Tamers* Revisited: New Approaches to the History of Women in the American West." *Pacific Historical Review* 49 (May 1980): 173–213.

Jensen, Joan M., and Darlis A. Miller. *New Mexico Women: Intercultural Perspectives*. Albuquerque: University of New Mexico Press, 1986.

Jones, Dennis. "Immigrant Women in Kansas in the Early Days." *Kansas Quarterly* 18 (Summer 1986): 5–17.

Kaufman, Polly Welts. *Women Teachers on the Frontier*. New Haven: Yale University Press, 1984.

Keep, Rosalind A. *Fourscore and Ten Years: A History of Mills College*. Mills College, California, 1945.

Kelly, Joan. *Women, History, and Theory*. Chicago: The University of Chicago Press, 1984.

Kerber, Linda K. "Separate Spheres, Female Worlds, Woman's Place: The Rhetoric of Women's History." *Journal of American History* (June 1988): 1–39.

—. *Women of the Republic: Intellect and Ideology in Revolutionary America*. Chapel Hill: University of North Carolina Press, 1980.

Kessler-Harris, Alice. *Out to Work: A History of Wage-Earning Women in the United States*. New York: Oxford University Press, 1982.

Kolodny, Annette. *The Land Before Her: Fantasy and Experience of the American Frontiers, 1630–1860*. Chapel Hill: The University of North Carolina Press, 1984.

Larson, T. A. "Dolls, Vassals and Drudges: Pioneer Women in the West." *Western Historical Quarterly* 3 (January 1972): 4–16.

—. "Woman Suffrage in Wyoming." *Pacific Northwest Quarterly* 56 (April 1965): 58–61.

—. "Women's Role in the American West." *Montana, the Magazine of Western History* 24 (Summer 1974): 3–11.

Leibhardt, Barbara. "Interpretations and Causal Analysis: Theories in Environmental History." *Environmental Review* 12 (Spring 1988): 23–36.

Limerick, Patricia Nelson. *The Legacy of Conquest: The Unbroken Past of the American West*. New York: W.W. Norton & Company, 1987.

Malone, Michael P. *Historians and the American West*. Lincoln: University of Nebraska Press, 1983.

Marburg, Sandra Lin. "Women and Environment, Subsistence Paradigms, 1850–1950." *Environmental Review* 8 (Spring 1984): 7–22.

Massie, Michael A. "Reform is Where You Find It: The Roots of Woman Suffrage in Wyoming." *Annals of Wyoming* 62 (Spring 1990): 2–21.

Matsuda, Mari J. "The West and the Legal Status of Women: Explanations of Frontier Feminism." *Journal of the West* 24 (January 1985): 47–56.

May, Elaine Tyler. "Expanding the Past: Recent Scholarship on Women in Politics and Work." *Reviews in American History* (December 1986): 216–233.

Mead, Margaret. *Culture and Commitment: The New Relationships Between the Generations in the 1970s*. The Natural History Press, Doubleday & Co., Inc., 1970. Reprint. New York: Columbia University Press, 1978.

Monk, Janice. "Approaches to the Study of Women and Landscape." *Environmental Review* 8 (Spring 1984): 23–33.

Myers, Sandra. *Westering Women and the Frontier Experience 1800–1915*. Histories of the American Frontier. Albuquerque: University of New Mexico Press, 1982.

Nash, Gerald D. *Creating the West: Historical Interpretations 1890–1990*. Albuquerque: University of New Mexico Press, 1991.

—-. "The West as Utopia and Myth." *Montana, the Magazine of Western History* 41 (Winter 1991): 69–75.

Newcomer, Mabel. *A Century of Higher Education for Women*. New York: Harper & Row, 1959.

Norton, Mary Beth. *Liberty's Daughters: The Revolutionary Experience of American Women, 1750–1800*. Boston: Little, Brown and Company, 1980.

Norwood, Vera L. "Heroines of Nature: Four Women Respond to the American Landscape." *Environmental Review* 8 (Spring 1984): 34–56.

Offen, Karen. "Defining Feminism: A Comparative Historical Approach." *SIGNS* 14, 1 (1988): 119–157.

Opie, John. "Frederick Jackson Turner, the Old West, and the Formation of a National Mythology." *Environmental Review* 5 (Fall 1981): 79–91.

Parker, Samuel Chester. *The History of Modern Elementary Education*. Totowa, N.J.: Littlefield, Adams & Co., 1970.

Pascoe, Peggy. *Relations of Rescue: The Search for Female Moral Authority in the American West, 1874–1939*. New York: Oxford University Press, 1990.

Patterson-Black, Sheryll. "Women Homesteaders on the Great Plains Frontier." *Frontiers* 1 (Spring 1976): 67–88.

Petrik, Paula. "The Gentle Tamers in Transition: Women in the Trans-Mississippi West." *Feminist Studies* 11 (1985): 677–94.

—-. *No Step Backward: Women and Family on the Rocky Mountain Mining Frontier, Helena Montana 1865–1900*. Helena: Montana Historical Society Press, 1987.

Phelps, Edith M., ed. *Selected Articles on Woman Suffrage*. Debaters' Handbook
series. 3rd ed. White Plains, N.Y.: The H. W. Wilson Company, 1916.

Platt, Horace. *The Law as to the Property Rights of Married Women, as Contained
in California, Texas and Nevada*. San Francisco: Sumner Whitney &
Co., 1885.

Poling-Kempes, Lesley. *The Harvey Girls: Women Who Opened the West*. New
York: Paragon House, 1989.

Pomeroy, Earl. "The Significance of Continuity." 1955. Reprint. In *The Frontier
Thesis: Valid Interpretations of American History?* Edited by Ray Allen
Billington. New York: Holt, Rinehart and Winston.

Potter, David M. "American Women and American Character." In *History and
American Society: Essays of David M. Potter*. Edited by Don E.
Fehrenbacher. New York: Oxford University Press, 1973, 278–303.

Propst, Nell Brown. *Those Strenuous Dames of the Colorado Prairie*. Boulder,
Colorado: Pruett Publishing Co., 1982.

Rabkin, Peggy A. *Father to Daughters: The Legal Foundations of Female
Emancipation*. Westport, Conn.: Greenwood Press, 1980.

Riegel, Robert. *American Feminists*. Lawrence: University of Kansas Press, 1963.

Riley, Glenda. *The Female Frontier: A Comparative View of Women on the Prairie
and the Plains*. Lawrence, KS: University Press of Kansas, 1988.

—. *Frontierswomen: The Iowa Experience*. Ames: Iowa State University Press,
1981.

—. *Inventing the American Woman: A Perspective on Women's History*. Arlington
Heights: Harlan Davidson, 1987.

Ross, Nancy Wilson. *Westward the Women*. New York: Random House, Inc.,
1944. Reprint. San Francisco: North Point Press, 1985.

Ryan, Mary P. *Cradle of the Middle Class: The Family in Oneida County, New
York 1790–1865*. New York: Cambridge University Press, 1981.

Sales, Fred John. "A History of the Superintendency of Public Instruction in the
State of California, 1850–1932." Ph.D. diss., University of Southern
California. 1935.

Scharff, Virginia. *Twenty Thousand Roads: Women, Movement, and the West*.
Berkeley: University of California Press, 2003.

Schlissel, Lillian. *Women's Diaries of the Westward Journey*. New York: Schocken
Books, 1982.

—. "Women's Diaries on the Western Frontier." *American Studies* 18 (Spring
1977): 87–100.

Schlissel, Lillian, Byrd Gibbens, and Elizabeth Hampsten. *Far From Home:
Families of the Westward Journey*. New York: Schocken Books, 1989.

Schlissel, Lillian, Vicki L. Ruiz, and Janice Monk, eds. *Western Women: Their Land, Their Lives.* Albuquerque: University of New Mexico Press, 1988.

Scott, Joan Wallach. "Gender: A Useful Category of Historical Analysis." *American Historical Review* (December 1986): 1053–1075. Reprint. In *Gender and the Politics of History.* New York: Columbia University Press, 1988, 42–43.

Senier, Siobhan. *Voices of American Indian Assimilation and Resistance: Helen Hunt Jackson, Sarah Winnemucca, and Victoria Howard.* Norman: University of Oklahoma Press, 2001.

Solomon, Barbara Miller. *In the Company of Educated Women: A History of Women and Higher Education in America.* New Haven: Yale University Press, 1985.

Smith, Henry Nash. *Virgin Land: The American West as Symbol and Myth.* 1950. Reprint. Cambridge, Mass.: Harvard University Press, 1970.

Smith-Rosenberg, Carroll. "The Female World of Love and Ritual: Relations Between Women in Nineteenth Century America." *SIGNS* 1 (Autumn 1975): 1–19.

—-. "The New Woman as Androgyne: Social Disorder and Gender Crisis, 1870–1936." In *Disorderly Conduct: Visions of Gender in Victorian America.* New York: Oxford University Press, 1985, 245–296.

—-. "Sex as Symbol in Victorian America." *Prospects* 5 (1980): 51–70.

Solomon, Barbara Miller. *In the Company of Educated Women: A History of Women and Higher Education in America.* New Haven: Yale University Press, 1985.

Sprague, William Forrest. *Women and the West: A Short Social History.* Boston: The Christopher Publishing House, 1940.

Spruill, Julia Cherry. *Women's Life and Work in the Southern Colonies.* University of North Carolina Press, 1938. Reprint. New York: W. W. Norton & Company, Inc., 1972.

Stansell, Christine. "Women on the Great Plains 1865–1890." *Women's Studies* (1976): 87–98.

Stanton, Elizabeth Cady, Susan B. Anthony, and Matilda Joslyn Gage, eds. *History of Woman Suffrage 1876–1885.* N.Y.: Arno & The New York Times, 1969.

Stefanco-Schill. "Women on the American Frontier: An Historiographical Essay." Paper presented at the Social Science-History Conference, Nashville, October 30, 1981.

Stoeltje, Beverly J. "'A Helpmate for Man Indeed': The Image of the Frontier Woman." *Journal of American Folklore* 88 (January-March 1975): 25–41.

Stratton, Joanna L. *Pioneer Women: Voices from the Kansas Frontier.* New York: Simon & Schuster, 1981.

Thompson, John. *Closing the Frontier: Radical Response in Oklahoma, 1889–1923.* Norman: University of Oklahoma Press, 1986.

Tilly, Louise. "Gender, Women's History, and Social History." *Social Science History* 13 (Winter 1989): 439–80.

Tilly, Louise, and Joan W. Scott. *Women, Work and Family.* New York: Holt, Rinehart and Winston, 1978.

Turner, Frederick Jackson. "The Problem of the West." *Atlantic Monthly* 78 (September 1896): 289–297. Reprint. In *Frontier and Section: Selected Essays of Frederick Jackson Turner.* Edited by Ray Allen Billington. Englewood Cliffs, NJ: Prentice Hall, Inc., 1961.

—. "The Significance of History." Presented at the Chicago meeting of the American Historyical Associateion, 1891. In *Frontier and Section: Selected Essays of Frederick Jackson Turner.*

—. "The Significance of the Frontier in American History." Presented at the Chicago meeting of the American Historical Association, 1893.

Unruh, John D., Jr. *The Plains Across: The Overland Emigrants and the Trans-Mississippi West, 1840–60.* Urbana: University of Illinois Press, 1979.

Van Kirk, Sylvia. *Many Tender Ties: Women in the Fur Trade Society, 1670–1870.* Norman: University of Oklahoma Press, 1983.

Webb, Walter Prescott. *The Great Plains: A Study in Institutions and Environment.* Boston: Ginn, 1931. Reprint. Lincoln: University of Nebraska Press, Bison Book Printing, 1981.

Webster, Rev. Thomas. *Woman, Man's Equal.* Cincinnati & NY: Nelson & Phillips, Hitchcock & Walden, 1873.

Welter, Barbara. "The Cult of True Womanhood: 1820–1860." *American Quarterly,* 18 (Summer, 1966): 151–74.

—. *Dimity Convictions: The American Woman in the Nineteenth Century.* Athens: Ohio University Press, 1976.

Wertheimer, Barbara Mayer. *We Were There: The Story of Working Women in America.* N.Y.: Pantheon Books, 1977.

West, Elliott. "Cowboys and Indians and Artists and Liars and Schoolmarms and Tom Mix: New Ways to Teach the American West." In *Essays on Walter Prescott Webb and the Teaching of History.* Edited by Dennis Reinhartz and Stephan E. Maizlish. Arlington: Texas A & M University Press, 1985, 36–60.

—. *Growing Up with the Country: Childhood on the Far Western Frontier.* Histories of the American Frontier. Albuquerque: University of New Mexico Press, 1989.

Wherry, Peg. "At Home on the Range: Reactions of Pioneer Women to Plains Landscape." *Kansas Quarterly* 18 (Summer 1986): 71–79.

Wilson, Joan Hoff. "The Illusion of Change: Women and the American Revolution." In *The American Revolution, Explorations in the History of American Radicalism*. Edited by Alfred F. Young. Dekalb: Northern Illinois University Press, 1976.

PSYCHOANALYTIC LITERATURE

Benjamin, Jessica. *Bonds of Love: Psychoanalysis, Feminism, and the Problem of Domination*. New York: Pantheon Books, 1988.

—. "Father and Daughter: Identification with Difference—A Contribution to Gender Heterodoxy." Paper presented at the Los Angeles Psychoanalytic Society and Institute, Los Angeles, February 21, 1991.

Bernay, Toni, and Dorothy W. Cantor, eds. *The Psychology of Today's Women: New Psychoanalytic Visions*. Hillsdale, NJ: The Analytic Press, 1986.

Cath, Stanley H., Alan Gurwitt, and Linda Gunsberg, eds. *Fathers and Their Families*. Hillsdale, NJ: The Analytic Press, 1989.

Chodorow, Nancy. *The Reproduction of Mothering: Psychoanalysis and the Sociology of Gender*. Berkeley: University of California Press, 1978.

Denford, John. "Going Away." *International Review of Psycho-Analysis* 8, 3 (1981): 325–332.

Erikson, Erik H. *Childhood and Society*. 2nd ed. New York: W. W. Norton & Co., Inc., 1963.

Feuer, Lewis S. *The Conflict of Generations: The Character and Significance of Student Movements*. New York: Basic Books, Inc., 1969.

Freud, Sigmund. "Some Psychical Consequences of the Anatomical Distinction Between the Sexes." Reprinted in Jean Strouse, ed., *Women & Analysis: Dialogues on Psychoanalytic View of Femininity*. N.Y.: Dell Publishing Co., Inc., 1974.

Gilligan, Carol. *In a Different Voice: Psychological Theory and Women's Development*. Cambridge: Harvard University Press, 1982.

Greenberg, Jay R., and Stephen A. Mitchell. *Object Relations on Psychoanalytic Theory*. Cambridge: Harvard University Press, 1983.

Grinberg, Leon, M.D., and Rebeca Grinberg, M.D. *Psychoanalytic Perspectives on Migration and Exile*. New Haven: Yale University Press, 1989.

Hartmann, Heinz. *Ego Psychology and the Problem of Adaptation*. Translated by David Rapaport. 1939. Reprint. New York: International Universities Press, Inc., 1958.

Horney, Karen. *The Neurotic Personality of Our Time.* New York: W. W. Norton & Co., Inc., 1937.

Johoda, Marie. "Note on Work." In *Psychoanalysis—A General Psychology: Essays in Honor of Heinz Hartmann.* Edited by Rudolph M. Loewenstein, Lottie m. Newman, Max Schur, and Albert J. Solnit. New York: International Universities Press, 1966, 622–633.

Keniston, Kenneth. *Young Radicals: Notes on Committed Youth.* New York: Harcourt, Brace & World, Inc., 1968.

Klein, Melanie. *The Psycho-Analysis of Children.* Translated by Alix Strachey. Vol. 2 of *The Writings of Melanie Klein.* Edited by Roger Money-Kyrle. London: Hogarth, 1975.

Kohut, Heinz. *The Analysis of the Self: A Systematic Approach to the Psychoanalytic Treatment of Marcissistic Personality Disorders.* The Psychoanalytic Study of the Child Monograph No. 4. Madison, Conn.: International Universities Press, Inc., 1971.

—-. *The Restoration of the Self.* Madison: International Universities Press, Inc., 1977.

—-. *Self Psychology and the Humanities: Reflections on a New Psychoanalytic Approach.* Edited by Charles B. Strozier. New York: W. W. Norton & Company, 1985.

Masterson, James F., M.D. *The Search for the Real Self: Unmasking the Personality Disorders of Our Age.* New York: The Free Press, 1988.

Miller, Alice. *Prisoners of Childhood: The Drama of the Gifted Child and the Search for the True Self.* New York: Basic Books, Inc., 1981.

Storr, Anthony. *Solitude: A Return to the Self.* New York: Ballantine Books, 1988.

Strouse, Jean, ed. *Women and Analysis: Dialogues on Psycholanalytical Views of Femininity.* New York: Dell Publishing Co., Inc., 1974.

Thompson, Clara M. "The Role of Women in This Culture." *Psychiatry* 4 (1941): 1–8.

Wakerman, Elyce. *Father Loss: Daughters Discuss the Man That Got Away.* New York: Henry Holt and Company, 1984.

Winnicott, D. W. *The Maturational Processes and the Facilitating Environment: Studies in the Theory of Emotional Development.* Madison: International Universities Press, Inc., 1965.

Wolf, Ernest S., M.D. *Treating the Self: Elements of Clinical Self Psychology.* New York: The Guilford Press, 1986.

Index

978-0-595-38702-1
0-595-38702-0